The Afterlives of Frankenstein

The Afterlives of Frankenstein

Popular and Artistic Adaptations and Reimaginings

Edited by
Robert I. Lublin and Elizabeth A. Fay

BLOOMSBURY ACADEMIC
LONDON • NEW YORK • OXFORD • NEW DELHI • SYDNEY

BLOOMSBURY ACADEMIC

Bloomsbury Publishing Plc, 50 Bedford Square, London, WC1B 3DP, UK
Bloomsbury Publishing Inc, 1359 Broadway, New York, NY 10018, USA
Bloomsbury Publishing Ireland, 29 Earlsfort Terrace, Dublin 2, D02 AY28, Ireland

BLOOMSBURY, BLOOMSBURY ACADEMIC and the Diana logo are trademarks of
Bloomsbury Publishing Plc

First published in Great Britain 2024
Paperback edition published in 2025

Copyright © Robert I. Lublin and Elizabeth A. Fay, and Contributors, 2024

Robert I. Lublin and Elizabeth A. Fay, and Contributors have asserted their right under
the Copyright, Designs and Patents Act, 1988, to be identified as Authors of this work.

For legal purposes the Acknowledgments on p.xi constitute an extension
of this copyright page.

Cover image © "Amorous Libation", reproduced with the permission of the artist, Mike Bell.

All rights reserved. No part of this publication may be: i) reproduced or transmitted
in any form, electronic or mechanical, including photocopying, recording or by
means of any information storage or retrieval system without prior permission in
writing from the publishers; or ii) used or reproduced in any way for the training,
development or operation of artificial intelligence (AI) technologies, including
generative AI technologies. The rights holders expressly reserve this publication
from the text and data mining exception as per Article 4(3) of the Digital Single
Market Directive (EU) 2019/790.

Bloomsbury Publishing Plc does not have any control over, or responsibility for,
any third-party websites referred to or in this book. All internet addresses given
in this book were correct at the time of going to press. The author and publisher
regret any inconvenience caused if addresses have changed or sites have
ceased to exist, but can accept no responsibility for any such changes.

A catalogue record for this book is available from the British Library.

Library of Congress Cataloging-in-Publication Data

Names: Lublin, Robert I., editor. | Fay, Elizabeth A., 1957– editor.
Title: The afterlives of Frankenstein : popular and artistic adaptations and reimaginings /
edited by Robert Lublin and Elizabeth Fay.
Description: London ; New York : Bloomsbury Academic, 2024. |
Includes bibliographical references and index.
Identifiers: LCCN 2023030747 (print) | LCCN 2023030748 (ebook) |
ISBN 9781350351561 (hardback) | ISBN 9781350351578 (adobe pdf) |
ISBN 9781350351585 (epub)
Subjects: LCSH: Shelley, Mary Wollstonecraft, 1797–1851. Frankenstein. |
Shelley, Mary Wollstonecraft, 1797–1851–Characters. |
Frankenstein, Victor (Fictitious character) | Frankenstein's monster (Fictitious character) |
Shelley, Mary Wollstonecraft, 1797-1851.–Adaptations.
Classification: LCC PR5397.F73 A335 2024 (print) | LCC PR5397.F73 (ebook) |
DDC 823/.7—dc23/eng/20230818
LC record available at https://lccn.loc.gov/2023030747
LC ebook record available at https://lccn.loc.gov/2023030748

ISBN: HB: 978-1-3503-5156-1
       PB: 978-1-3503-5160-8
       ePDF: 978-1-3503-5157-8
       eBook: 978-1-3503-5158-5

Typeset by RefineCatch Limited, Bungay, Suffolk

For product safety related questions contact productsafety@bloomsbury.com.

To find out more about our authors and books visit
www.bloomsbury.com and sign up for our newsletters.

Contents

Notes on Contributors   vii
Acknowledgments   xi

Introduction   *Robert I. Lublin and Elizabeth A. Fay*   1

Part One   Cultural Reinventions

1. "Only from the future": *Frankenstein*, *The Mummy!*, and the Ontology of Revolution   19
   David Baulch
2. Frankens-Time: *Frankenstein* and the Temporality of Artificial Life   29
   Tobias Wilson-Bates
3. Meiji Japan Responds to *Frankenstein*: The 1889–1890 translation "The New Creator" and the Illustrations   40
   Tomoko Nakagawa
4. *Frankenstein* Goes Global: Returning the Necropolitical Gaze with *Frankenstein in Baghdad*   54
   Hugh Charles O'Connell

Part Two   Frankensteinia

5. Frankenstein in the Popular Imagination   67
   Sidney E. Berger
6. Frankenstein Masks: Perpetuating the Monster Assemblage   85
   Taylor Hagood
7. "Machines Within the Machine": Definitions of Humanity in Victor LaValle's and Dietrich Smith's *Destroyer* (2017)   97
   W. Andrew Shephard

Part Three   Playing Frankenstein

8. *Mary Enters*: Staging Shelley in Contemporary *Frankenstein* Biodramas   111
   Brittany Reid

9	The Frankenstein Myth in Twenty-First-Century Film *Robert I. Lublin*	121
10	The Water and the Corpse: Exploring Nature, Shelley's Echoes, and Twenty-First Century Cultural Anxieties in *The Frankenstein Chronicles* *Lorna Piatti-Farnell*	131
11	The Aesthetics of Digital Naturecultures in La Belle Games's *The Wanderer: Frankenstein's Creature* (2019) *Andrew Burkett*	139

Part Four Artists Talk Back

12	*A Monstrous Circus on* Frankenstein: Mediating Shelley's Novel through John Cage's Multimedia Strategies *R. L. Silver and Miriam Wallace*	155
13	Frankenstein in Three Chords *Elizabeth A. Fay and James McGirr*	171
14	From *Frankenstein* to Writing Sci-Fi to Collage *Margaret Hart*	184

Coda: Frankenstein Continued *Daniel Cook*	199
Notes	205
Index	230

Contributors

David Baulch is an Associate Professor of English at the University of West Florida, where he teaches courses in British Romanticism, the Gothic, and Critical Theory. His most recent publications are "'Living Form': William Blake's Gothic Relations" in *William Blake's Gothic Imagination* (2018) and "The Sublime" in *William Blake in Context* (2019). Baulch is revising his manuscript, "Being at the Limit: William Blake, the Sublime, and Repetition."

Sidney E. Berger is on the faculties of the library schools at the University of Illinois, Urbana-Champaign and Simmons University in Boston where he teaches a variety of classes on rare books. His volume *Rare Books and Special Collections* won the ABC Clio / American Library Association Award for The Best Book in Library Literature for 2014. The second edition of his book *The Dictionary of the Book* is at press. His present research interests are in book history, papermaking and paper decoration, and publishing.

Andrew Burkett is Associate Professor of English and Director of the Science, Technology, and Society Program at Union College. His research and teaching interests center on the intersections among imaginative literature, technology, and science during the British Romantic period. He is the author of *Romantic Mediations: Media Theory and British Romanticism* (2016).

Daniel Cook is Reader in English Literature at the University of Dundee, UK. He is the author of *Thomas Chatterton and Neglected Genius, 1760–1830* (2013), *Reading Swift's Poetry* (2020), and *Walter Scott and Short Fiction* (2021). He is also the editor or co-editor of a dozen more books, including *The Afterlives of Eighteenth-Century Fiction* (2015; with Nicholas Seager), *Austen After 200: New Reading Spaces* (2022; with Kerry Sinanan and Annika Bautz), and editions of *Gulliver's Travels*, *Frankenstein* and *The Private Memoirs and Confessions of a Justified Sinner*. His creative practice includes comic-book and theatrical reworkings of *Gulliver's Travels* and *Frankenstein*.

Elizabeth A. Fay is Professor of English at the University of Massachusetts Boston. She has published seven books on British Romantic literature, including *Romantic Egypt: Abyssal Ground of British Romanticism*, *Fashioning Faces: The Portraitive Mode in British Romanticism*, *Romantic Medievalism: History and the Romantic Literary Ideal*, and *Romantic Immanence: Interventions in Alterity, 1780–1840*.

Taylor Hagood is Professor of American Literature at Florida Atlantic University. His publications include *Faulkner's Imperialism: Space, Place, and the Materiality of Myth* (2008) and *Faulkner, Writer of Disability* (2014, winner of the C. Hugh Holman Award for Best Book in Southern Studies), and the co-edited volume, *Undead Souths: The Gothic and Beyond in Southern Literature and Culture* (2015). His current work includes a biography of novelist Theodore Pratt and a book of philosophy/theory/criticism on rurality.

Margaret Hart is Professor at the University of Massachusetts, Boston in the Art and Art History Department. Her creative research interests focus on posthumanism, speculative fiction, and feminist theory. Her collage artworks are informed by these interests and visually explore the intersections between them. Her work is collected and exhibited internationally.

Robert I. Lublin is Professor of Theatre Arts at the University of Massachusetts Boston. He is the author of *Costuming the Shakespearean Stage: Visual Codes of Representation in Early Modern Theatre and Culture* and contributing co-editor of *Reinventing the Renaissance: Shakespeare and His Contemporaries in Adaptation and Performance*.

James McGirr is a professional musician residing in Portland, Maine, USA. He holds a MA in music from Brooklyn College and instructs in trumpet and bass. His performance schedule is currently focused on playing bass and trumpet in pit orchestras of musical theater productions. Most recently he has performed for productions of "The Rocky Horror Show," "Jekyll & Hyde" and "Little Shop of Horrors."

Tomoko Nakagawa is Professor of English Literature at the University of the Sacred Heart, Tokyo, Japan. She is the author of *Aspects of Daily Lives in the British Novel* (2011, in Japanese) and the co-editor of four books in Japanese, including *Frankenstein* (2006) and *The British Novel and Representation of Food* (2004). Her research interests focus on female writers of the Romantic era, Anglo-Japanese cultural exchanges in the nineteenth century, modernist literature and physical realities, and literature and environment.

Hugh C. O'Connell is Associate Professor of English at the University of Massachusetts Boston. His current research focuses on the utopian valences of Africanfuturism and the relationship between speculative fiction and speculative finance. He is the editor of *Disputing the Deluge* by Darko Suvin, and co-editor with David M. Higgins of *Speculative Finance/Speculative Fiction* a special issue of *CR: The New Centennial Review* 19(1).

Lorna Piatti-Farnell is Professor of Film, Media, and Cultural Studies at Auckland University of Technology, where she is also the Director of the Popular Culture Research Centre. She is President of the Gothic Association of New Zealand and Australia (GANZA), and Coordinator of Australasian Horror Studies Network

(AHSN). Her research interests lie at the intersection of popular media and cultural history, with a focus on Gothic Studies. She has published widely in these areas, including (among others) *Consuming Gothic: Food and Horror in Film* (2017), *The Vampire in Contemporary Popular Literature* (Routledge, 2014), and *Gothic Afterlives: Reincarnations of Horror in Film and Popular Media* (editor, Lexington, 2019). She is currently working on a new edited project entitled *Disney's Gothic Kingdom: Dark Shadows in the House of Mouse* (in conjunction with Prof. Jeffrey Weinstock; Lexington), while also completing her latest monograph, entitled *Poison and the Popular Imagination: Narratives, Aesthetics, and Cultural Legacies*. Prof. Piatti-Farnell is sole editor of the 'Routledge Advances in Popular Culture Studies' book series, as well as co-editor (with Prof. Carl Sederholm) of the 'Horror Studies' book series for Lexington.

Brittany Reid is an Adjunct Professor in the Department of English Language and Literature at Brock University. Her research interests include Gothic and Romantic literature, theater history, performance studies, and sport literature. Her recent projects explore Romantic gravesites, Taylor Swift's new Romanticism, the 1972 Summit Series between Canada and the USSR, and *sidelines* (2021): a collection of sporting memories.

W. Andrew Shephard is Assistant Professor of African American Literature and Culture at the University of Utah, specializing in modes of genre fiction. His work has been featured in *The Cambridge History of Science Fiction*, *New Critical Review*, Wiley-Blackwell's *Encyclopedia of Contemporary Fiction, 1980-2020*, and the forthcoming volume, *Again, Lingua Cosmica*. His current book project, *Temples for Tomorrow: African American Speculative Fiction and Historical Narrative*, interrogates Black speculative fiction writers' engagements with history.

R. L. Silver is Producer and Interim Director of New Music New College at New College of Florida. He has composed for and performed at many NMNC concerts over the years and has presented and led workshop performances at the New Music Gathering and at Social Theory, Politics, and the Arts conferences.

Miriam L. Wallace is Professor of English & Gender Studies at New College of Florida. Her scholarship focuses on late eighteenth/early nineteenth-century Britain, exploring common or every day "speaking subjects" and orators. Most recently she published "The Everyday Celebrity of 'Sir' Jeffrey Dunstan, Mayor of Garrat," for *Making Stars: Biography and Eighteenth-Century Celebrity* (2022) and "Embodying Rhetoric: Oration and Society in Eighteenth-Century Britain," for *The Cambridge History of Rhetoric* (in press).

Tobias Wilson-Bates is Assistant Professor in the English department at Georgia Gwinnett College. He researches the technological and narrative history of Time as a means of understanding how industrialization changed the storytelling practices of the nineteenth century. He is especially interested in the ecological impacts of the global standardization of time in relation to transportation, extraction, and communication. He has published on the temporality of education, time travel in anime, illustrations of clocks in Dickens, and Anthropocene time. His current book project on time machines and extraction is titled, *Holes in Time*.

Acknowledgments

Robert wishes to thank his co-editor Libby for two decades of mentorship and friendship. He would also like to thank the late Professor Lynn Morrow of Albright College, who taught him how to write. Personal thanks go to his wife, Elina Cymerman, a brilliant strong woman, for her love, support, and sometimes her exceptional editing skills. He notes especially that "together, we raise our daughters, Sara and Julia, already brilliant and strong, whom I love with all my heart."

We would like to thank each other for an unusually enjoyable partnership, the culminating experience of our long friendship and shared projects. It has been an honor and a joy to work together on this volume. Included in our collaborations is UMass Boston's participation in *Frankenreads* sponsored by the Keats-Shelley Association of America, a global project of collaboratively reading aloud Mary Shelley's novel.

We would also like to extend thanks to our editor at Bloomsbury Lucy Brown, for supporting our efforts throughout the challenges of the Covid-19 pandemic and for her critical role in bringing this volume to print. The late Dean David Terkla and the CLA Dean's Office at UMass Boston provided a grant to cover costs of the volume's color illustrations, and we are grateful for this support. Dean Terkla was also one of our Frankenreaders, a treasured memory for us now that he has passed.

INTRODUCTION

Frankenstein in the Cultural Imagination

Robert I. Lublin and Elizabeth A. Fay

For the last 200 years, Frankenstein has been ubiquitous.[1] Since it was first published in 1818, *Frankenstein* has received nearly constant attention, being republished continuously, translated across the world, written and rewritten for the stage repeatedly throughout the nineteenth century, and then rendered into film near the start of the twentieth century. Since then, new cinematic versions have appeared at an unprecedented (and almost unbelievable) rate, with more than 200 films appealing directly to the novel for their title and premise. If we consider movies that simply borrow Mary Shelley's basic story of a scientist seeking to create life with disastrous consequences, the number of films indebted to the novel leaps to the thousands.[2] In addition to these films, dozens of original novels have taken up the story of Frankenstein as well as comic books, television programs, computer games, and more. Much more. The great majority of these new works do not attempt to recreate Mary Shelley's work with any fidelity. Instead, they reimagine the Frankenstein myth and explore its ramifications in ways that are of immediate relevance to the time and location of their instantiation. *Frankenstein* has been the subject of endless adaptations that creatively respond to their moment using Shelley's story as their central motif and motivating myth.

The Afterlives of Frankenstein treats the popular culture and artistic engagements with both Mary Shelley's novel and the myth it spawned, ranging from serious novels to comics and graphic novels; Hollywood movies to visual artworks; video games and music to television series and plays; popular culture kitsch to monster masks. The myth of monstrous creation, or creation run amuck, proves an immensely fertile one for the creative imagination. It can transform into a critique of creative possession (Can a creature or artwork be possessed? Does it have a life of its own?) or become a subject ripe for parody (Bobby "Boris" Pickett's 1962 hit song "Monster Mash" is a good example). *Frankenstein* and its monstrous myth have been the germ seed and touchstone for so much of what touches on the uncanny or fearful, and artistic responses can be edgy, silly, or unnerving—but they are always revealing. They manifest something terrible or hard to look at, just as the "normal" humans in Shelley's *Frankenstein* react fearfully at seeing Victor's "abnormal," transhuman creature.

Except for Shakespeare's plays, no other author or single work has drawn such continual attention as Mary Shelley and *Frankenstein*. Since the novel's original publication, more than perhaps any other single work, *Frankenstein* has served as a cultural seismograph in terms of gauging the tenor of the times. This has been true from the start. When Mary Shelley wrote *Frankenstein*, beyond telling an extraordinary horror story that has been credited as the first work of science fiction, she engaged and explored the immediate concerns of literature, politics, philosophy, biology, chemistry, and religion that fascinated the period. In the novel, Victor Frankenstein begins his tale by stating "I am by birth a Genevese." With this succinct opening, he poignantly cites the location where the author was living when she first conceived of the idea for her novel, but *Frankenstein* also invokes the extraordinary associations the city carried at the time. Geneva was the intellectual birthplace of the French Revolution. Jean-Jacques Rousseau, whose political writings provided the philosophical basis for revolution, had been born nearby and was honored by an obelisk outside the city which Mary Shelley had seen. Beyond political philosophy, Rousseau also wrote an important and widely read book on the raising and proper education of children, *Emile, or On Education*. In *Frankenstein*, Victor's failure to nurture and educate the life he created takes on a particular resonance when considered in light of Rousseau's work, which specifically highlights the role that a father or tutor plays in raising a child to have a moral compass. Thus, with his first words, Victor situates his efforts to create a life in the place where personal freedom and effective child rearing had been deeply theorized, yet he denies his "child" both. The result is disastrous for everyone, an important lesson in a time reeling from the French Revolution (fought to bring personal freedom to the masses) and its aftermath, the Napoleonic Wars (which brought destruction instead). Frankenstein's creature embodies both that hope and that despair; its story has proved germinative for both critiques and parodies of society's hypocritical smashing of political ideals, especially at historical moments when critique, but also parodic laughter, strikes the right tone.

As much as *Frankenstein* touches on deeply human issues of insiders and outsiders, the recognizable and the alien, it is also steeped in the cultural moment in which it was composed. The galvanic force that animated Frankenstein's creation and brought it to life, for instance, was drawn directly from the experiments with electricity that were being conducted and widely discussed at the time.[3] Mary Shelley's aptitude for engaging the issues of the moment served as literary galvanism, motivating *Frankenstein*'s form and substance at the deepest levels and rendering her novel into a cultural phenomenon. The work's vital connection to the time and place of its authorship was not lost on its readers. A contemporary review states that the book has "an air of reality attached to it, by being connected with the favourite projects and passions of the times."[4] The novel's distinctive ability to engage and articulate the period's scientific, artistic, philosophical, and political fascinations carried over to the later works that rewrote, revised, and adapted *Frankenstein*. Received as a piece of popular fiction, the book was not deemed high art, and no one held the notion that it needed to be strictly adhered to in any adaptive work. What resulted were new works that were indebted to the reigning ideals and ideas of their particular moment every bit as much as they were beholden to Mary Shelley's original work; the same is true of adaptive works being produced today.

Theatrical Reimaginings

The capacity of a new "Frankenstein" adaptation to suit the tenor and the tastes of the time was demonstrated shortly after the novel was published. The first dramatic version of *Frankenstein*, Richard Brinsley Peake's *Presumption; or the Fate of Frankenstein*, opened on the London stage on July 28, 1823. The play was an immediate success, offering a very new notion of Victor Frankenstein and his creation. For the stage, *Frankenstein* morphed to engage the particular expectations of the sensational melodramas that were popular at the time. Unlike Mary Shelley's novel, in Peake's play Frankenstein's creation was an inarticulate creature. This makes sense, since, as Steven Forry has noted, melodramas "concerned as they were with action, did not really desire to exhibit the mind of the Creature coming into Lockean awareness."[5] Peake's play was not a singular phenomenon—by the end of the year, five different *Frankenstein* plays had been staged in London, and within three years, the number of new works based on the novel had risen to fourteen, including popular productions in New York and Paris.

In these theatrical productions, Frankenstein's creation remained a large, threatening, unspeaking brute, introducing the expectation that Universal Pictures followed more than a century later when it presented the iconic image of the creature as "monster" with its 1931 film. The theatrical versions of *Frankenstein* that proliferated after 1823 shared additional traits beyond its silent antagonist, many of which lived on in the Universal film, including the tradition of having a vengeful mob hunt down the creature. The new theatrical monsters also, inevitably, loved music and were drawn to it in production after production. New *Frankenstein* plays tended to discard the narrative frame of Walton's Arctic voyage entirely. They offered a linear plot that eschewed the novel's use of flashbacks. These new plays also presented Victor Frankenstein as a mature scientist rather than a rising schoolboy and made little mention of Victor's formative, boyhood experiences. Finally, theatrical versions introduced an assistant for Victor, a comic foil he could speak with about his experiments as the play had no access to narrative and replaced it with dialogue to introduce key information.[6] In *Presumption*, Victor's assistant was Fritz, and it was the assistant's reaction to the creation of the creature that guided the audience's first response: "Oh, dear! Oh, dear! Oh, dear! There's a hob—hobgoblin, seven-and-twenty feet high!" A century later, Igor was a fixture of *Frankenstein* productions when he appeared on film.[7]

Beyond these shared characteristics, the theatrical versions of *Frankenstein* that proliferated after Peake's *Presumption* and remained popular onstage throughout the nineteenth century also exhibited striking differences. Comic versions of the play started to appear onstage before the end of 1823, with Peake himself introducing the practice by offering a burlesque of his own work. *Another Piece of Presumption* opened at the Adelphi Theatre in the Strand on October 20, less than three months after the premier of Peak's earlier play. In this work, Fritz becomes Frizzy and helps the master Tailor, Mr. Frankinstitch, sew together body parts from yeoman tailors to create a monstrosity named Hobgoblin. The large audiences that attended the original production returned for Peake's farce, and the ability of the Frankenstein myth to assume comic form began its own history. Before the end of 1823, *Humgumption; or, Dr. Frankenstein and the Hobgoblin of Hoxton* was staged at the New Surrey Theatre, and in 1824, *Frank-in-Steam; or, The Modern Promise to Pay* appeared at the Olympic Theatre. In less than a year, the London stage determinedly established the extraordinary flexibility of the Frankenstein myth, and it has demonstrated and expanded that vaunted potential ever since.

Mary Shelley had the chance to see the original production of Peake's *Presumption*, attending the theatre on 28 August 1823, and she was delighted to see her work take on new life. In a letter to Leigh Hunt, she writes "lo & behold! I found myself famous!— Frankenstein had prodigious success as a drama & was about to be repeated for the 23rd night at the English opera house.... I was much amused, & it appeared to excite a breathless eagerness in the audience—it was a third piece a scanty pit filled at half price—& all stayed till it was over. They continue to play it even now ... On the strength of the drama my father had published for my benefit a new edition of F."[8] In the years before the "long run," twenty-three consecutive performances of a play represented an extraordinarily successful production, and the show went on to the remarkable total of thirty-seven. And yet, it is the final line of Shelley's letter to Hunt that is most important to the project of this collection, for it marks *Frankenstein*'s introduction into cultural circulation from which it never left. The theatrical success of Peake's play reinvigorated interest in the novel; a second edition was published which, for the first time, had the author's name listed on the title page. Subsequently, the novel received numerous new editions and reprints throughout the nineteenth century and, to date, there have been more than 300 editions.

Literary and Graphic Reimaginings

Although the general consensus is to understand Mary Shelley's *Frankenstein* as envisioning the future of technologically enabled subjects, the cyborg that Donna Haraway argues that we have become, the novel was the opposite: a contribution to a contemporary literary debate about a world gone awry due to humanity's endless ego-driven striving, represented by Napoleon and his revision of the French Republic into a pan-European empire. The debate's themes were worked out in texts such as Shelley's father William Godwin's *St. Leon: A Tale of the Sixteenth Century* that she later sketched out further herself in short stories like "The Mortal Immortal" and "Transformation." In all or most of these works alchemy looms large. The works of Paracelsus that young Victor imbibes in his father's library, putting him on the path to a medical project not of Promethean stature so much as overblown ego, stands in for the West's abuse of science to enlarge its franchise on the natural *and* the superhuman. Novels and short stories that adapt *Frankenstein* either follow this formula or Shelley's critique of it. More recent adaptations, such as Ahmed Saadawi's 2013 *Frankenstein in Baghdad*, tend to take the second line, whereas earlier writers were more concerned to provide variants on Shelley's story and cast of characters without examining too closely her astute cultural critique.

An example of such variants followed fast on the heels of Peake's 1823 play *Presumption; or the Fate of Frankenstein* which was published anonymously as "The Monster Made by Man; or, the Punishment of Presumption" in 1826. It was first issued even earlier in pamphlet form in the serial *Endless Entertainment*, June 17, 1825, revealing how much it was the creature, rather than his egotistical creator, who captivated audiences.[9] Today, fascination with the novel itself rather than Hollywood reinventions of it remains strong. Evidence is widely available, from the global *Frankenreads* project of simultaneous group readings of the novel on the Halloween Day of the novel's bicentennial to the recent auction sale of a signed copy of a first edition for £350,000.[10]

The relation of the Frankenstein myth to A.I. technology, futuristic genres such as steampunk, and young adult fiction are some of the topics taken up by Francesca Saggini and Anna Enrichetta Soccio's volume, *Transmedia Creatures*. The essays collected there include an excellent treatment of Frankenstein comics by Frederico Meschini, who makes clear the natural path from Shelley's novel to comic book adaptations: if the first adaptation of the novel was, very naturally, a stage play that visualized the plot and characters, the next visual forms would be cinema and graphic adaptations. Moreover, "cinema and comics . . . were introduced into the world the same year, 1895, by the renowned Lumière brothers as well as Richard Outcalt and his *Yellow Kid*; they share a basic grammar . . . and their mutual influences are well known."[11] Andrew McInnes' chapter on youth fiction complements Meschini's by showing how Shelley's visually rich story compels the imagination regardless of whether the pictorial element is there or not. Young readers are drawn to the visual whether this is verbal or imagistic. Cinema, comics, and youth fiction all find common ground in dwelling on the problem of monstrosity as presented by Shelley's novel, and for young readers, monstrosity directly feeds "childhood anxieties and desires."[12] Claire Nally's "Staging Steampunk Aesthetics in *Frankenstein* Adaptations" discusses the intriguing intersection of the nineteenth-century myth of Frankenstein with steampunk's retrofuturistic vision, and neo-Victorianism in two very popular stage and film adaptations of the novel (the National Theatre's 2011 production directed by Danny Boyle, and the 2015 film *Victor Frankenstein* directed by Paul McGuigan).[13]

The Frankenstein myth as Shelley created it has proved so robust that an historical line can be drawn so that, even in the last half of the twentieth century, literary adaptations hewed fairly close to the science-gone-mad formulation, albeit with the early theatrical and literary reduction of the complexly transhuman creature to Victor's unjust characterization of him as a hellish "fiend." For a French horror series in the vein of the London serial anthology *Endless Entertainment; or Comic, Terrific, and Legendary Tales*, Jean-Claude Carrière rapidly produced six continuations of the Frankenstein story between 1957 and 1959 with titles like *The Tower of Frankenstein*, *The Step of Frankenstein*, and *Frankenstein Prowls*. These spinoffs follow the nearly immortal creature after the Iceland incident as he continues his revenge on humanity, wreaking havoc at every turn. Frank Schildiner produced two more short novels in this popular series: *The Quest of Frankenstein* and *The Triumph of Frankenstein*. Another series published by Popular Library is *The Frankenstein Horror Series*, however only the first of the nine novels concerns Victor's creature: Paul W. Fairman's *The Frankenstein Wheel* (1972).

The next year, Brian Aldiss published *Frankenstein Unbound* (1973), a more ambitious project focusing on the circumstances surrounding the writing of the novel rather than Victor's creature. Aldiss imaginatively yokes Mary Shelley's novel and Percy Shelley's epic poem *Prometheus Unbound* into a tale of time travel back to 1816 Geneva and the creation of *Frankenstein*. The 1970s seem to have found special resonance in the Frankenstein story, perhaps because of the critique of world dominance inspired by anti-war sentiment. Just two years later, in 1975, Robert Myers published a sequel to the original novel titled *The Cross of Frankenstein* that returns the focus to the creature but first complicates Victor's guilt by giving him an illegitimate son. It is this delegitimized hero who encounters the creature in America where it continues its revenge on mankind. Myers published a second sequel the next year, *The Slave of Frankenstein*, in which the creature is a confirmed racist as well as misanthrope as he plots to create a race of slaves to do his bidding. As these titles show, by this time "Frankenstein" has irrevocably come to designate the creature rather than Victor himself. It's not until ten years later that an author felt the story to be relevant again as literature rather than film: Fred Saberhagen's *The Frankenstein Papers* appeared in 1986, telling the story entirely from the creature's perspective.

The Frankenstein Papers takes the myth into science fiction more properly, signaling a turn to cultural critique rather than formulaic versions of the original story. In it, the being taken to be Victor's creature is an alien suffering from amnesia and disfigured by an electrical explosion in Victor's lab; ironically, Victor's creation was a failure, with the electrical spark of life having no effect on its assembled body. It was almost another twenty years before Peter Ackroyd's 2008 *The Casebook of Victor Frankenstein* appeared; Ackroyd rejected science fiction in favor of a postmodern adaptation, proving the ongoing relevance of the Frankenstein myth. In Ackroyd's story, Victor Frankenstein and Percy Shelley encounter each other while university students in London. Robert Harris introduces the science-postmodern hybrid of artificial intelligence and the Frankenstein myth with 2012's *The Fear Index*. However, the first line of formulaic imitation and adaptation has not died out: William Chanler's 2017 sequel, *Son of Terror: Frankenstein Continued*, begins in the Arctic after Victor dies, the starting point of so many of the adaptations mentioned above.

Frankenstein has also served as a potent metaphor for exploring race within literature and popular culture. H. L. Malchow has argued that, in *Frankenstein*, "Shelley's portrayal of her monster drew upon contemporary attitudes towards non-whites, in particular on fears and hopes of the abolition of slavery in the West Indies."[14] Elizabeth Young notes that Frankenstein has served since the early nineteenth century as a pervasive American metaphor that condemns the institution of slavery and the notion of black monstrosity in works of popular literature, film, and performance. In her book *Black Frankenstein: The Making of an American Metaphor*, she writes "Black Frankenstein stories ... effected four kinds of antiracist critique: they humanized the slave, they explained, if not justified, his violence; they condemned the slaveowner; and they exposed the instability of white power."[15] To make her argument, Young traces a genealogy of black Frankenstein stories in America from the 1830s to the present and from literature into film, and beyond.

Mary Shelley's masterpiece was incredibly attuned to its times in additional ways that proved prospective. Within less than a decade of its publication what may be the first comic book was issued: *The Glasgow Looking Glass* (1826).[16] The affinity between

Frankenstein and graphic illustration was quickly discovered, perhaps because the theatrical adaptations inspired visual representation of the creature's appearance. But the development of widespread comic books, which occurred in Britain in the 1860s with publications like *Ally Sloper's Half Holiday* (1867) was in response to working-class readers' desire for humor in an easily accessible form.[17] It was not until the wartime boom in comic books, beginning with Action Comics' Superman in 1938, that the association between horror, villains, and illustrated narrative connected the dots between the Frankenstein myth and the graphic genre. After the end of the Second World War, the same occurred in Japan with the publication of manga. The full account of comic book and manga adaptations of *Frankenstein* cannot be given here or even summarized. A few key examples will give the flavor, however. And yes, there was a Frankenstein superhero comic book (the 1961 "Bizarro Meets Frankenstein!").

In 1939 DC Comics issued its first *Movie Comics* that included a short adaptation of the third Boris Karloff film, *Son of Frankenstein*, which premiered that same year. In 1940 Dick Briefer produced a horror version of the Frankenstein myth but then revised it as a comedic one in 1945, titled *Frankenstein Comics*. This strain is visible in the mid-1960s television series *The Munsters*. Other comic book treatments followed less quickly, with a serious treatment of the creature in its Arctic exile in 1973: DC Comics' "Spawn of Frankenstein." In the same year, Marvel Comics released *The Monster of Frankenstein*, a non-comedic graphic version of Shelley's story for five issues. The sixth issue changed direction with a somewhat ridiculous transfer of the creature to a present-day James Bond-style plot. Even more ridiculous uses of the creature-as-monster appeared as his encounter with the X-Men (Marvel, 1968) and Batman and Superman stories in the 1990s (DC Comics). Dell Comics issued their own Frankenstein superhero version in 1966–1967. Other entanglements of the Frankenstein myth and popular heroes and villains similar to these are too numerous to include except for the creature's appearance in video gamess such as *Monster in My Pocket* (1991), which was also a comic book and animated special.

The history of manga adaptations of Shelley's novel is just as complex, beginning with Junji Ito's *Frankenstein,* an earnest adaptation of the novel that was published with his other manga for English audiences in 1999. Others include Atsushi Ōkubo's adaptation of the novel as part of his 2004 *Soul Eater*; in it a character named Franken Stein, who combines both Victor and the creature, is a scientist and doctor whose body is covered with stitches, and although he succeeds in creating a zombie-like being, he is also deranged, a strong departure from both of Shelley's characters. In 2001, Mitsukazu Mihara produced six stories as *Beautiful People*; the title story interrogates our emotional assumptions about beings like Shelley's creature. Shueisha created a manga series based on the novel in 2007 entitled *Embalming—Another Tale of Frankenstein*, which questions the nature of fiction by treating Victor as an historical person whose lab notes scientists are still using to recreate his experiment, while characters also read Shelley's novel for guidance and inspiration. Manga adaptations, as these examples show, provide another lens on artistic reimaginings of the Frankenstein myth by invoking a variety of ethical issues surrounding the question of revitalizing or creating beings from dead body parts.

Manga artists are not alone in responding visually to the novel. Recent graphic novels such as the 2019 *Tales of Frankenstein* by Donald F. Glut, Mike Vosburg, et al., which takes the gothic horror approach, to the fairy tale version, *Rapunzel vs. Frankenstein: A Graphic Novel* by Martin Powell and Omar Lozano, published the same year, reveal an ongoing attraction to the myth. Visual artists have likewise responded. In 2018 a gallery show opened in Los Angeles featuring 100 artists responding to Shelley's novel and film adaptations of it, *Frankenstein 200*. Curated by the Ecuadorian illustrator Chogrin, the list of artists includes such impressive names as Carly Janine Mazur, Caitlin McCormack, Marc Scheff, and Jared Flores. In an interview Chogrin notes that "It is the quintessential story of creator and creation, which is why I think many artists and scientists are immediately attracted to it."[18]

Frankenstein on Screen

Throughout the twentieth century and into the twenty-first, scholars and critics have periodically argued that the Frankenstein myth no longer fascinates or that it has worn out its ability to captivate audiences. Chris Baldick wrote in 1987:

> Myths are also susceptible to "closure," or to adaptations which constrain their further development into fixed channels. In the case of the Frankenstein myth, this moment of closure arrived in 1931 in the shape of William Henry Pratt (better known as Boris Karloff), whose rectangular face and bolt-adorned neck have fixed our idea of the monster into a universally known image from which it is hard to see further revisions breaking free.[19]

This statement seems patently true but is demonstrably false. The monster Boris Karloff made famous certainly lives on in our collective imagination to this day as the preeminent visual representation of Shelley's creature.[20] It is undoubtedly the first image that comes to mind when Frankenstein is mentioned. But the myth has by no means experienced closure. Our fascination and undiminished interest in *Frankenstein* can be witnessed most clearly in the sheer number and extraordinary range of movies that addressed the scientist and his creation in the twentieth century, and the twenty-first has actually seen an increase in the rapid pace of producing Frankenstein films, most of which display no visual indebtedness to Karloff's legacy.[21]

A few short years after the Universal Pictures films made Karloff's visage the dominant visual expectation for Frankenstein's creature, the type was challenged by Hammer Studios' *The Curse of Frankenstein* in 1957. Offering a creature that looked very different, this film was a resounding popular (if not necessarily critical) success, recouping its production costs more than 70 times over, and spawning its own series of films with very different stories and original creatures that were not indebted to Karloff's image.[22]

The financial success of the Hammer films demonstrated that the Frankenstein myth was not closed, but ripe with potential for creative interpretation and financial exploitation. Other production companies began to offer their own Frankenstein films and, since the release of *Curse*, few years have gone by without seeing the production of at least one new Frankenstein film, and most years saw more. Frankenstein films have engaged every genre of filmmaking including science fiction, musical, experimental, shock-horror, comedy, Blaxploitation, pornographic, children's, and even, less frequently, sober attempts to recreate the novel. Credit is due to Donald F. Glut for tracking the great proliferation of Frankenstein films and Frankenstein in popular culture long before books such as this one took the topic seriously. In his work, Glut catalogs all of the films indebted to *Frankenstein* and summarizes their plots, noting the genres to which they belong.[23] But beyond merely appearing in a great range of cinematic forms, Frankenstein films have helped to establish and inform how we understand the genres themselves.[24] Frankenstein has proven adaptable over and over in film, providing a potent artistic opportunity for our culture to reflect upon its own fears and fascinations.

Other Artistic and Popular Culture Responses to *Frankenstein*

Serious and popular artists have not confined themselves to theatrical, literary, cinematic, and graphic responses to and interventions in the Frankenstein story. Artists have additionally responded through music, from musical theatre and opera to lyric song, and through multimodal projects. The story lends itself to multiple interpretative and adaptive strategies regardless of medium in the ongoing fascination with creation, recreation, and self-invention. Popular culture tends to riff on this theme through Halloween masks that allow one to "become" the creature in its Boris Karloff identity, toys that allow children to play in a safe environment with the monstrous, and cartoons that mock the creature's capacity for harm.

Generalizations are dangerous, but we can nevertheless detect among serious artistic engagement an attraction to the creature's humanity and a sympathy for its humiliations and unjust treatment, whereas popular artistic productions tend to engage the horrific or spoof it à la the Karloff rendition. Fred Gwynne's iconic portrayal of the Karloffian creature as a gentle, bleeding-heart liberal and devoted family man allows for continuous punning on the visual undermining of his personality, which might seem to put *The Munsters* firmly in the popular cultural spoof category, except that the slights, mistakes, and comedic innuendos reflect a faithful rendering of Shelley's creature's treatment at the hands of "real" humans based on its appearance. Edmund Munster makes the viewer question the concept of a "common humanity," when a character cannot accept him as fully human. The show is revelatory in its gentle, or not-so gentle, rewriting of Shelley's novel. Similarly, the more recent *Frankenweenie* films of 1984 and 2012, both by Tim Burton, trade on the disjunction between entertainment and Mary Shelley's tragic novel. This tension is intertextually marked in Burton's two parodies, one a live-action short film starring Shelley Duvall, Sofia Coppola, and Daniel Stern with Barret Oliver as Victor, and the other a stop-motion animated feature-length film. The original choice of Shelley Duvall to play Victor's mother allows a visual reminder, through Duvall's fragile slenderness, of the novel's depiction of the frail Caroline Frankenstein. The 2012 stop motion film massages tensions between fragility and love, the distress and trauma of death, miscommunication, fear, and interspecies entanglements. Classed as a horror comedy, *Frankenweenie*'s bite is sharper than that of *The Munsters* series, and like so much of what this volume covers, these popular culture parodies of Mary Shelley's *Frankenstein* put aspects of that novel on the table that otherwise would find no expressive outlet. Giving life to these aspects is what this collection hopes to achieve.

The Afterlives of Frankenstein

This collection seeks to explore the resonant ways *Frankenstein* has transformed and been received at significant historical moments. For more than 200 years, *Frankenstein* has proven to be more than a novel or a play or a film or a breakfast cereal. It is a cultural phenomenon that has obsessed us since it first appeared in English and then reached an increasingly global readership. *The Afterlives of Frankenstein* addresses key junctures in the evolution of the Frankenstein myth, to illuminate the ways that Mary Shelley's novel has engaged the concerns of the culture that continues to be mesmerized Victor and his creation. To pursue this project, *The Afterlives of Frankenstein* is divided into four sections: (1) Cultural Reinventions, (2) Frankensteinia (also the title of a blog that constantly posts updates on all things Frankenstein[25]), (3) Playing Frankenstein, and (4) Artists Talk Back. In the first, scholars consider the cultural dialog that Mary Shelley's novel engaged with its historical moment. In the second, we look at extraordinary examples of how *Frankenstein* has suffused our cultural consciousness. The third explores how the Frankenstein myth has become something to play with, a locus for reinvention and imaginative interpretation. In the fourth section, artists respond to the Frankenstein myth today, putting it into cultural circulation in new ways that speak creatively to current anxieties and concerns.

The first section, "Cultural Reinventions," begins with David Baulch's essay which takes on the nineteenth-century reception of *Frankenstein* with Jane Louden's *The Mummy! A Tale of the Twenty-Second Century* (1827), which he describes as "already a conscious, politically informed response to Mary Shelley's *Frankenstein* (1818)." Louden's reading of Shelley's novel transforms the creaturely conception of a living, albeit reanimated, being into the nightmare of a walking corpse. What connects the two novels is less their gambit that the future may be grimmer because of its science than that it is haunted by its "zombie" past. This past surfaces in both novels through "the problem of revolutionary subjectivity," animated by psychic drives—specifically, the return of the repressed and the problem of difference. Baulch draws on the writer Damien Leone's 2015 film *Frankenstein vs The Mummy* in order to illuminate the ways in which the two novels speak to the same politico-cultural impulses. Arguing for a reading of these impulses through Marx's analysis of the French Revolution, Baulch claims that both novels illustrate Marx's theory that revolutionaries, like those of this political uprising, fail because they are unable to free themselves of the ideologies in which they were raised. Marx insists that, instead, "a truly revolutionary subject comes 'only from the future.'" Comparing these two future-oriented novels allows Baulch to locate "the faint outlines for a radically revolutionary subject divulged in the conversation between Shelley's *Frankenstein* and Louden's *The Mummy!*"

In "Frankens-Time: Frankenstein and the Temporal Origins of Artificial Life" Tobias Wilson-Bates explores the implicit connections between Shelley's imagining of an artificially constructed man as a saviour for the human race and the ongoing development of AI that also elicits anxieties over how new technologies can go awry in ways prefigured by Victor Frankenstein's creation. Connecting the industrial elements of *Frankenstein* to the contemporaneous development of Charles Babbage's prototype for computers, Wilson-Bates shows how conversant Shelley was with concurrent scientific debates about artificially produced thought and memory. He also argues that both industry and Romantic-era poetics imagined standardized time as what produces consciousness, and with it, intelligence.

In "Meiji Japan Responds to *Frankenstein*: The 1889–90 Translation 'The New Creator,' and the Illustrations" Tomoko Nakagawa reveals the fraught circumstances surrounding the first Japanese translation of *Frankenstein*. Shelley's novel first appeared in Japanese in serialized form as *Atarashiki Zobutsu-sha*, which translates as "The New Creator." The work's content and publication, Nakagawa argues, is rooted in the political and ideological debates that surrounded female education in Japan in the late nineteenth century. The magazine in which "The New Creator" appeared was founded by the teachers of the state-of-the-art Tokyo Koto Jogakko, a girls' middle school established in 1886. While the work was appearing in print, the school was summarily closed by traditionalists opposed to women's liberal education. This halted the publication of the magazine, and a truncated conclusion was printed but, to this day, the translator's identity is uncertain. Considering textual, biographical, and historical evidence, Nakagawa suggests the most likely translator. She then considers the illustrations that were included in the original translation and explicates how they engaged Shelley's novel by manipulating Japanese images to enable the reader to bridge the worlds of *Frankenstein* and late-nineteenth-century Japan.

At the other end of the historical spectrum, Hugh O'Connell treats a recent novel that also appropriates and adapts Shelley's concern with the failed past and yet the terrible prospects of the future, *Frankenstein in Baghdad* by Ahmed Saadawi. Here too the revolutionary subject of the stitched-together creature is uncontrollable, an unstable differential in the lives and society of those who created and interact with him. In "Frankenstein Goes Global: Returning the Necropolitical Gaze with *Frankenstein in Baghdad*" O'Connell explores the novel in terms of "a burgeoning Arabic science fiction (SF) tradition that mediates the complex, overlapping discursive ends of oil boom development and hi-tech modernization, neo-imperial invasion, governmental destabilization, sectarian violence, and the democratic political upheavals of the Arab Spring." He argues that because the novel adapts the "mother-text" of science fiction, *Frankenstein,* Saadawi's work allows us to rethink the implications of Shelley's work with its open geopolitical and temporal borders through "its emphasis on the bodies that comprise the creature, and its rewriting of the narrative/readerly gaze in the final scene," and the ways these focus on the necropolitics of our own globalized world.

In the volume's second section, "Frankensteinia," Sidney Berger examines the extraordinary collection of popular culture artifacts relating to the Frankenstein myth held in the Smith College rare books library in his chapter "Frankenstein in the Popular

Imagination." Smith boasts one of the premier collections of works, both literary and pop culture, dedicated to Shelley's novel and its afterlives, collectively expressing the mind-boggling ways that Frankenstein has grown as a cultural phenomenon. In his chapter, Berger surveys the ways that Boris Karloff's famous monster has dominated the visual landscape of Frankenstein merchandise as well as the exceptions that introduce Frankenstein into broader cultural discussions.

"Frankenstein Masks: Perpetuating the Monster Assemblage," by Taylor Hagood surveys and theorizes the history of Frankenstein's monster's masks. Noting that Frankenstein's creation is an assemblage of disparate body parts, Hagood explores the effect of a monster mask, itself an iconic part of the assemblage. This reaches beyond the confines of the cinematic world and is both malleable and marketable. The history of Frankenstein masks begins with one artfully designed to invoke Boris Karloff, but which actually presents the visage of Glenn Strange, the fourth actor to play the iconic monster. A mask designed to present Karloff's actual visage as the monster followed two decades later, but the purpose had changed from wearing to collecting. Cheap Halloween costumes followed, introducing masks that appealed to Karloff's legacy but with a strategic lack of fidelity for purposes of eluding copyright infringement and making money. Hagood traces the history of Frankenstein masks further to explore some of the creative ways they were made to effectively engage the myth and the marketplace.

In "'Machines Within the Machine': Definitions of Humanity in Victor LaValle's and Dietrich Smith's *Destroyer* (2017)," Andrew Shephard discusses this sequel to Mary Shelley's proto-science fictional classic *Frankenstein*. *Destroyer* reimagines many of its predecessor's concerns for our contemporary moment: LaValle and Smith reinvent the mad scientist archetype in the form of Dr. Josephine Baker, a black woman driven to resurrect her son with nanotechnology after he is gunned down by the police. Her quest contrasts with that of Frankenstein's monster, who has been driven from his arctic sanctuary of the last two centuries by humanity's lack of respect for both the environment and the living creatures which inhabit it. Both of these parallel narratives build upon the original novel's concerns with scientific ethics, the ongoing question of how we define the human, and the often troubling ways in which we, as a species, treat those we deem to be less than human.

Beginning the third section, "Playing Frankenstein," Brittany Reid's chapter "Staging Mary Shelley in Contemporary *Frankenstein* Biodramas" explores the increasingly common practice in recent theatrical productions of prominently featuring Mary Shelley herself as a character. These new dramatic works creatively blend elements of fact from Shelley's life with fiction to blur the line between Romantic lives and writing, highlighting the parallels between real and fictionalized acts of creation. Reid notes that following the string of plays written about Mary Shelley's life in the 1970s and 1980s, there was a burst of dramatic work that considered Mary and her various roles as creator: as the author of *Frankenstein*, but also as mother, collaborator, editor, and legacy builder. She introduces the term *Frankenstein* biodrama to collectively examine works that integrate elements of both *Frankenstein* and Mary Shelley's own life to collapse the traditional life/writing binary.

Robert I. Lublin provides a filmography of recent screen adaptations of the Frankenstein myth in his chapter, "The Frankenstein Myth in Twenty-First-Century

Film." From 1910 to the present day, directors and screenwriters have had a heyday with Shelley's novel, creatively introducing adaptations that fit every genre of film. The essay begins chronologically where most other studies of *Frankenstein* films end, with Kenneth Branagh's influential *Mary Shelley's Frankenstein* (1994). It then explores the extraordinary range of new films that expand and transform the Frankenstein myth on screen. The first two decades of the twenty-first century have seen two new productions that attempt to follow the basic storyline of Shelley's novel and many that offer wild departures. Looking at such films as *I, Frankenstein, FRANK3N5T31N, Victor Frankenstein*, and many more, Lublin's essay surveys and theorizes the ways these films engage a vibrant, living myth and creatively adapt it to their particular cinematic purposes.

In "The Water and the Corpse: Exploring Nature, Shelley's Echoes, and Twenty-First Century Cultural Anxieties in *The Frankenstein Chronicles*," Lorna Piatti-Farnell argues that London's Thames River is thematically central to the unfolding mystery that structures the television adaptation of *Frankenstein*. Set in 1827, the story is predicated on the creature's monstrosity rather than its humanness; the river enables monstrosity to take center stage by functioning as "an entity that within the narrative acts as both a physical placing and a symbolic channel." Insisting that "As it flows, the river brings to the surface a critical focus on preoccupations connected to ecological concerns and the continuous perils of experimental science," Piatti-Farnell explores the liminal nature of a river historically associated with floating and submerged corpses, hidden crimes, and the workings of tortured imaginations.

In Andrew Burkett's chapter on video games, "The Aesthetics of Digital Naturecultures in La Belle Games's *The Wanderer: Frankenstein's Creature* (2019)" the focus is on this experimental art game, available on the Steam/Valve platform. This narrative adventure walking simulator game allows users to take on the role of Shelley's creature as player character and witness the world through its eyes as it wakes to life and discovers the beauties as well as harsh realities of its environment. As in the original novel on which the game is based, the natural world plays an absolutely critical role in the digital game, and developers at La Belle Games worked carefully with the public humanities media network ARTE to base the design worlds of the game not only on the gothic traditions so crucial to Shelley's novel but also on representations of nature issuing from European Romantic visual artists such as Caspar David Friedrich. Burkett argues that this allows the play to problematize rather than resolve the narrative conclusively; the game world's complex, artful representation of nature becomes a dynamic experimental space rather than digital backdrop or aesthetic player surround.

The fourth section, "Artists Talk Back," begins with "*A Monstrous Circus on Frankenstein*: Mediating Shelley's Novel through John Cage's Multimedia Strategies," in which Miriam Wallace and R. L. Silver detail the performance of *Frankenstein* they created using the conventions of chance introduced by John Cage. Working with their students at the New College of Florida, Wallace and Silver rendered *Frankenstein* into mesostics, a series of poetic phrases. They then developed the mesostics into a script, and collaborated with professional musicians and actors to create a multimedia event that included a live performance, recorded and live sound, multiple performance spaces, and projected images. The result was an opportunity for performers and audiences to approach *Frankenstein* in an entirely original way that created new points of access to Shelley's work.

In "Frankenstein in Three Chords," Elizabeth Fay and James McGirr examine the different musical treatments of the Frankenstein myth from genre, harmonic, artistic, and literary perspectives. Ranging from Bob Dylan's "My Own Version of You" to operatic and popular musical treatments, the starting point for the chapter is Dylan's reimagining of the Frankenstein myth in a song that also folds in other major cultural myths operative in our contemporary moment. This deep critique then informs the subsequent comparison of other generic treatments, putting it in conversation with bands like Electric Frankenstein, teams like Edgar Winter and Rick Derringer ("Frankenstein"), productions like Richard Campbell's *Frankenstein: The Metal Opera*, and the Royal Opera House's ballet *Frankenstein*. Musicians have created both parodic and serious musical interpretations that give voice to both creator and creature, provoking questions concerning subject and object in ways that often elevate the emotional force of these entanglements to a greater degree than can be conveyed through text or image alone.

"From Frankenstein to Writing SciFi to Collage" is the artist Kate Hart's exploration of *Frankenstein*'s influence on her imagination and creative activity. The major portion of her chapter is dedicated to an examination of a series of her collage works that engage science fiction with creative activity. Working with the rich possibilities of "Shelley's medical, marvelous monster," Hart strives for "greater insight into the human condition." Using what she calls "a private science fiction writing practice" in combination with collage, Hart shows how these two creative practices allow her "to achieve artworks infused with that vital warmth Shelley pursued in the creation of her novel." The collaged creature that Victor Frankenstein brings to life has a direct analogy to Hart's art of text-and-material form collage. In discussing her own work, Hart's chapter offers the reader insight into the creative imagination in a way that helps us understand something new about Shelley's *Frankenstein*.

Conclusion and Coda

In the Coda, "Frankenstein Continued," Daniel Cook weighs in on the afterlives of a novel of astounding generativity. As he notes, Shelley's *Frankenstein* has provided creative room "for many Frankensteins. Many Monsters. Many Brides. Many sons and daughters." Cook also hoists the term "Frankenstein Network," coined by Dennis Cutchins and Dennis Perry in 2018, to cover the collective shapings of the Frankenstein myth as these extend beyond the literary, with all its attendant sequels, coquels and other forms of paranarratives, into visual art, commodity products, and wearables.[26] These all deserve to be considered Frankenfictions. Shelley's novel is murderous, Cook observes, but even so, "the Frankenstein Story is deathly but undying." *Frankenstein*'s afterlives will continue to be produced, lived into, and enjoyed for a long time to come.

With these essays we envision a more thorough engagement with readers' interest and participation in the Frankenstein myth. As a deep-seated component of our cultural imaginary, the Frankenstein myth is introduced to children at an early age through Halloween festivities, TV cartoons, toys, and games. As adults ours is a willing participation in this myth—from using "Frankenstein" adjectivally ("Frankenfruit" for GMO-modified produce) or as a synonym for "monster" to decry someone—and extends to absorbing filmic, musical, artistic, graphic novel, and fictional adaptations. These adaptations across genres of either *Frankenstein* or the Frankenstein myth ensure that "Frankenstein" emblematizes our cultural vision of past errors and future mistakes as one that will continue to haunt us and to fascinate us. We hope that if this volume does anything, it will be to spawn more conversations and more creative projects with ever-new treatments or adaptations of *Frankenstein; or The Modern Prometheus*.

Part One

Cultural Reinventions

1

"Only from the future": *Frankenstein*, *The Mummy!*, and the Ontology of Revolution

David Baulch

The Elusive Subject of Revolution

Writer, director, and make-up artist Damien Leone's direct-to-video *Frankenstein vs The Mummy* (2015) stages an unprecedented cinematic meeting between two of the most marketable and widely adapted figures in film history. Equally remarkable, the climactic battle between the film's two creatures is almost an afterthought. As brief as it is violent, there is nothing at stake historically or politically in this final showdown. Instead, *Frankenstein vs the Mummy* focuses on a romance between a Professor of the Philosophy of Medicine, who identifies himself as "Victor F_____" (Max Rhyser), and Egyptologist, Naihla Kahalil (Ashton Leigh).[1] Wresting its creatures from historical context and political purpose alike, Leone's obscure film recommends a reconsideration of Jane Louden's long-overlooked, *The Mummy! A Tale of the Twenty-Second Century* (1827)—already a conscious, politically informed response to Mary Shelley's *Frankenstein* (1818).

Leone's film replaces the problem of revolutionary subjectivity that haunts *Frankenstein* and *The Mummy!* with darkly inescapable Freudian drives that trap its characters in their respective pasts. Even though Victor's concise philosophy of medicine ("Gods [. . . .] We are them, and they are us") somehow keeps him employed as an academic, he can only satisfy his deepest yearnings for the secret of life by stitching together the dead bodies that a lascivious university janitor (and eventual involuntary brain donor) delivers to his abandoned laboratory.[2] Swept up by Victor's iconoclastic speculations on life, but sexually assaulted by its libidinally uninhibited incarnation (doubtlessly the janitor's posthumous revenge), Naihla, in turn, reveals her enduring belief in the immortal divinity of the pharaohs she dissects in a basement storeroom inexplicably labeled "Nursing Clinic Laboratory." Why? An Electra complex compels her to seek her Egyptologist grandfather, while Victor must Oedipally avenge his mother's suicide.[3] With the gruesome deaths of Victor, his creature, and the mummy, only Naihla remains alive. A Walton-like, knowing-survivor, Naihla endures as a traumatized testament to the two clichés *Frankenstein vs the Mummy* adapts from past iterations of Frankenstein and mummy narratives: man is not god, and the despotic forces that ruled ancient Egypt are still with us. Yet even this clichéd, incoherent takeaway is more about a certain repetition that defines *Frankenstein vs the Mummy*'s conception of human existence than the potential of the inhuman monsters they produce. As a story of inevitable human limitations in the face of the inhuman forces they bring into being, *Frankenstein vs the Mummy* is a testament to the political malaise endemic to the Freudian subject.

By contrast, *Frankenstein* and *The Mummy!* engage the problem of the past through a distinctly Marxist lens. As in Marx's *The Eighteenth Brumaire of Louis Bonaparte* (1851), these novels regard the emergence of revolutionary subjectivity as the prerequisite for a political revolution released from the compulsive repetition of the past.[4] *Frankenstein* and *The Mummy!* are experiments in the formation of revolutionary subjects and the strange future-oriented temporality Marx identifies as the necessary precondition for the emergence of a subject capable of revolutionary action in the nineteenth century.[5] Anticipating Marx's *The Eighteenth Brumaire*, Shelley's *Frankenstein* and Louden's *The Mummy!* emphasize that revolution in the nineteenth century is a gothic problem in search of a science-fiction solution.

In *The Eighteenth Brumaire*, Marx critiques political revolutions of the nineteenth century for their inability to conceive of subjects that escape the ideological grip of the past. For Marx, the two French revolutions fail precisely because they depend upon subjects defined by pre-existing ideologies; thus, their revolutionary efforts are always/already draped in the failures of that past. Marx delineates the conundrum in two key statements:

(1) The tradition of all dead generations weighs like a nightmare on the brains of the living.[6]
(2) The social revolution of the nineteenth century cannot take its poetry from the past but only from the future.[7]

Marx tells us that we must break from ideological repetition to free the future from the zombie hordes of ideologies past. We cannot take the content of a revolutionary future from the past; a truly revolutionary subject comes "only from the future." Thus, *Frankenstein vs the Mummy* is inert as a film because it is both possessed by Marx's first statement, and it cannot begin the formidable task of envisioning the second. *Frankenstein vs the Mummy*'s unprecedented meeting of monsters conveys nothing more than the feeling that we have been here before; Marx assures us that we have. By going back to *The Eighteenth Brumaire* to think about the future of revolution, however, I recover the faint outlines for a radically revolutionary subject divulged in the conversation between Shelley's *Frankenstein* and Louden's *The Mummy!*

Marx's gothic/sci-fi poetics of revolution finds its precursor and narrative elaboration in the very genres his text invokes to describe the failures of the French Revolutions of 1789 and 1848. While Marx's gothic zombies are mere figures for the embodied force of ideology, however, Shelley's *Frankenstein* and Loudon's *The Mummy!* present the revolutionary prospect of difference, rather than the gothic uncanny of the reanimated dead. *Frankenstein* and *The Mummy!* show us that the problem Marx grapples with is ontological as much as it is ideological. These novels thus suggest that effectively resisting the ideological circularity of revolution is only possible through the immanent emergence of ontological difference. For Shelley, Louden, and Marx, a revolutionary subject capable of resisting the ideological grip of the past is not—cannot be—human.

"'The path of my departure was free'"

In Shelley's *Frankenstein*, Victor's desire to create a creature has little to do with expanding the frontiers of the emerging sciences. Notice Victor's specific interest in creating life: "A new species would bless me as its creator and source; many happy and excellent natures would owe their being to me. No father could claim the gratitude of his child so completely as I should deserve theirs."[8] Rather than fathering a race, Leone's film entails an essentialist reanimation of the dead, rife with Freudian undertones.[9] From the viewpoint of *The Eighteenth Brumaire*, Victor's project has everything to do with the production of a revolutionary political subject unallied with the ideological entanglements of a human history: "a new species" that owes nothing to anyone but Victor. This does not mean that Frankenstein's creature is free from historically specific ideologies or, what Louis Althusser calls "ideology in general;" it does, however, mean that Shelley's novel presents its creature as an intolerable gap in the ideological "double constitution" that allows individuals to "hail" and "interpellate" each other as human subjects in the novel's late-eighteenth-century setting.[10] The creature is excluded from the ideological rituals of society, which is to say, human political order. He is not a *lusis naturae* of humanity to be shunned, but tolerated as an object of secret, self-conscious fascination. Indeed, the presence of Frankenstein's creature is almost unbearable. Victor's "new species" is cut free from the weight of Marx's "dead generations." Rather than the recovery of a deceased individual, Shelley's novel presents Victor's creature as a different kind of being altogether. As the creature tells us,

> I was dependent on none, and related to none. 'The path of my departure was free'; and there was none to lament my annihilation. My person was hideous, and my stature gigantic: What did this mean? Who was I? What was I? Whence did I come? What was my destination? These questions continually recurred, but I was unable to solve them.[11]

While Frankenstein's creature possesses the distinctly Romantic idealism and emotional intensity of his creator, this intensity does not derive from the past, for the creature literally has no past. It is not merely the case that Frankenstein's creature is produced outside of viviparous reproduction, friendless because he is hideous, and a victim of bad parenting. He is specifically inhuman. Thus, the creature is exactly right when, after studying the De Laceys, Volney, Milton, Goethe, and Plutarch, he concludes, "I was not even of the same nature as man."[12] Because he has no place in the Human origin myths or ideological rituals that constitute the experience of the Enlightenment individual, Victor's creature never achieves a retroactive subjectivation within the ideological field of the novel's historically revolutionary setting. Hence his tragic exclusion. However, precisely because he is unassimilable to the human, the creature is all the more revolutionary.

From the perspective of *The Eighteenth Brumaire*, Shelley's novel presents the temporal prolepsis necessary for Marx's "social revolution of the nineteenth century"; the creature takes the poetry of his politics "only from the future" in one key instance. First, though made from the body parts of the dead, he emerges from Victor's lab a perfect Lockean *tabula rasa*. Secondly, he takes his poetry from a verse that Percy Bysshe Shelley had yet to write in the 1790s setting of the novel's action. Recognizing that his ontological difference necessitates a revolutionary political difference from humanity, the creature quotes "Mutability," declaring, "'The path of my departure was free.'"[13] The creature forms his political identity in a single line of poetry that is literarily, if not literally, from the future, for "Mutability" is not published until 1816.[14] Note carefully how the creature's "my" takes the place of Percy's "its."[15] This revealing pronoun substitution grammatically signals his absolute difference from humanity. With "my," the creature identifies himself as the mutable inhuman of Percy's poem. Even before the creature's telling misquotation, Victor correctly quotes the entire last half of "Mutability" as he scales Mont Blanc, thereby occupying the position of the human narrator of the poem. Here, Victor recognizes mutability as an inhuman agency directing the future of humanity. It is easy to imagine why this particular sentiment is important to Victor. If humanity is neither responsible nor able to control the unpredictable changes wrought by mutability, then hope for a change for the better after the deaths of William and Justine is not completely irrational. Ironically, the mutability he invokes, in the form of the creature he created, awaits him nearby with a humanitarian supplication that is also a revolutionary political proposition that could eventually displace humanity altogether.

Through Frankenstein's creature, Percy's abstractly ideal Platonic mutability takes on a body and a concrete political purpose apart from, and antithetical to, humanity. The political threat of ontological difference suggested by the play of quotation and misquotation becomes manifest in the creature's desire for an opposite-sexed partner of his "species" with whom he can forge a social-political existence apart from that of mankind. As we know, Victor initially assents to the creature's request. For a moment, Victor and the creature replay the retelling of the scene of God granting Adam a partner in *Paradise Lost*.[16] Here, it is worth recognizing just how savvy a reader of Milton the creature is. Like Milton's God, Victor's promise of a female is a way to make "amends" for the creature's isolation.[17] The creature also exploits the moment by briefly rekindling Victor's enthusiasm for a "new species" composed of "many happy and excellent natures," but Victor's second thoughts are evidence that he realizes that the specter of revolutionary, inhuman, geo-political domination are at stake in the creature's proposition.

Anticipating Victor's political fears, the creature offers something like a non-competition clause—"If you consent [to create a female creature], neither you nor any other human shall ever see us again: I will go to the vast wilds of South America."[18] This is not a politically inconsequential choice on the creature's part. South America is a continent where British colonization was never entirely successful. Indeed, the creature's proposition resonates with the political inflection South America receives in Anna Laetitia Barbauld's *Eighteen Hundred and Eleven, A Poem*. After setting forth the image of a future London in ruins and overrun by tourists from North America,

Barbauld's prophecy turns to South America as a site for a revolutionary future. The poem echoes contemporaneous "independence movements among the Spanish colonies" to conclude "thy world, Columbus, shall be free."[19] Here, Barbauld glosses South America as the emerging challenger to European ideological and political dominance. These two popular literary references suggest that "the vast wilds of South America" are a politically loaded destination, a site from which the creature and his "species" can challenge European domination.

Victor's more politically attuned second thoughts fear a female creature who can produce a race of superior competitors engaged in colonizing the Earth. As Victor speculates, "one of the first results of those sympathies for which the daemon thirsted would be children, and a race of devils would be propagated upon the earth, who might make the very existence of the species of man a condition precarious and full of terror."[20] We should take Victor's reservation seriously—not because a race propagated by the creature would be "devils," but because a race of vegetarian beings of superior size and strength, unaffected by heat and cold, could easily displace humanity through their more sustainable and robust existence. Certainly, the creature finds his unbridgeable difference from humanity a clear cause for concern for his own political future. Given the creature's superior abilities, he sees no reason why he should be subservient to human political control: "the human senses are insurmountable barriers to our union. Yet mine shall not be the submission of abject slavery."[21] Doubtlessly, the human "sense" which is "insurmountable" to such a "union" is humanity's anthropocentric myth of its own insurmountability as a species. In short, the creature realizes any potential partnership with mankind would never be on an equal footing, and hence he refuses to be a lesser partner.

Realizing the creature's desire for a mate is so politically fraught, Frankenstein prevents Marx's "social revolution of the nineteenth century" from taking place even before Marx formalizes the necessary preconditions for such a revolution. What is lost in the revolutionary potentiality Victor forecloses by denying his creature a mate? This, we can say, is the subject of Louden's *The Mummy!* With a clear eye on Mary Shelley's first and third novels, Louden's *The Mummy!* traces out the long-term implications of a post-*Frankenstein* British history that fails to produce a revolutionary situation in *The Eighteenth Brumaire*'s sense of the term. And without the inhuman, Louden's novel confirms, there will be no revolution free from the ideological burden of humanity's past.

"The Chronicle of a Future Age"

Critics habitually understand Louden's *The Mummy!* as a conservative, moralistic satire of Shelley's *Frankenstein* and *The Last Man*.[22] Despite the absence of evidence, analyses of the novel speculate, or simply take for granted, that this was Louden's intention. As a result, the distinctly radical implications of Louden's lengthy, complex, and oblique adaptation of Shelley's *Frankenstein* have remained obscure. Plot-wise, the major difference between the potentially revolutionary monster/subjects in *Frankenstein* and *The Mummy!* lies paradoxically in their greatest thematic similarity: the reanimation of dead flesh into inhuman creatures. While Victor's composite creature really is a scientific breakthrough in the novel, the goal, and only apparent success, of Louden's Edric is the reanimation of Cheops's mummified remains. Moreover, Edric's failure to actually reanimate the mummy of Cheops produces the final sense of moral certainty in *The Mummy!*. By contrast, Victor's success is the root of all of *Frankenstein*'s moral ambiguity. The particular difference in these texts is nonetheless indicative of a similar position with regard to human life. Even as these novels agree that humanity should neither seek nor employ the secret of life, they render explicit the political potentiality of ontological difference implicit in Marx's *The Eighteenth Brumaire*. Thus, on the crucial question of the morality of bestowing or restoring life, *The Mummy!* aligns with *Frankenstein*: The secret of life is beyond human wisdom because it is in excess of human experience, and, in *The Mummy!*, at least, even the grasp, of humanity.

For Lisa Hopkins, the mummy of Cheops is a moral and political embodiment of Louden's political opposition to *Frankenstein*: "*The Mummy!* at times seems like a quasi-comic inversion of *Frankenstein* in which, so far from being ostracized, the revenant immediately becomes immersed in British political affairs."[23] Even as a "quasi-comic inversion," Hopkins' reading of the novel simultaneously depends on the Mummy also being recognizable as the authentic voice of timeless moral truth in the novel. Such a reading, however, overlooks the extent to which *The Mummy!* satirically doubles down on the conservative politics, monarchy, and morality its author is presumed to advocate. *The Mummy!* is a satire of the legacy of revolution that repeats its own political past— the satire of a future British monarchy that must be saved from corruption by a singularly nefarious despot from the past. It is as if things are so politically bad in Britain in the twenty-second century that a corrupt pharaoh must return from the past to save them. At the same time, the novel functions as a farce of the timelessness of the morality it appears to endorse through Cheops. In this sense, *The Mummy!* underscores the necessity of linking radical revolutionary potential and ontological difference, just as *Frankenstein* does. Waiting for moral salvation from a transcendent being that ultimately works through Cheops is as cruel as it is laughable.

A reading of *The Mummy!* that gives its satire free rein reveals a text that extends *Frankenstein*'s anticipation of Marx's stipulation that the revolution of the nineteenth century can take its content "only from the future" by presenting a future that fails to break the past's ideological grip. Revolution fails to break with the past in *The Mummy!* because the "tradition of all the dead generations," in the form of the Mummy himself, literally "weighs like a nightmare on the brain of the living" within Louden's novel. To take one's poetry or prose from the future, it must be, as Marx says, "*only* from the future." The satirical point of *The Mummy!* is that the political form of a revolutionary future is probably not going to be established by a despot from the past brought back to life to perform the terms of his own personal redemption. Why, if the moral tone of nineteenth-century politics is disappointing to Louden personally, does her novel insist on an even more disappointing and absurd resolution to the problem of reestablishing moral standards as something its author, according to Hopkins "ultimately...endorses"? Such a position depends on delimiting the scope of its satire under the aegis of Louden's presumed beliefs.

My argument hence suggests that the satiric impulse of *The Mummy!* should be read as more comprehensive and harder hitting with regard to monarchy than critics such as Hopkins and Alan Rauch suspect. Rather than making monarchy more attractive by implicitly contrasting it with the difficult moral questions of *Frankenstein*, *The Mummy!* begins by making a joke of what can be accomplished by revolution in the first place. If, as *The Mummy!* maintains, human nature remains the same throughout time, then there is little we can hope for from political revolution. In fact, hopes for a revolutionary future are dashed in the second sentence of the novel: "Numerous changes had taken place for some centuries in the political state of the country, and several forms of government had been adopted and destroyed, till, as is generally the case after violent revolutions, they all settled down into an absolute monarchy."[24]

The first paragraphs of *The Mummy!* describe British history between the nineteenth and twenty-first centuries as a series of "violent revolutions" that eventually return the country to something like its late-fifteenth-century political condition, when power was firmly in the hands of the sovereign, and Catholicism reigned as the state religion.[25] Here, the first paragraph is key. It provides a defense of Great Britain's status quo in 2126, just before the crisis of succession brought on by the death of Queen Claudia, even though she is described as one who "never perform[ed] an action worthy of being recorded."[26] The very terms of this defense suggest satire masquerading as future wisdom. According to the narrator of *The Mummy!*, the British political ideal is one wherein the country has only come to enjoy "peace and tranquility under the absolute domain of a female sovereign."[27] The narrator's opening move is to state that political and moral repression is the chief source of social harmony. If British "peace and tranquility" can only be achieved by the absolute rule of a virgin female sovereign, then it is worth considering whether the narrator herself is not also an object of the novel's satire, rather than Louden's surrogate; after all, Britain's sovereign at the novel's end is King Roderick of Ireland, married to Elvira of England.[28] The novel follows this paradox immediately with one that is even more glaring: religious certainty can only be achieved through a return to Catholicism. Of the British church/state relationship in 2126, the narrator observes the following:

> The religion of the country was as mutable as its government; and in the end, by adopting Catholicism, it seemed to have arrived at nearly the same result: despotism in the state, indeed, naturally produces despotism in religion; the implicit faith and passive obedience in the one case, being the best of all possible preparatives for the absolute submission of mind and body necessary in the other.[29]

The narrator's history of the future claims 2126 as a nearly perfect state insofar as it returns to its pre-1534 condition.[30] While the importance of monarchy is a legitimate and widely held social concern in 1826, it is hard to imagine that a return to Catholicism or an Irish king would seem even remotely plausible. Regardless of whatever sentimental attachments to the long-term future of the monarchy or a return to Catholicism are concerned, the novel's invocation of both is clearly satirical; these institutions are heralded specifically because they have proven themselves to be extremely effective as ideological and repressive state apparatuses.

Granted, the narrator's shocking advocacy of despotism in religion and politics as the recipe for social tranquility in the first paragraph is balanced by a several-page comic send up of the dangers of the French Revolutionary program and a classless society. In *The Mummy!*'s satire, however, the real root of Britain's future social corruption is universal education. After education becomes compulsory, the lower classes echo Frankenstein's creature as they refuse enslavement: "We will be slaves no longer; we will all be masters."[31] Thus, education is a problem specifically when it becomes a potential conduit to the political emancipation of lower-class subjects. Education produces two main political results: (1) the lower classes become increasingly aware that differences in social class are an arbitrary political imposition, and (2) as they become aware of the arbitrary nature of British social order, they become less willing to provide menial labor to support the social structure without enjoying its benefits. Education turns servants into Marx's revolutionary class. For these reasons, the narrator concludes that "a division of labour and a distinction of ranks were absolutely necessary to civilization; and sought out their ancient nobility, to endeavor to restore something like order to society."[32] The effort to thwart the effects of education is at the center of the satirical political return to monarchy enforced in *The Mummy!*

The active repression of the desire to learn is no small part of what makes *Frankenstein*'s political vision tragic and *The Mummy!*'s political vision thoroughly farcical. Robert Walton's eventual resistance to the desire for new knowledge is crucial to the tragedy of *Frankenstein*. Fascinated by Victor's claim to know the secret of life, Walton "endeavoured to gain from Frankenstein the particulars of his creature's formation."[33] Victor refuses, and Walton never records himself as asking a second time. Victor successfully teaches Walton to sublimate his desire for knowledge and power into submission in exchange for the certainties of hearth and home. This is the lesson that prepares Walton for his ultimately sympathetic response to the threat of mutiny among his crew.

Likewise, in the last pages of *The Mummy!*, Edric's desire for knowledge, like Walton's, is suppressed. As Edric tells Cheops, "I do still desire to know the secrets of the tomb."[34] The Mummy's response resembles Frankenstein's response to Walton: "Has anything but misery attended your former researches? And can anything but misery attend the knowledge you now covet? ... Seek not to pry into secrets denied to man!"[35] What follows is fascinating. Even though the secret of life is "denied to man," Cheops now nonetheless tauntingly offers this forbidden knowledge to Edric. Why would Cheops offer Edric the knowledge forbidden to his species? Because Cheops senses that he has already won the argument. Of course, Edric refuses. As he tells the Mummy, "Then I no longer seek to hear them; for, even weak as you esteem me, I can learn wisdom from experience. Thus, then, I tear the tormenting doubts, which so long have haunted me, from my mind, and bid them farewell for ever!"[36] Comically, Edric is willing to be persuaded out of thought. If he has surrendered the potential to create life, he has also foreclosed the possibility of the emergence of an unprecedented being, like Frankenstein's creature, who is no longer an inheritor of the "nightmare" of ideology's enslavement to the past. Thus, not only has Cheops overseen Elvira's rightful succession to the British Throne, but he has also effectively sealed off the potential for the emergence of an ontologically different and revolutionary subject in 2126. Rather than looking to an unprecedented future, to a political subject who is "only from the future," Edric's future is now firmly defined by the past. Instead of experiencing the ideological persistence of the political past as a "nightmare," as Marx puts it, Edric has resolved not to feel "haunted" by "tormenting doubts."[37] Abjuring his quest for the secret of life, Edric also forsakes the potential for the emergence of a political alternative to monarchy.

If, in most of *The Mummy!*, Cheops' mission appears to secure the rightful Elvira on the throne, in the last pages of the novel his true purpose is suddenly revealed as more politically sinister. It is not until Edric surrenders his ambitions for knowledge that Cheops considers his task complete. When Edric refuses the secret of life that Cheops offers, the Pharaoh's eyes respond by "beaming with joy."[38] Only at this point does he announce, "my task is accomplished. I have at last found a reasonable man. I honour you, for you can command yourself, and now you may command me."[39] It is hard to miss the satirical twist. The man of "reason" is the man who seeks neither knowledge nor social change. Precisely because he does not seek change, Cheops determines that Edric is fit to "command." This freedom to "command" amounts to asking two questions before Cheops returns to an inert state. First, Edric asks Cheops to relate his sordid personal history as a despot. Here, Cheops reveals that, even now—after his redemptive mission is accomplished—he is driven by a "never-dying fiend" and that he internally "burns with unquenchable and never-ceasing torment."[40] Second, seeming to forget he appeared to raise Cheops, Edric asks, "Was it a human power that dragged you from the tomb?"[41] Just as Cheops reenters his sarcophagus, he gives Edric the answer; the experiment failed: "The power that gave me life could alone restore it."[42] Cheops reveals Edric's scientific failure as humanity's moral and political triumph. It is a dark triumph, for the British political landscape of 2126 is every bit as entombed by the gothic nightmare of repetition as Marx described in 1851. By contrast, the story of Mary Shelley's creature is the literal embodiment of Marx's revolutionary subject, a subject of ontological difference and mutability. The tragedy of the creature is the loss of this potential. *Frankenstein*'s science-fiction vision of the tragic loss of a politically revolutionary subject who takes his "poetry only from the future" repeats itself as the satire of revolution as recurrence in *The Mummy!*

Inconclusive Endings: The Future of Revolution

I have labored over the through-going satire of *The Mummy!* precisely because it underscores the novel's intervention in revolutionary discourse as an oblique adaptation of *Frankenstein*, rather than its satirical disavowal. As read through the lens of Marx's enigmatic formulation of the revolutionary subject in *The Eighteenth Brumaire*, Louden's adaptation of the Frankensteinian problem of the revolutionary subject suggests that the problem of revolution in the nineteenth century is ontological, as well as ideological. For revolution to be an ideological departure from the past, it must take its subject, as well as its political content, "only from the future."

Leone's *Frankenstein vs the Mummy*, however, founds its adaptation of both Frankenstein and Mummy narratives in terms of a Freudian subject that expresses the dark, barely unconscious motivations of its characters as the driving forces of an inevitable repetition that is never quite engaged with material/political history. This is a theoretical limitation internal to *Frankenstein vs the Mummy*, and it is a symptom of our cultural moment, for in the era of "capitalist realism," it is impossible to imagine alternatives to capitalism that are not already subsumed by its forces and commoditized by its most enthusiastic resistors.[43] The psycho-analytics of this repetition are clearly on display in the final scene the film. Here, William, one of the students Victor has inspired in his lectures yet personally spurned, locates Victor's secret abandoned laboratory, but only after Naihla has burned and largely destroyed the equipment.[44] William picks up Victor's lab notes, burned to illegibility. Then, he finds Victor's battered digital voice recorder. He presses the play button, and the whole story starts to repeat itself. William listens, enraptured. In a sense, he has already reanimated Victor: "Tuesday January 14, 2013. My name is Victor Frankenstein, and I'm about to embark on a journey of discovery that will change the world forever . . . ."[45] Walton's experiences foreclose the revolutionary potential of a creature like that of Mary Shelley's Victor, just as Edric does in Louden's *The Mummy!*, but *Frankenstein vs The Mummy* does not have to. Two hundred years later, down the seemingly endless adaptive chain of classic monster films, *Frankenstein vs The Mummy* exists to reproduce itself.

Because *Frankenstein vs the Mummy* focuses upon the Freudian narratives of its human principles, it misses the radical potential of Victor's creation. The battle royal between Frankenstein's creature and the Mummy is meaningless because the film invests nothing in either of these monsters as subjects. *Pace* Leone, then, it is not *Frankenstein vs the Mummy* that should interest us, but rather *Frankenstein and The Mummy!* that should command our attention, for together they confirm the truly monstrous dimensions of the proposition of revolution in *The Eighteenth Brumaire*. If there is a politically revolutionary movement in Marx's terms, then it is certain that these revolutionaries will be inhuman, unassimilable to the ideological fields of past or present.

2

Frankens-Time: *Frankenstein* and the Temporality of Artificial Life

Tobias Wilson-Bates

Recent studies like Eileen Hunt Botting's *Artificial Life After Frankenstein* (2021) have made it increasingly clear how much our current discourse on artificial life owes to the ideas amplified by Mary Shelley's landmark novel. The story now operates as a *de facto* intertext for almost all conversations about science, technology, and the ethical obligations of creation. However, Shelley's novel does not only present the topic of artificial life, but also engages with its foundational cultural structures. By examining how Shelley manipulates Time in the novel via its found text frame, layered story structure, and temporal intertexts, we can also begin to understand how this novel on artificial being was *itself* programmed. Megan Ward describes the algorithmic processes involved in the production of realist characters as a corrective to the notion that artificiality is necessarily inhuman: "To be like a human is not the antithesis of the machine but one form of its embodiment."[1] In *Frankenstein* (1818), both Shelley's creature and the novel act as mirrors to this process of artificially producing the human, a concern that was becoming popular in the period. There is a long tradition of reading *Frankenstein* as a "birth myth" in which Victor Frankenstein seeks to become a new form of mother by creating a race to whom "No father could claim the gratitude of his child so completely as I should deserve their's."[2] The novel, however, can also be read as an initial foray into the intentional manufacture of a thinking object, an intelligent machine.

In 1824 the President of the Astronomical Society of London, Henry Colebrooke, commended the efforts of the society's controversial mathematician, Charles Babbage. Babbage was undertaking the creation of his Difference Engine, which Colebrooke imagined would usher in a new technological era: "In other cases, mechanical devices have substituted machines for simpler tools or for bodily labour ... But the invention to which I am adverting comes in place of mental exertion: it substitutes mechanical performance for an intellectual process." In other words, "Mr. Babbage's invention puts an engine in place of the computer."[3] In his study of Babbage and artificial intelligence, Simon Schaffer notes the interesting etymological inversion at the end of this quote, remarking that "computer" in this instance actually means human.[4] Implicit in the creation of the Difference Engine and in his later Analytical Engine is Babbage's claim that a meaningful portion of human thought may be replicated through algorithmic calculations.[5] If not a fully fledged mechanical brain, Schaffer illustrates how Babbage and his later collaborator, Ada Lovelace, continually anthropomorphized the machine's actions. In 1838 Babbage conceded that "in substituting mechanism for the performance of operations hitherto executed by intellectual labour ... the analogy between these acts and the operations of mind almost forced upon me the figurative employment of the same terms. They were found at once convenient and expressive, and I prefer to continue their use."[6] Hence he was committed to phrases such as "the engine knows" to describe its predetermined move from one calculation to the next. The machine might be an automaton, but it carried intelligence. Lovelace put the issue like this: "although it is not itself the being that reflects, it may yet be considered as the being which executes the conceptions of intelligence."[7] This quote, from Lovelace's notes on Luigi Menabrea's writing on the analytical engine, was part of a larger project of Lovelace's that sought to develop the concept of "'Poetical Science,' in which scientific logic would be driven by the imagination."[8] The code that Lovelace developed to illustrate her ideas concerning the analytical engine has often been referred to as the first computer language, but her underlying assumptions echo the task that Shelley took on in her novel: the representation of intelligence and the ethical dilemmas over the production of an operational mind.

Lovelace was not alone in imagining ways that the human mind could be understood and replicated via analysis. John Herschel, Babbage's longtime collaborator, focused on time as the constant capable of laying bare a formula for the activity of the mind. Thought and memory, for Herschel, involved the extension of intention over time. A schematic of his theory reveals the conceptual fixity of time in examining thought[9] (see Table 2.1). As the denominator in these equations, time produces the illusion of memory and intention as extra-temporal elements. What Herschel obscures in such an equation is a parallel theory of temporality, time as clock time, measurable and standard in its operations and effects on human experience.[10]

In the double existence of "artificial intelligence" as signifying both a conversation about computing and emergent consciousness, one may find the unsettled question of time in the industrial period. By flattening time so as to combine experience with a unit of measurement, the industrial era's "annihilation of space with time" coopted abstract notions of time into a denominator for the purpose of equating previously unlike units.

Frankenstein is a story that wrestles with the rapid transformations in science and industry that were altering the dimensions of early nineteenth-century culture and representation. In the novel, Shelley confronted the difficulty of not just representing the production of new life, but also how that creation would be expressed as textual

Table 2.1 Herschel's formula for consciousness

1. Mental (Motive) → Memory X Time = Physical (Force) → Matter X Time
         — Action →   — Movement →
2. Intention → Will → Effort
3. Intention (carrying Motive) = Motion (carrying Force)
         — Time →   — Time →

information. Each of the novel's frames executes proto-scientific forms of knowing that are irreparably compromised by their simultaneous existence as self-reported *Bildung* narratives. Central to this difficulty is the problem of representing new modes of industrial time, the organizing principle of the competing media that make up the novel's found-text framework. The novel's polemic, then, is not merely the question of creation; it also illuminates how existence under new forms of temporality undermine the possibility of rendering that creation objectively. The new scientific frontiers of galvanism and polar exploration do not offer the reader speculative futures, but rather resurface unanswered polemics about authorship, realism, and comprehending human perception of time. By figuring time into the text as a problem, the novel highlights the patterns that came to regulate the lived and imagined experience of technological modernity.

These practices are presented throughout the text as an issue of representation. Readers receive the creature's narrative of emergent self-awareness third- or even fourth-hand via a series of transcribed letters reporting past conversations and experiences. One is asked to understand the creature's nature only through recitations of its thoughts and actions, and to recognize, as Mikhail Bakhtin describes the novel genre generally, "the image of man in the process of becoming."[11] The novel, though, only describes an *image* of a process, a phrase fraught with the paradox of a two-dimensional medium describing an ongoing action. Shelley coordinates an intersection between the representational goal of the *Bildung* genre, the artistic production of represented human growth, and the Romantic notion that poetic expression, as described by Samuel Taylor Coleridge, is an echo of a primary and original act of creation.[12] By writing a formation novel about a new, technological act of creation, Shelley creates a text that interrogates mechanical reproduction, the *Bildung* genre, and the Romantic imaginary at once.

The Politics of Non-Linear Time

Shelley's construction of the complex layers of temporal structure in *Frankenstein* highlights how time as an idea and time as a practice in both the public and private spheres were undergoing conceptual shifts recognizably present in both industrialism and Romanticism. The latter engaged this subject with a series of thought experiments that sought to speculatively explore the reducible characteristics of human thought. In his notebooks, Coleridge postulates "What is Nature? Multeity coerced into Number and Rhythm ... How? ... by the WORD, and by Every Word that Proceedeth in and thro' the same—Call the Words Numbers numerant, Living Numbers; or Ideas; or Laws; or Spirits; or ministrant Angels;—if you please & which you please. The terms are all equivalent."[13] By flattening these terms, Coleridge reiterates the familiar transcendentalism of the Romantic movement. At the same time, he proposes the mind as a mechanism that produces meaning intelligible across a range of informational modes. Inherent in this proposition is the germ idea of computational intelligence. All expression is ultimately information, and organized mechanical expressions of numbers are explicitly the equivalent of words, ideas, laws, spirits, or angels. By placing

Nature prior to its expressive vehicle, Coleridge makes the human mind only an incidental participant in the manifestation of intelligence.

While, for Coleridge, the conversion of words, ideas, and numbers into a single code allowed for potential access to and expression of a higher spiritual realm of creation, more empirical thinkers like Babbage and Herschel explicitly imagined such an equivalence as a new form of industrial philosophy. They made a project of visiting factories and developing an analytical belief that language and thought could be translated into a set of mathematic symbols. As William Ashworth describes in his work on the industrial mind, their studies led them to the conclusions that "the mind was rendered visible and open to empirical scrutiny in exactly the same way as any other object of scientific study or manufacturing site. The way was then opened to the possibility of artificially building the same kind of intelligence into a machine."[14] The Romantics were likewise interested in what it meant to render the mind visible. Wordsworth's seminal project *The Prelude, or, Growth of a Poet's Mind* (1850) attempts to reveal the workings of his own consciousness stretched out across the canvas of his first three decades. While no one would mistake Wordsworth's poetry for Babbage's diagrammed factory operations, the Romantics nonetheless wrestled with a parallel form of inscribing thoughts as information.

In "Mediating Monstrosity: Media, Information, and Mary Shelley's *Frankenstein*," Andrew Burkett describes the central scientific discovery of the novel as focused on media and equivalence. Burkett argues that for Victor Frankenstein "information is best understood as a virtuality abstracted from (though indeed connected complexly to) the material substrates that may variously embody it. Resultantly, Victor understands information as dematerialized and abstract (though nonetheless 'real'). Otherwise stated, Victor perceives *matter as a medium* for embodying information."[15] This realization of matter as a medium is materially echoed by the novel itself. Burkett describes the "parallels between the monster's fragmented body and the textual body of the novel as a sutured-together information structure and mediated narrative apparatus."[16] Extending Burkett's thinking further, the novel also constitutes an initial foray into a form of realism that predicates its reality on the Romantic and industrial temporality built out of a conscious equivalence between various sets of information that proposes time not as storytelling time, but as self-conscious groupings of data. Victor's various meditations on life, electricity, and information constitute one level of the novel's diegesis, while Shelley also organizes these various materials into a material substrate via the intentional artificial production of time. Her narrative experiment pays careful attention to the production of the sutures that hold together the text even while exposing its artificiality. The pauses for epistolary time cues, transitions of narrator, and layered recitations of memories within memories create what Elisha Cohn describes as subtle disturbances "in received categories of thinking, knowing, and doing that organize development."[17] Time in the novel is never only developmental, but always also influenced by the presence of the storyteller's perspective and the heavy materiality of the found-text framing device of the novel.

When reading *Frankenstein*, we must be aware that the novel's argumentative work extends beyond the character and story all the way out to Shelley's structural decision making, and that these decisions held further weight given their relation to fictional and cultural intertextual forms. Criscilla Benford argues that the novel's multilevel structure intentionally resists interpretive closure and traditional strategies of coherence. At stake in this resistance is a form of reading that is recursive as opposed to linear.[18] Recursion is a mathematical concept that signals a structure which prompts a meta-numerical response to itself at the level of material. The page numbers, letter dates and time cues of the novel are immediately objects drawn into question by a structure that challenges linear readings. Benford claims that time in the novel and the distinct modes of temporality emerging from its non-linear rhythms form an additional level of textual meaning. To read *Frankenstein* is to become incorporated in alternate notions of temporality.

Broadly speaking, the Romantics were fascinated by the effect of temporal patterns on the reader.[19] Elizabeth Freeman traces the way that the "virtual coherence" of the family letter-writing that makes up the body of the novel is undermined by the temporal gap between the moment of writing and the moment of receiving and reading a letter, such that adjacent pages may contain both Justine Moritz's happy inclusion into the family and her imprisonment for the murder of William.[20] Challenging normative representations of time in a text is also a way to reveal the social pressures inherent in representing self and family as information structures. The novel's temporal structure signals one of Shelley's intentional interventions, and the politics of time were clearly planned extensively and minutely, as Essaka Joshua makes clear in her exhaustive study of diegetic time in the novel: "Aside from the issue of communication the novel's narrative structure raises anxieties about time."[21] Joshua pushes back against Elizabeth Nitchie's suggestion that Mary Shelley "had difficulty sustaining a long, involved plot" by displaying the novel's clarity as an organized resistance to linearity that proposes a complex form of realism.[22] Shelley includes references to extrinsic historical events as well as contemporary publications such as Coleridge's *Rime of the Ancient Mariner* to initiate tension between situating the novel's temporality as existing in relation to "real" non-fictive time in conjunction with the closed number system of the novel. Such a system, Joshua posits, moves beyond the biographical arguments that have been proposed by critics to a system that challenges the reader to reconsider time via extensive calculation and hypothesis.[23] Far from creating a complex coherence, though, Shelley's extensive planning seems to intentionally create a form of textually destabilizing fragmentation.[24]

The Fallibility of Time in *Frankenstein*

Every page of *Frankenstein* is coordinated within the novel as a whole via letter dates and cues that create repetition in meaningful temporal departures and dissonances. These marks are inadequate for understanding the novel's temporal play, or rather, their failure to function as "real" representations of the time of Captain Walton's inscriptions serves to illustrate how careful representation of experience is always contingent upon the means of its representation. At one point Walton remarks that "Frankenstein discovered that I made notes concerning his history: he asked to see them, and then himself corrected and augmented them in many places."[25] Victor carries letters with him as well that are directly transcribed into Walton's textual record, but that indicate precisely the disconnection between the moments of transmission, reception, and consumption that fragment the particular temporal moment of a letter. These do more than disrupt a simple notion of time; they posit a modern relationship to time as a representation insistently masking and homogenizing an underlying heterogeneity.

At the end of Volume II, Chapter II, the creature pleads for Frankenstein's patience: "Listen to my tale; when you have heard that, abandon or commiserate me, as you shall judge that I deserve. But hear me."[26] When his creator rages against the sight of him, the creature places his hands over the scientist's eyes. The erasure of Victor's vision in relation to the creature's speech prefaces the upcoming shift of narrative frame as the story transitions from Frankenstein as the first-person speaker to the creature. For the reader, this is the third autobiographic fragment, following the growth and maturation stories of Walton and Victor. The creature's description of its own formation narrative is initiated by a plea to forego visual for oral information. In other words, the creature seeks to replace Victor's immediate experience of the moment with his own represented experience of the past.

This substitution of representation for immediate experience performs a proto-version of Alan Turing's "imitation game," what we now call a Turing Test. In his paper, "Computing Machinery and Intelligence," Turing proposes that we should move past the impossible question to prove "Can machines think?" to the verifiable experiment of whether a person is able to pass a blind test differentiating human and machine thought as it is expressed in language.[27] In an aside oddly reminiscent of the monster's plea, Turing remarks that the study must be done blindly because "we do not wish to penalize the machine for its inability to shine in beauty competitions."[28] Implicit in Turing's essay is a conceptual division between the information that can be conveyed via a tool of representation and the hazy metaphysical difficulty of recognizing "real" thought in another being. Burkett postulates that Victor's essential recognition is that matter *is* medium, which would naturally imply that lightning *is* life and speech *is* thought. Implicit in this combination is the collapsing of Cartesian mind-body dualism, and an echoing of Coleridge's equation of manifold terms with their underlying identity. The machine that acts is the mind that thinks. This simple conflation continues into our contemporary technological fields in which thinkers like Rodney Brooks, former head of MIT's Artificial Intelligence Laboratory, intentionally describe the human mind as hardware and software, while offering the term "specialness" to denote the false binary that separates humans from machines.[29] Shelley's novel accepts a version of this idea by allowing that a fully cognitive creation can exist, and speculates further about how it would enter into reflection about the nature of its own existence and how to represent its "life." Niculae Gheran reviews at length the indebtedness of the idea of the robot and artificial life to the publication and dissemination of *Frankenstein* not only in the literary tradition, but also in public and scientific debate discussing the ethics and pragmatic concerns of scientific creation.[30] As a predecessor to modern ideas of creations that threaten the "specialness" of human beings, *Frankenstein* is a foundational text for its technological framing and its ethical complexity.

The creature, attempting to communicate to Victor his ethical duty to his creation, must first navigate its own convoluted relationship to time. After coming to terms with its tangle of sensory perception, the creature relates its primary impressions as varying between light and dark. It then comes to terms with the sun as "the gentle light" that "stole over the heavens." Followed by a larger perception of how "Several changes of day and night passed, and the orb of night had greatly lessened when I began to distinguish my sensations from each other."[31] The use of the first person places the reader inside the creature's consciousness, which still displays a primitive relationship with time several pages later when the creature has come to live in the hovel alongside his beloved exiles, "having remained during the space of several revolutions of the moon in my hovel."[32] This diurnal understanding of time emerges as the creature develops a seasonal knowledge: "As the sun became warmer, and the light of day longer, the snow vanished, and I beheld the bare trees and the black earth."[33] Finally, as the creature's "thoughts become more active" in relation to continued experience of itself and its voyeuristic empathy with the French exiles, "the past was blotted from my memory, the present was tranquil, and future gilded by bright rays of hope."[34] While these conceptions of temporality are reported to us from the position of the mature creature reiterating its production in time, they also propose alternative forms of temporal experience and perception. The patterns of light and darkness or the sensations of snow, trees, and earth are counter-temporalities to the dated material of the novel's found texts or even the regular page numbers that organize the reader's linear motion.

In her careful representation of the creature's recitation, Shelley offers the reader the problem of information and transmission from yet another perspective. Readers are forced to become concerned with time as they find themselves sensually confronted with its plasticity. Herschel's equation, which assumes the movement of consciousness occurring above a denominator of standard time, is contradicted in the text by a time that is only ever relational via sensation and contingency, uncertain in its communication. The problem of Victor's reduction of life to electricity is echoed by the problem of reducing the novel's information to the linear passage of time, or even to a recognizable pattern of time that would establish a consistent rhythm. Thus, readers enact the position of beings concerned with time's plasticity even as they are reading a first-person account of a being coming into an awareness of time as relational.

The reader's own experience is controlled by the presumed frame beyond the outermost framing device of the novel, the receiver of Walton's letters. Margaret's and the reader's interaction with the text is tightly bound to the performance of narrative time, most notably the moments when Walton signs off on any particular letter or journal entry. This interaction can be graphed so that we could imagine distinct units of text laid out over a graph with x-y axes of narrative length (roughly number of words) and in-narrative linear time (from December 11 when Walton writes his first letter to September 12 when he concludes his writing). This graph allows us a very simple narratological representation of how time is paced in the novel in proportion to the physical or embodied time necessarily expended in the act of reading. This time spent, the necessary pace of consumption and its interruptions, is the base experience shared between the reader and Margaret and organizes the focus and intensity placed on particular moments in the text. In other words, we are made forcefully aware of the dissonance between times inside and outside the text. A quick calculation of the ratios created in such a scheme reveals the underlying pacing of the text (see Table 2.2). There are 11 letter dates (Dec 11, Mar 28, Jul 7, Aug 5, Aug 13, Aug 19, Aug 26, Sept 2, Sept 5,

Sept 7, Sept 12) which we may organize in ratio to the 11 divisions of words (1,195 words, 1,307 words, 296 words, 1,377 words, 808 words, 64,788 words, 1,179 words, 318 words, 779 words, 42 words, and 2,922 words).

Table 2.2 Number of words per letter

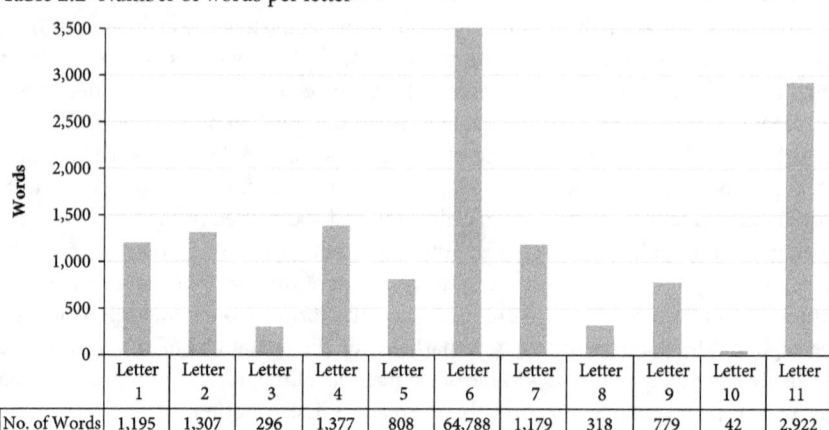

	Letter 1	Letter 2	Letter 3	Letter 4	Letter 5	Letter 6	Letter 7	Letter 8	Letter 9	Letter 10	Letter 11
No. of Words	1,195	1,307	296	1,377	808	64,788	1,179	318	779	42	2,922

Letters in chronological order

The massively disproportionate data point that appears in the middle of the graph is the piece that changes the temporal arch of the story from a simple movement through a feeling of beginning, middle, and end to a frame for a central moment of stasis. Letter 6, the letter that contains the creature's story, dwarfs the other ten letters that comprise the novel combined. The other letters contain 10,223 words in comparison to the 64,788 of letter 6. A close view of the graph reveals the relative stability of the other letters' contents over the course of the novel. The letters even appear to have a general pattern of rising and falling lengths. Resizing the graph to accommodate the outlier, Letter 6, reveals another interpretation of the novel's patterned temporality (Table 2.3).

Table 2.3 Number of words per letter: Resized

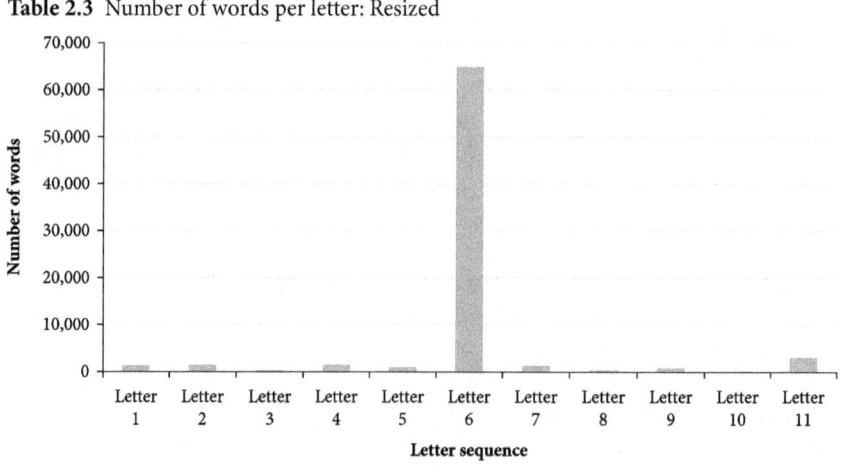

Resized to accommodate Letter 6, the other letters lose almost all relative character as distinct time frames. Instead, the novel becomes dominated by the stories of Victor and the creature. The reader spends such a disproportionate amount of time with this element of the text that the frame narrative seems to disappear entirely. What small fragments remain visible on the chart appear relatively uniform. In other words, Shelley's temporal choices create an underlying emphasis not just on the act and consequences of creation, but also on the effect this event has on the novel's relationship to time that may have appeared to be narratively significant prior to the event. To put this in perspective, if the novel were a poem, it would contain a stanza six times as long as the rest of the poem combined, and this single stanza would likely compromise the reader's ability to identify the significant rhythms of the poem.

Table 2.4 Words per day

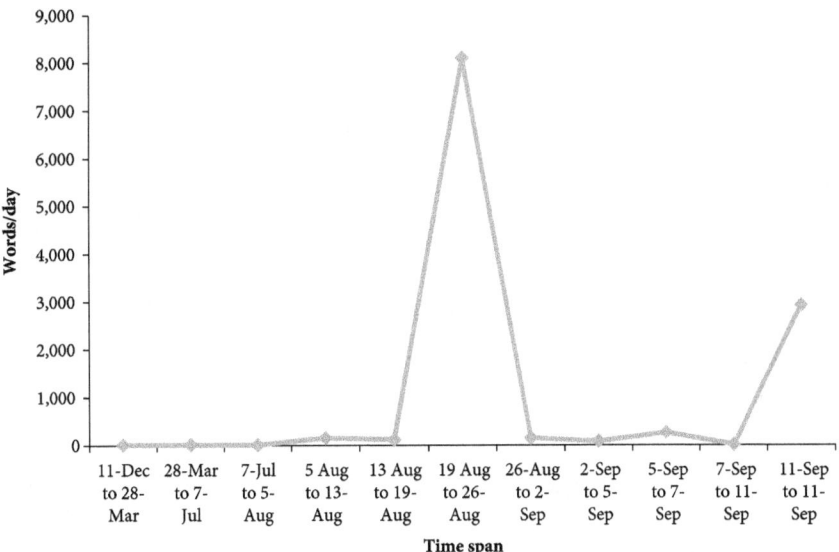

The other major effect of Letter 6 is an immense shift in the relationship between the rate of diegetic time that passes over its allotted number of pages (Table 2.4). Since time passes over the course of each letter, the text constructs a speed out of the spatialized time of the page that may be loosely calculated by words measured against days. Once again Letter 6 skews the graph, but this time the chart does not simply measure the size of the letter in relation to the other letters, but rather the slowness of time within the central letter of the novel. Time passes at a relatively stable rate, especially through the first five letters of the text (Letter 1: 11.06 words per day, Letter 2: 12.81 w/d, Letter 3: 9.87 w/d, Letter 4: 153 w/d, Letter 5: 115.43 w/d) before slowing down immensely to 8,098.5 words per day in Letter 6. The graph also reveals that the final letter, written in a single day, only comprised of that day and also mentioning the creature, ends the novel by once again stretching out time over a relatively large number of words. This makes clear one of Shelley's central aesthetic strategies in the novel:

controlling the reader's experience of time by creating both temporal rhythms that define an identifiable pace for the text, and then reorganizing the reader's relationship to time by intentionally inserting temporalities that bring such a rhythmic, standard temporal order into creative tension with the massively discordant temporality of creating a new being. The new being is, in a sense, a new temporality that forces the reader into a drastically new relationship with time. By graphing the deceleration of time as the reader transitions from the speed of one letter to the speed of the next, it becomes apparent that a meaningful element of Shelley's emplotment is exactly the gradient (an increase in the magnitude of a property in passing from one point to another) obtained in the relative deceleration from Letter 5 to Letter 6 and the massive acceleration that occurs between Letter 6 and Letter 7 (see Table 2.5).

Table 2.5 Acceleration and deceleration of letters

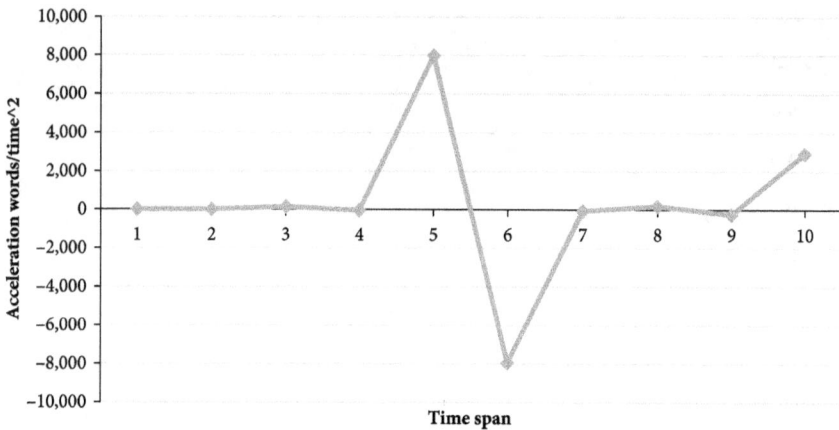

Numerically, we might imagine the overwhelming nature of this shift by checking the gradient (in this case the increase or decrease in the magnitude of speed when passing from one point to another). The acceleration and deceleration of time between letters moves at rates of: 1.75, -2.94, 143.13, -37.57, 7,983.07, -7,951.13, -67.88, 180.17, -252.67, and 2,915. The two central points, our transition from Walton's normal correspondence into telling Frankenstein's story and then the shift from the story back to the letters, display the abrupt and enormous shift in time. Within the slowed temporality of Letter 6, the reader comes to terms with the creature's acclimation to time and his equivalent acquisition of intelligence, consciousness, and language. When the reader transitions to Letter 7, there is a sudden return to Walton's ship, mutiny, and the climactic decision to turn back from the expedition. The reader can comprehend the rapidly amplifying pace of time, but that comprehension, the imaginative work necessary to perceive such a drastic shift in duration, forces the reader into a new relationship with the lived experience of the text.

These sudden leaps and grinding stillnesses are coded into readers' experience. Readers are forced to become concerned with time as they find themselves sensually confronted with its plasticity. Herschel's equation that assumes the movement of consciousness occurring above a denominator of standard time is contradicted in the text by time that is only ever relational via variable speeds that are mapped out irregularly over the text's correspondence. The birth of this new subjectivity is always foregrounded by the actual creation of a being who, from birth, acts as a foil to the scientific notion of life and intelligence as information.

The novel's form does not offer a unified reality or even a set of identifiable subjective lenses through which to view its movement. Its blocks of disproportionate time, sudden deaths and reversals, and scattered perspectives seem to support Georg Lukács' claim about the novel form, that it "can be systematized only in abstract terms, which is why any system that could be established in the novel ... had to be one of abstract concepts and therefore not directly suitable for aesthetic form-giving."[35] Shelley's novel stresses its own deformity and, in laying claim to its instability, questions what is lost when qualitative experience becomes quantitative information. Lukacs defines the *Bildungsroman* as the biographical form "that portrays a protagonist's inward growth and acquisition of social identity."[36] *Frankenstein* is a *Bildungsroman* shot through with the pressures exerted by the rapid industrialization of time and experience. Rather than man becoming in conjunction with his temporal and spatial historical location, and acquiring social identity, the central characters reject or are rejected by the social scenes they seek to occupy.[37] The novel is not only told by different narrators reflecting on events from different overlapping times that include letters and stories of even more implicit bibliographic timelines, but the laboratories, ships, and classrooms of the text suggest that each utterance is imbricated with forms of modern knowledge production.

3

Meiji Japan Responds to *Frankenstein*: The 1889–1890 translation "The New Creator" and the Illustrations

Tomoko Nakagawa

The first Japanese translation of Mary Shelley's *Frankenstein*, *Atarashiki Zōbutsu-sha* (hereafter referred to by its literal translation: "The New Creator") (1889–1890), was published in a serialized form in a magazine called *Kuni no Motoi* (Foundation of the Nation). The magazine was founded by the teachers at a girls' middle school called Tokyo Kōtō Jogakkō, based on an Enlightened ideal of female education. This chapter explores the historical context of the publication of "The New Creator" and makes the argument that a time-place specific political and ideological scuffle over female education left indelible marks on the translation. This historical context led to the textual and graphic representations of the creature—a construct of modern science and technology embodying the Enlightenment—as a monstrous other, a similar turn Mary Shelley's original had taken. Simultaneously, both the translator and the illustrator tried to make the text relevant to the reader, employing devices that would facilitate its reception among the Japanese public.

The publication history of "The New Creator" has several mysteries: why they chose to translate *Frankenstein*; which edition the translator used; who the translator was; why the translation abruptly ended in March 1890. The first section will discuss how the assassination of Mori Arinori, Japan's first Minister of Education, possibly precipitated but, in the end, frustrated the translation. Particular attention will be paid to the mid-Meiji scandal called the "Tokyo Kōtō Jogakkō incident," now scarcely known, that fills in a hitherto unknown historical gap in the background to the publication of "The New Creator." The second section will deliberate the identity of its translator and the source text. It will also discuss how the translator tried to make the text relevant to the reader, employing devices that would facilitate its reception among the public, accompanied by a brief discussion about the creature's monikers in both "The New Creator" and Mary Shelley's *Frankenstein*. The final section will clarify how Kobayashi Kiyochika, the chief illustrator, incorporated in his illustrations of Western characters and settings images indigenous to the Japanese culture. It will explore how Kiyochika, a ukiyo-e woodblock print artist and caricaturist, made implicit comments on the political situation surrounding the magazine in which "The New Creator" appeared.

Murder Behind the Translation: "The New Creator"

After more than 200 years of Japan's international isolation, the Meiji era started in 1867. Enlightenment was the key to the new era, with the name Meiji meaning "Enlightened rule." From an early stage, there was conflict between those who endorsed Western values and those who upheld traditional Japanese and Confucian values. Nevertheless, neither challenged the necessity of Western learning in higher education for male students. Modernization of the nation was paramount over all other considerations to avoid Japan becoming a tributary to Western power(s). The country's two representative slogans of the time demonstrate this priority: "*Fukoku kyōhei* (A rich country with a strong army)" and "*Shokusan kōgyō* (Increase production, promote new industry)."

The persistent conflict between traditional and Enlightenment factions played out significantly in the discussion of female education and education for the general public.[1] Education for girls or the general public was less urgent than education for male students, and therefore, more susceptible to ideological and political battles. At the start of the Meiji era, the Western scholars, the main driving force of the new government, promoted girls' education based on liberal arts and gender equality through the new knowledge imported from the West, frustrating the traditionalists' Confucian model that only allowed a secondary status to women, limiting female education to conventional morals and household skills. Soon afterward, however, a counterthrust began, followed by a power struggle between the two factions. When *Kuni no Motoi* was inaugurated in April 1889, the Western scholars found themselves on the defensive for the second time.

"The New Creator" appeared in the monthly magazine in June 1889, twenty-two years into the Meiji era. The founders of the magazine were the teachers of Tokyo Kōtō Jogakkō, the state-of-the-art girls' middle school established in 1886 (Meiji 19). The school was the brainchild of the first Minister of Education, Mori Arinori (1847–1889), a leader of the pro-Western faction, whom Ito Hirofumi, the first Prime Minister, called "the Westerner that Japan had given birth to."[2] The school aimed to provide girls between thirteen and eighteen with as much learning as necessary to strengthen the nation's foundation. The curriculum illustrated Mori's ambition to provide women with the same level of liberal arts education as male students rather than continue limiting female education to the subjects related to Confucian morals and household duties.

English learning, central to the curriculum, was the distinctive feature of Tokyo Kōtō Jogakkō. It enhanced ideological differences from its predecessor, Fuzoku Kōtō Jogakkō, affiliated to Girls' Higher Normal School (the word *fuzoku* means affiliation).[3] The curriculum of Tokyo Kōtō Jogakkō was designed to focus on learning English: during their four-year study, students learned English for nine hours per week in the first two years, and eight hours per week in the last two, with the number of class hours for sewing, manners, and home economy significantly reduced.[4] Even if the number of English classes was, by the time "The New Creator" began to be serialized, reduced to six hours per week for all students, there remained a clear contrast with the education of the predecessor, Fuzoku Kōtō Jogakkō, where English was totally absent from the curriculum.

Around the time Mori launched Tokyo Kōtō Jogakkō, the conflict between the factions had intensified; reactionary conservatism, opposing excessive Westernization, was taking a firm hold among the Japanese. Mori's assassination occurred on the morning of February 11, 1889, the day of promulgating the Great Japan Imperial Constitution. The assassin was a nationalist who believed the false allegation that Mori had desecrated the Grand Ise Shrine, counted among the most revered of the Shinto shrines in Japan, by striding into its hall of worship with his shoes on.

The inaugural issue of *Kuni no Motoi* was published six weeks later. The congratulatory messages that appeared within revealed disharmony surrounding Tokyo Kōtō Jogakkō and the magazine. The honored contributor was Hiroyuki Katō, an influential educator and political theorist, who was once close to Mori but had abandoned his former views about Japan's need for Westernization. Katō purposefully congratulates the school's policy as the one to prepare "good wives and good mothers," while disparagingly criticizing "a certain school that educates girls so that they will be flagrantly pro-Western."[5]

Public reproach gained force soon after Mori's death, leading to what is called the "Tokyo Kōtō Jogakkō incident." A series of invented scandals were reported in the national newspapers and magazines to undermine the school's reputation and its enlightened ideals. Scandalous reports about female students' immorality, not limited to those at Tokyo Kōtō Jogakkō, followed. There even appeared a serialized *roman à clef* targeting the girls' school.[6] Mori's death and the political situation regarding female education in the mid-Meiji period were crucially, if indirectly, relevant to the first Japanese translation of *Frankenstein*. In March 1890, Tokyo Kōtō Jogakkō virtually vanished from history by an abrupt affiliation with Tokyo Girls' Higher Normal School. Yatabe Ryokichi, the school's principal, was not aware of, and therefore wholly unprepared for, the announcement. On the morning of March 25, 1890, Yatabe learned of the school's closure through a brief notice in the government gazette.[7] It announced the news as a simple matter of affiliation. *Kuni no Motoi* was discontinued along with the disappearance of Tokyo Kōtō Jogakkō. The incident had a severe impact on girls' emerging secondary education, dramatically reducing the number of girls attending middle schools.[8]

Interestingly, the incident, in a way, repeated the history of another girls' school, Tokyo Jogakkō, established in 1872, a trailblazer in Japan's formal education for girls. The founding spirit of Tokyo Kōtō Jogakkō, in fact, revived that of Tokyo Jogakkō. The two schools shared the same ideals for female education, namely, gender equality and liberal education. Like Tokyo Kōtō Jogakkō, Tokyo Jogakkō placed great emphasis on English learning; it was also abruptly closed in the face of opposition from traditionalists. Both cases happened ostensibly not as closure, but as affiliation with the same normal school for girls.

Aoyama Nao's historical research of girls' middle schools during the Meiji era traces the lineage of Tokyo Kōtō Jogakkō back to Tokyo Jogakkō. It provides a historical context to Mori's scheme and the traditionalists' deep-rooted antagonism towards female education, both secondary and tertiary, during the Meiji era.[9] The enlightened ideals for female education seem to have been premature, both in the case of Tokyo Jogakkō (1872–1877) and Tokyo Kōtō Jogakkō (1886–1890). The lineage, obfuscated through affiliation and marginalization, demonstrates the ideological and political conflict over female education in the first half of the Meiji era. "The New Creator" is best understood as an ironic metaphor of conflicted modernization of Japan in the Meiji era, as will be demonstrated in the next two sections.

In 1886 [Meiji 19], Mori, as Minister of Education, tried once again to direct female education towards the enlightened ideal. He started the reform by severing the affiliation of *Fuzoku Kōtō Jogakkō* (which was formerly *Tokyo Jogakkō*) to Tokyo Girls' Higher Normal School, subsequently placing the former under the direct control of the government. The school was first called *Kōtō Jogakkō*, with the word *fuzoku* (meaning affiliation) removed, but was soon renamed as Tokyo Kōtō Jogakkō. However, Mori's untimely death triggered a chain of events strongly reminiscent of the fate of Tokyo Jogakkō. At the end of March 1890, Tokyo Kōtō Jogakkō was once again affiliated to Tokyo Girls' Higher Normal School, terminating the publication of *Kuni no Motoi*, and therefore, curtailing the serialized translation of *Frankenstein*.

The Unidentified Translator and the Nameless Creature

The Tokyo Kōtō Jogakkō incident left traces in the translated text of *Frankenstein* in more than one way. The first installment of the translation was published in the June issue of *Kuni no Motoi* in 1889, to be followed monthly until November that year. The first six installments, apart from the omission of the first two letters of Robert Walton at the beginning, mostly followed the original *Frankenstein* chapter by chapter, ending with Justine Moritz's execution and Victor's lament over her death. After three months' suspension from December 1889 to February 1890, the last installment appeared in March 1890, after which the magazine was discontinued without any notice. The last installment summed up the whole of the second volume of Mary Shelley's original at one go, ending with the creature's plea for Victor to create a female companion for him and Victor's determination to perform this request.

To this day, the first translator of *Frankenstein* remains unidentified. Nowhere in the translated text does the the translator's actual name appear, nor does that of the original author. Before 1899 when Japan joined the Berne Convention, it was common in Japan that the translator's name or pen name replaced the author's name. Also, it was customary for a novelist to use five or six pen names; for example, Tsubouchi Shōyō, a pioneering novelist known to have translated all of Shakespeare's works into Japanese during the Meiji era, used several pen names. In the case of "The New Creator," the title was only accompanied by the phrase "Hisago-no-ya shujin kō," which means "Written by the master of the gourd's house."

None of the leading translators at the time is known to have used this name or anything like it. Only two lesser-known writers are known to have used a pen name related to the gourd before 1889.[10] A more likely candidate is Tanabe Tatsuko, who used a literary pseudonym "Gourd" when writing her stories published in *Jogaku Zasshi*, a literary magazine, in the 1890s.[11] Tatsuko later married and came to be known as Miyake Kaho. Several other facts suggest that Kaho was likely to be the unidentified translator of *Frankenstein*: her affiliation with Tokyo Kōtō Jogakkō; her interest in the English language;

her profile as an emerging author and her career as a translator; her familiarity with the Western culture through her family; and her acquaintance with Tsubouchi Shōyō.

Kaho translated at least three stories in 1891–1893.[12] More significant is that, in 1888, Kaho had published her first novel, *Yabu no Uguisu* (*A Warbler in the Bush*, hereafter referred to as *Warbler*). She made her name as the first female to write a modern novel in Japan. The dialogue in *Warbler* is in a new vernacular Japanese style that Tsubouchi Shōyō, the first male author of the modern novel in Japan, innovatively employed in his *Tōsei Shosei Katagi* (The Character of Present-Day Students), published in 1885–1886. In *Warbler*, a 16-year-old student at Tokyo Kōtō Jogakkō mingles English words and idioms in her cheerful exchanges with her schoolmates, who respond to her in a similar manner. The speeches of other educated characters are also interspersed with the English vocabulary.

Kaho's first novel *Warbler* presents an interesting parallel with the publication history of "The New Creator." The story depicts the characters', and possibly the author's, ironic attitudes to Western values, with a male protagonist choosing a young woman with traditional graces over his excessively Westernized fiancée. The story develops with the return of a young man, Shinohara, from his five-year study in Europe. Shinohara is engaged to Hamako, the daughter of a senior government official who financed his study. Soon after his return, he finds Hamako, a student at Tokyo Kōtō Jogakkō, too Westernized for his taste; she is vivacious, sociable, and an enthusiastic learner of English. Hamako conveniently falls in love with and is allowed to marry her impoverished private English tutor, Yamanaka. Yamanaka then abandons his wife for an old lover, having robbed her of all her wealth. In the end, Hamako, now destitute, turns to Christianity; Shinohara meets and marries Hideko, a young woman who has lost her parents and now supports herself and her young brother in her unpresuming, yet, dignified and honest way.

Although the plot summary appears to suggest a schematic triumph of conventional female virtues, the text presents different values that remain conflicted to the end. Despite the simplistic condemnation of Western values in the plot, the novel's strength is in the lively portraits of young women attending Tokyo Kōtō Jogakkō. For all her failings, Hamako is an attractive young woman; vivacious, brilliant, and sociable. Her strengths are an exact match with what one critic of Mori's educational policy condemned. In Uchida Roan's view, Mori initiated the excessive Westernization of Japanese young women, in protest of traditional principles based on neo-Confucian teachings prescribed in *Onna Daigaku* (Greater Learning for Women); Mori made more of "vivacity than elegance; brilliance than obedience; sociability than domestic chores; learning than handcrafts" in young women.[13]

"The New Creator" is based on the revised 1831 version of *Frankenstein*, as is clear from the fact that Elizabeth, Frankenstein's fiancée, is described as an adopted orphan. It does not translate Mary Shelley's original text word for word; the narrator summarizes parts of the story, cuts down on details, and includes additional phrases or sentences to facilitate the reading of the novel set in a context quite foreign to that of her readers.

At first glance, this may appear to be the result of so-called *goketsu-yaku* or audacious translation prevalent in the early years of Meiji, which freely adapts the original text. However, a close examination of the first six installments reveals that this deficiency is attributable to its source text, which shows significant omissions of paragraphs and passages. The most notable omission in the translation of "The New Creator" is Robert Walton's two letters at the outset of the novel, which the translator replaced with a preface. Also, specific sentences or episodes that seem essential to the novel are missing. For example, the episode of young Victor Frankenstein watching a beautiful oak struck down by a bolt of lightning is missing, together with the references—the only ones in the original novel—to electricity and galvanism in the subsequent passage.

These omissions in "The New Creator" seem to have derived from its source text: the "Routledge World Library" edition (hereafter referred to as the RWL). The RWL was one of a series of inexpensive editions published by Routledge to educate lower-middle and working-class readers, along with other editions published in the second half of the nineteenth century, including Routledge's Pocket Library, Sixpenny Library, and Railway Library.[14] While the other editions printed the unabridged 1818 edition of *Frankenstein*, the RWL edition presented an abridged 1831 edition. The text of "The New Creator" does not include any part of the 1831 *Frankenstein* left out of the RWL edition. Extensive cuts in the second installment of "The New Creator," which translated Volume I, Chapter 1 of *Frankenstein* (1831), exactly correspond to those cut in the RWL edition, including the entire six paragraphs from the second to seventh paragraphs of the chapter.[15]

"The New Creator" had further omissions, for example, two crucial sentences expressing Victor's first reaction to the creature, included in the RWL edition, are missing in "The New Creator": "How can I describe my emotions at this catastrophe, or how delineate the wretch whom with such infinite pains and care I had endeavoured to form?" and "Beautiful!—Great God!".

The translator demonstrates striking originality in her use of a variety of monikers employed for the creature, which helps to retain the ambiguity and complexity of the original text. The translator highlights the creature's indefinability, which is embedded in the original, using different Chinese characters to designate it. The creature is indefinable because it is simultaneously both an object and an animal, a human and monster, created out of the dead bodies of humans and animals.

The ghostly, supernatural elements are played up in "The New Creator" by the Chinese characters used to refer to the creature. As I have discussed elsewhere, the equivalent of the word "monster"—"bake-mono" — is repeated throughout the Japanese translation. The translator uses three different combinations of Chinese characters 怪物 化物 and 妖物 in many cases, with the specification that they should read as "bake-mono" or monster. The second character of all three, corresponding to the sound *mono*, represents a "thing" while each of the first characters, corresponding to the sound *bake*, all enact the ghostliness of the creature (as the ghost is called "o-bake" in Japanese) with slightly different connotations: the character 化 signifies "to transform" or "to bewitch"; while the character 妖 generally used as an adjective root is related to "seducing" or "fascinating"; the character 怪 signifies "to doubt" or "to suspect." The word "bake-mono," in this way, points to the creature's monstrosity ("bake") and its materiality (mono) while the variety of Chinese characters used for *bake* indicate the creature's indefinability as well as monstrosity.[16] The shift in Chinese notations in the translation makes the reader more perceptive about the creature's designation in the original.

"The monster" is not the designation most often used in the original text; most frequently used is "the creature," followed by the words "wretch" and "fiend." As the story progresses, the use of "creature" decreases, while the use of "wretch" or "fiend" becomes more common; however, the creation's humanity is held in view to the very end of the novel as something attainable.[17] It is true that "The New Creator" simplifies Shelley's *Frankenstein* in many ways, but it also helps us look at Shelley's text with a fresh eye. The translation creates complexity of another kind, which enhances some aspects that remained unrecognized by the reader of the original text.

Kiyochika's Creature Transformed into a Caricature

"The New Creator" was accompanied by seven illustrations. Kobayashi Kiyochika, a samurai-turned ukiyo-e artist, who, by this time, was also a leading caricaturist, did four out of the seven illustrations.[18] His representations of the creature help the reader see Frankenstein's creation as something that cannot be conceived or visualized as a specific *persona*, defined and unalterable.

Kiyochika illustrated all three representations of the nameless creature. In each, the creature has flowing hair, a gigantic physique, and strained muscles in its long limbs and torso, which conspire to emphasize its strength and agility, following Shelley's descriptions. However, the confrontations between the creature and other characters

Figure 3.1 Kobayashi Kiyochika, "Bakemono hito wo odorokasu (The monster surprises people)". *Kuni no Motoi* II, no. 12 (1890). Courtesy Waseda University Library.

are rendered using Western and Japanese elements in varying proportions, seemingly suggesting an increasing irreconcilability between the two cultures. Of the three representations of the creature, the most puzzling is the last one in the final issue of *Kuni no Motoi* (see Figure 3.1).[19] The contrast between the Western and Eastern elements is striking. The colossal torso of the creature on the left seems to represent a traditional Japanese demon, with the mouth open from ear to ear, the eyes glaring, the muscles in the arms bulging. The iconicity of these features is evident if compared with the ukiyo-e prints like the indigenous demon depicted by Tsukioka Yoshitoshi (see Figure 3.2).[20] By contrast, Kiyochika renders the De Laceys in Western style. Old De Lacey, to whom the creature confides his predicament, sits pathetically on a stool at the center in the manner of illustrations of sentimental novels; Felix is rushing forward with his top hat flying behind; Agatha is flabbergasted in the manner of Western caricature.

What is it that lies behind this disparity between the Western and Japanese/Asian elements in the last illustration? Kiyochika, a caricaturist, employed two distinct styles to signify the conflicting political forces at work behind the scenes: old traditionalism and Western Enlightenment. In his two other representations of the creature, Kiyochika suggests the possibility of new eclecticism emerging from the dynamic juxtaposition of the Western and Japanese/Asian elements.[21]

Figure 3.3 celebrates the creature's birth, with the dark background and the bright foreground enhancing the luminosity that surrounds and glorifies the creature.[22] For those familiar with the paintings of Cranach the elder, the creature may look like Christ in Resurrection. The similarities between the two are recognizable: a long flowing drapery wraps around both the body of Christ and the creature; the soldiers running off in surprise in Cranach are replaced in Kiyochika by Victor, who cannot stand up.

At the same time, the creature standing tall could remind the viewer of the figure of Ni-oh, the guardian god placed in many Buddhist temples in Japan. The viewer may even find, superimposed onto the Ni-oh-like representation, a highly stylized confrontation scene of villain Sadakurō and staggering Yoichibei in Act V of *Chūshingura* (*The Storehouse of Loyal Retainers* or *Forty-Seven Ronins*), a well-known Kabuki play performed to this day.[23]

Kiyochika renders the creature in an entirely different style in the next scene. Victor imagines himself to be fighting with the creature, as Henry Clerval looks on in surprise (see Figure 3.4).[24] Unlike the other two of Kiyochika's illustrations discussed so far, this scene seems overwhelmingly Western; however, there are some conflicting elements: the representation of the creature immediately suggests the image of Hercules in his labors, the motif recreated by European artists in sculptures, engravings, and paintings, whereas the figures of Victor and Henry are comic in the style of a caricature. Henry's wide-open eyes, fingers spread out, straightened leg, dropped jaw, and flying top hat all exaggerate his surprise while Victor looks diminutive, almost child-like against the sheer mass of the creature's body.

Figure 3.4 contains two mysteries that at first appear indecipherable. Although it illustrates a serious, if imagined, fight, the fighters' right arms are crooked in a way that makes it impractical for them to strike their opponents. Curiously, the fighters remain

Figure 3.2 Ikkaisai(Tsukioka) Yoshitoshi, "Raiko Shitennō Ōeyama Kijin Taiji no Zu" (Raiko and the Best Four Disposing of the Oeyama Monster)" (detail), 1864.

Figure 3.3 Kobayashi Kiyochika, "Aratani tsukurishi hito ni tamashii wo iretaru zu (Picture of a newly created man infused with soul)", *Kuni no Motoi* I, no. 5 (1889). Courtesy Waseda University Library.

Figure 3.4 Kobayashi Kiyochika, "Aratani tsukuritaru hito to kenka wo naseru zu (Picture of a fight with a newly created man)". *Kuni no Motoi* I, no. 4 (1889). Courtesy Waseda University Library.

empty-handed, with no sword or weapon, and the creature is looking past Victor at Henry in the doorway. Moreover, their right legs seem to be in the air; the creature is even on tiptoe. Their postures make the duel look more like a duet; the two are dancing to the same beat; the creature's posture mirrors Victor and vice versa. Harmony, rather than conflict, dominates the scene. Another mystery is the feminizing elements of the frame of the fight scene: the flowered trellis and the butterflies flying in.

Two woodblock prints of Yoshitoshi, Kiyochika's contemporary artist, based on stylized *Kabuki* combat provide the clue to both. The first print depicts the fight between Ushiwaka-maru and Benkei.[25]

Ushiwaka-maru was the childhood name of Minamoto Yoshitsune, a legendary twelfth-century Japanese warrior who inspired major traditional performing arts like *Noh* plays, *Kabuki* and *Bunraku*. Many stories have been created and recreated about Yoshitsune. He still is the inspiration for TV dramas or *manga*s today. In the mid-Meiji era, Yoshitsune's stories became popular *Kabuki* programs, with some *ukiyo-e* artists featuring him in their woodblock prints. His popularity is attributable to the fact that he was a defeated hero: being a brilliant military strategist, Yoshitsune won the crucial final battle with the rival clan on behalf of his elder brother, Yoritomo, the head of the *Genji* clan; however, Yoritomo grew suspicious of the younger man's loyalty and decided to destroy him.

Figure 3.5 Tsukioka Yoshitoshi. Dainihon meishō-kagami: Saitō Musashibō Benkei Onzōshi Ushiwaka-maru nochi no Iyo Minamoto-no-kami Yoshitsune (Catalogue of Illustrious Japanese Commanders: Saitō Musashibō Benkei, Prince Ushiwaka-maru, later to become Iyo Minamaoto-no-kami Yoshitsune)", 1878. Courtesy Tokyo Metropolitan Library.

Yoshitoshi's print (Figure 3.5) combines some iconic elements of this tragic hero. It depicts a well-known duel between a young Ushiwaka-maru, disguised as a girl and wearing a female robe, with his future retainer, Benkei, a monk, on a bridge in Kyoto. The boy wins the fight with *ninja*-like agility; Benkei went on to serve Yoshitsune with a selfless loyalty until he was eventually killed while defending his master. Yoshitoshi emphasizes young Yoshitsune's femininity with his pink robe and a pattern of pinks in the loose red trousers. The coordinated movement of the fighters depicts harmony symbolizing the bond between the two. Kiyochika seems to have been inspired by Yoshitoshi's print and crystallized the feminine elements in the butterflies and flowers, two iconic symbols of femininity in Japan. He also used, as did Yoshitoshi, the highly stylized representation of the fight in *Kabuki*, characterized by their rhythmical foot movement. The pair look like shadows of the other, as inseparably bound as Victor and the creature.

Another print by Yoshitoshi is equally significant. In Figure 3.6, both Ushiwaka-maru and Kumasaka Chōhan, a bandit leader, have their arms crooked at sharp angles.[26] Here, the bandit has a long spear in hand, and Ushiwaka-maru, a sword. Like the creature in Kiyochika's print, parts of the opponent's face, a big eye and the tip of his nose, are visible under his right arm. Kiyochika's borrowing from Yoshitoshi's print also explains why the creature looks past his opponent Victor to Henry, an on-looker. In Yoshitoshi's print, the bandit is glaring straight at Ushiwaka-maru.

Kiyochika, as a caricaturist, seems to have purposely chosen and superimposed the images taken from the legendary Japanese tragedies, *Chushingura* and *Ushiwaka-maru*: legends that resonate with the readers' experience of a revolutionary turnover as the Meiji enlightenment era replaced the feudal Edo era. To those who fought for the Shogun and lost in the civil wars, the hero who dies for honor and loyalty must have been an endearing subject, which explains why Yoshitoshi, Kiyochika's contemporary, created these prints.

As discussed above, we see in Kiyochika's three illustrations a clear divide evolving between the world of old traditionalism and the world of Western arts, the latter encompassing both classical and modern elements. The illustrations invite the reader to see a vision of harmony between the East and the West (Figure 3.3), an intensifying but hidden conflict between traditional Japanese values and newly introduced Western values (Figure 3.4), ending in disintegration between the two (Figure 3.1).

We may regard the looming demon, strangely poised and aloof, of his last illustration (Figure 3.1) as Kiyochika's ironic self-portrait. He was one of many *samurai*s who lost their prerogatives at the collapse of the Shogunate. Kiyochika may well have tried to modernize himself by conforming to the new era of Enlightenment, only to be disillusioned by the political turmoil in modernized Japan. Kiyochika, however, is a caricaturist, capable of distancing himself from the situation to present comedic images of the situation to the public. What he may have seen behind the confrontation of an indigenous Japanese demon with the caricatured Western characters was an intensified conflict between newly introduced foreign values and traditional values at this particular juncture in Japan's modern history. When we consider the illustrations that fuse two distinct cultural elements, however, the demon no longer looks purely Japanese or Asian. The viewer simultaneously detects Western classical divine images

Figure 3.6 Taiso (Tsukioka) Yoshitoshi. "Yoshitoshi Mushaburui: Minamoto no Ushiwaka-maru, Kumasaka Chōhan" (Yoshitoshi's Warriors Trembling with Anticipation: Minamoto no Ushiwaka-maru and Kumasaka Chōhan)", 1883. Courtesy National Diet Library Digital.

in its dignified posture: a Roman senator sitting in an armchair or the river god Arno reclining in the waterbed.

Both the translated text of "The New Creator" and Kiyochika's illustrations were unique products of their time and place. The political turmoil of the mid-Meiji era, typified by Mori's assassination in 1889 and the closure of Tokyo Kōtō Jogakkō in 1890, provides a unique historical background to this first Japanese translation of *Frankenstein*. The translated text and the illustrations both may seem unrelated, or even bizarre, to Shelley's original. Yet, a close examination of the two encourages the reader's consideration of human response when faced with the cultural other, and they demonstrate how Mary Shelley's *Frankenstein* can resonate with readers' distinctive experience in different times and places.

This work was supported by JSPS KAKENHI Grant Number JP22K00490.

4

Frankenstein Goes Global: Returning the Necropolitical Gaze with *Frankenstein in Baghdad*

Hugh Charles O'Connell

Ahmed Saadawi's *Frankenstein in Baghdad* (originally published in Arabic in 2013 and translated into English in 2018) caused quite a stir in the science fiction (SF) community. Well ahead of its official translation it was already being discussed at SF conferences as early draft translations circulated among eager scholars. The enthusiasm that met *Frankenstein in Baghdad* can, in part, be explained through timing, since its date of English publication corresponds to the bicentennial of Mary Shelley's *Frankenstein: Or, The Modern Prometheus*. Shelley's *Frankenstein* has long held a paramount position in SF studies, often lauded as the founding SF work. However, the publication of Saadawi's novel also overlapped with a significant turn away from the Anglo-Euro spheres that have long dominated SF studies in favor of a more robustly global and postcolonial turn. Alongside its formal indebtedness to SF's founding mother-text, then, what excited scholars was a burgeoning Arabic SF tradition that mediates the complex, overlapping discursive ends of oil boom development and hi-tech modernization, neo-imperial invasion, governmental destabilization, sectarian violence, and the democratic political upheavals of the Arab Spring.

This chapter brings these two ends together and focuses on *Frankenstein*'s position within SF studies as both a progenitor for the genre's critical development and more recently as a touchstone for SF's global turn. Most broadly, it's concerned with the question of what it means to globalize SF through the Frankenstein narrative. As such, Saadawi's novel offers a unique perspective for rethinking the role of the Frankenstein mythos within the global SF imaginary, most notably through its emphasis on the bodies that comprise the creature, and its rewriting of the narrative/readerly gaze in the final scene. While many SF stories continue to revamp *Frankenstein*'s foundational narrative about the production of life, *Frankenstein in Baghdad* shifts the emphasis from biopolitical reproduction to what Achille Mbembe refers to as "necropolitics": the "contemporary forms of subjugation of life to the power of death."

Shelley's "workshop of filthy creation"

In order to appreciate *Frankenstein in Baghdad*'s intervention into SF studies through its globalization of the *Frankenstein* narrative, it's necessary to first consider the relationship between SF studies and Shelley's novel.¹ Doing so requires taking account of how the "hideous progeny" produced in this "workshop of filthy creation" points equally to (1) the very genre of SF, (2) the SF tropes that circulate under the name of *Frankenstein*, and (3) the monster's relation to the construction of the postcolonial Other—that is, the presence of the in/human monstrousness that haunts and defines Enlightenment rationality and subjectivity in the biopolitical sense and that is carried through the circulation of *Frankenstein*'s SF tropes.

It's not every day that an anonymously published book by a 20-year-old author creates an entirely new genre. But for many SF scholars, that's exactly what Mary Shelley's *Frankenstein* did. This, despite the fact that "science fiction" was not employed as a purposeful genre designation until 1926, some 108 years after the novel was first published in 1818. (Often considered the founder of modern SF, the inaugural SF editor Hugo Gernsback first employed the term scientifiction in 1926, itself a horrible attempt to stitch together "scientific" and "fiction" into a monstrous portmanteau, before he thankfully adopted "science fiction" in 1929).

It has therefore taken some intellectual heavy lifting by SF novelists, critics, and academics alike in order to retroactively establish *Frankenstein* as SF's founding text. Although it had been suggested by science fiction writers and critics for some time, it was SF-author-critic Brian Aldiss's 1973 genre-defining history *Billion Year Spree* that first formalized this origin myth. Aldiss writes, "Of course, it is in a way a Stone Age truth to say that SF began with Mary Shelley's *Frankenstein*."[2] Aldiss' own rhetoric betrays the fact that this is indeed not a "Stone Age truth," but one that he's very much attempting to establish. This identification of *Frankenstein* as the Ur-text from which SF sprang fully formed was also a mode of disavowal, a way of dis-identifying Gernsback and the pulp age, confining them, if not to the dustbin of history, then to a peripheral corner of SF production that is better forgotten. Indeed, his very definition of SF can be seen as directly derived from *Frankenstein* and pitted against Gernsback's favoring of scientific accuracy and faithful future extrapolation: "Science fiction is the search for a definition of [humankind] and [its] status in the universe which will stand in our advanced but confused state of knowledge (science), and is characteristically cast in the gothic or post-gothic mode."[3] Here, Gernsback's proto-STEM-oriented techno-optimistic notion of "a charming romance intermingled with scientific fact and prophetic vision" is displaced by the unsettling gothic, whereby scientific fact is constrained by confusion, and the techno-driven certainty of an extrapolative future is downplayed in favor of inward humanistic-philosophical rumination.

At the same time, *Frankenstein* has also been called upon to foreground SF's radical utopian drive. For Carl Freedman, Shelley's novel is "the first work in which the science fictional tendency reaches a certain level of self-consciousness, thus enabling a line of fiction, that at least in retrospect, can be construed as the early history of science fiction proper."[4] Significantly, it introduces what many would take to be the key hallmark of science fiction: the interest in radical futurity. For Freedman, such futurity is a notional foregrounding of the possibility of radical difference in our world, negating what we take for granted as the inviolable state of reality as we know it, and thereby reopening the "problematic of historicity"[5] by rendering our present and its certainties as a historical past. This is accomplished through *Frankenstein*'s very form, which marks the end of the spatial narrative (figured by the frame story's protagonist Walton and his travel plot) and the beginning of the narrative of time as Walton's story is subsumed by Victor's as soon as Walton become his amanuensis.

I highlight these instances, just two among many, of asserting *Frankenstein* as the progenitor SF text because they unite both the aesthetic and political strands involved in placing Shelley as the center from which SF sprang forth. By displacing the Gernsback era of the pulps with what by the late-twentieth century had been recovered by academic feminism and romanticist studies as serious literature, part of the motivation was surely to supply SF with a foundational source of literary merit, to help remove some of its stigma as "sad trash," the memorable term Victor's father uses to describe Victor's childlike interest in Cornelius Agrippa, a purveyor of the occult. By this same token, critics often employ a similar castigation of "sad trash" to differentiate SF from other non-mimetic genres via its purportedly singular political vocation. Here, Victor's father's elevation of science over the fantastic echoes many early SF critics' desire to raise SF above fantasy and horror—dismissed as "jiggery-pokery magic"—as well as trashy pulp SF, in order to inaugurate it as the inheritor of realism's crucial literary-historical-political vocation to historicize the present.[6]

Yet, as John Rieder remarks, this search for SF's single founding moment fundamentally misrepresents how genre works: "A genre cannot have an original member, because genres consist of relations between texts, so that texts do not belong to genres but rather use them. This use [...] emerges in the course of practices of imitation, echoing, allusion, parody, and so on, in the production of texts as well as practices of categorization, generalization, periodization, and so on, in the interpretation of texts."[7] What's important is how the text differentiates itself from other existing genre protocols—in this case the gothic—and what the text speaks to within the current socio-political conjuncture that makes it speak to new or emerging genres. That is, rather than purely gothic, or purely SF, *Frankenstein* exists within an inter-related matrix of genres that comprise the historically constituted mass cultural genre system.

As Rieder develops across his work, *Frankenstein*'s entanglement with SF was due to its historical situatedness. Initially published long before the burgeoning SF of the late Victorian period, it wasn't until *Frankenstein* went out of copyright in 1881 and print editions once again proliferated that the novel became widely read, by which time it began to circulate among a number of early SF texts, including lost race narratives, scientific romances, and extraordinary voyages.[8] It is at this time that, like the Martians or Morlocks of Wells, the technological marvels of Verne, or the evolutionary racial pseudoscience of Rider Haggard, Shelley's proto-scientist and thematic biopolitical concerns of a staunchly patriarchal science's desires for the control of life became firmly embedded in SF's genre-narrative DNA. Thus, Rieder contents that, "[i]t is not as a formal paradigm, but as an extraordinarily rich matrix of opportunities for response, that *Frankenstein* plays its part in the beginning of science fiction."[9]

Ultimately, what is most interesting, then, is the way that *Frankenstein* as an SF progenitor participates in what Rieder refers to as SF's ambivalent "colonial gaze" that swings between the poles of affirmation and critique.[10] As Rieder persuasively argues, the emergence of SF within the larger genre-system of mass culture is indelibly linked to the ideological protocols of colonialism through their shared ideologeme of progress and its attendant fantasies of discovery, missionary conversion, and anthropological race-thinking. Therefore, the way that Shelley's novel "speaks to the project of modernity, that is, the way it explores the project of reason or enlightenment and its limits"[11] needs to be fully embedded within modernity's own monstrous progenitor: imperialism. In other words, its circulation through SF needs to be seen from within global modernity.

Many critics have examined the colonial gaze of Shelley's *Frankenstein* in conjunction with the DeLacey family and the creature's acculturation to imperial geopolitics through its reading of Volney's *The Ruins, or Meditations on the Revolutions of Empires* (1791), as well as through the issue of biopolitics and the conservative desire for control of reproduction that underscores both a misogynistic and imperial desire. Within this context, the ambiguity of the colonial gaze can be seen at work in the contrasting responses it's garnered. For example, connecting *Frankenstein*'s politics to *Frankenstein in Baghdad*, Roger Luckhurst can quickly rehearse *Frankenstein*'s anti-imperialist bona fides as a given: "Shelley's *Frankenstein* was of course a secular, materialist, and stridently anticolonial book; her monster teaches itself to read with a copy of Volney's [*Ruins*]."[12] As he writes elsewhere in a review of *Frankenstein in Baghdad*, "Volney, like Gibbon in the *Decline and Fall of the Roman Empire*, offers a moral lecture over the ruins that line the Mediterranean on the delusions of imperial power. It is ruination that inspires the creature's rebellion against his master. These little touches bind *Frankenstein* and *Frankenstein in Baghdad* together as anti-imperial statements."[13]

Yet, for Claudia Gualtieri, the construction and acculturation of the creature reveal a staunchly anti-postcolonial position: "The Creature is a hybrid figure of the postcolony: a monster and scientifically constructed body, a migrant and a technologically enhanced human being, both subhuman and posthuman."[14] Although such a "postcolonial hybrid" generally evinces "a positive figure of mixing and change, and of future creative possibilities" by taking the power of representation and agency away from the imperial center, she argues that *Frankenstein* presents the opposite process whereby "the hybrid Creature gradually undergoes a twist towards the monstrous, following a typically Romantic arc process."[15] While my own reading falls closer in line with Luckhurst's, what's really significant here is the fact that the construction of the creature's subjectivity circulates around issues of colonial otherness and race that can be read as broadly biopolitical in the Foucaultian sense of technologies of social coherence predicated on mapping and policing otherness.[16]

It's these colonial and biopolitical themes that migrate from Shelley's text and become embedded within SF narrative tropes more broadly and begin to circulate with and through SF. As Sherryl Vint notes, "Certain prominent texts become dense centers of gravity, inevitably pulling the meaning of icons toward their influential formulations. For example, any created being in SF carries a trace of Frankenstein's Creature."[17] Thus *Frankenstein*'s afterlives through its continuing global circulation often have less to do with the particular novel *Frankenstein* and more with the trope of Frankenstein; this is captured by the appellation of "Frankensteinian" to nearly any narrative having to do with the re-animation of the dead by a mad scientist or, even less specifically, to the sense of folly and hubris attached to an over-reaching, over-confident rationality measured against such monstrosity. Yet despite the dislodging of the Frankensteinian SF trope from the originary text itself, I want to suggest that part of its continual circulation relates, at least ideologically, to the embedding of Shelley's narrative within the genre protocols of SF as it (e)merged with nineteenth- and twentieth-century imperialism.

In this sense, what is most interesting is the way Shelley's novel continues to circulate throughout SF via its various adaptations and reboots, signifying that its narrative dilemmas concerning the ambiguous colonial gaze have yet to be resolved. I argue that this is related to the fact that the tale itself never decisively resolves. That is, although the monster promises to destroy himself in flame far from civilization in the "most northern extremity of the globe,"[18] this end is never witnessed (and this in a novel that is all about witnessing, verifying, and reporting). Instead, we're left with the monster still possibly out there on the borders of civilization and as the border marker of our humanity—as the thing that separates humanity from the monstrous, but also humanity from godhead. As the monster haunts the periphery of humankind and civilization so, too, does the novel continue to haunt the periphery of SF and its globalization. That is, every repetition of the Frankensteinian SF trope carries with it the original's biopolitical threat and promise at some residual level.

From the Colonial to the Necropolitical Gaze

At this point, I want to turn to how *Frankenstein*'s mediation of the colonial gaze and biopolitical mastery of reproduction continues to circulate in the more recent global SF boom through Saadawi's novel. While many, particularly western cyberpunk and postcyberpunk SF narratives continue to revamp *Frankenstein*'s pioneering narrative (and warnings) about the production of life through cybernetics and artificial intelligence,[19] *Frankenstein in Baghdad* shifts the emphasis from the biopolitical production and control of life to a necropolitical focus on the production of death. This is achieved particularly through the attention to the dual production of corpses—both the corpse-body of the creature as well as the corpse-bodies that are employed to produce the creature.

Frankenstein in Baghdad takes place in in 2005–2006 and recounts the early years of the US occupation of Iraq and the growing sectarian violence that it unleashed. The narrative focuses on the lives of a group of people living in the Bataween neighborhood of Baghdad: Elishva an elderly woman grieving the disappearance of her son Daniel who was conscripted into the Iraq–Iran war; Hadi, a local junk dealer and creator of the creature; Abdu Anmar, a hotelier; and Faraj, a real estate investor. Most related to the circulation of Frankensteinian SF tropes is the strand of the narrative that recounts Hadi's construction of a new body out of the various body parts of bombing victims that he collects from the streets of Baghdad, and which one day, rather miraculously, comes to life—the soul of a recently killed hotel guard enters it—to seek revenge on the perpetrators of these bombings. The monster—whose exploits are tracked by journalists and the Iraqi military's "Tracking and Pursuit Department"—is then variously known throughout the novel as Citizen X, The One Who has No Name, Frankenstein (particularly in sensationalist journalist accounts) but, most frequently, the Whatsitsname (a translation of the Arabic *Shisma*).

The novel's form draws on many facets of the original *Frankenstein*—employing a framing narrative about the constitution of the novel itself, filtering the tale through three primary levels of narration, and providing an extended middle section where we get to hear the Whatitsname's story through its own voice. Moreover, on the thematic level, it turns to questions of guilt and remorse over the killing of innocent people along with the moral anguish that this entails. But really, it's all about the bodies and the endless supply of body parts that allow the creature to continually reconstitute itself and thus never having to resolve any of these questions.

Short-circuiting the biopolitical emphasis on subjectivity, *Frankenstein in Baghdad* skips the parts about acculturation and *Bildung* that are central to the creature's development in Shelley's text. Instead, it focuses on the other end of the novel: revenge against those that have already stripped it of its humanity. The Whatitsname thus kills those responsible for the death of each body part. However, in a nod to the recursive violence that plagues contemporary Iraq, the Whatsitsname needs to keep acquiring new body parts in order to carry out his missions, leading to an endless cycle of death and violence in which it becomes impossible to differentiate the "saints seeking justice" from the "terrorists." As we're told many times, it's an impossible distinction and "In truth, no one's innocent."

What does it mean to globalize *Frankenstein* through such a narrative? One way of understanding this simultaneous cultural and literary circulation is through the ongoing debates about world literature and globalization. We might insist that *Frankenstein* was always global through its diffuse locations and ruminations on imperial history. However, in *Frankenstein in Baghdad* the narrative and its tropes are globalized. That is, what appears as the periphery in *Frankenstein* (South American indigenous peoples, Turkey) is re-centered in *Frankenstein in Baghdad*. In this sense, we can begin to think of it as a returning of western SF's colonial gaze.

Emphasizing this doubling and return of the colonial gaze through the dual maneuver of the transfer of *Frankenstein* from the global north to Iraq and *Frankenstein in Baghdad* from Iraq to the global north through its translation, reading, and commentary might bring us to the notion of "world literature" in David Damrosch's conception. For Damrosch, world literature, rather than a canon of texts, underscores notions of cultural exchange and translation by emphasizing texts "that circulate beyond their culture of origin, either in translation or in their original language [...such that] a work only has an *effective life* as world literature whenever, and wherever, it is actively present within a literary system beyond that of its original culture."[20] This accords with the notion of the Frankensteinian trope, cut loose from its socio-historical mooring of Shelley's 1818 text.

Moreover, such notions of translation, circulation, and exchange are certainly at play in *Frankenstein in Baghdad*'s relation to Shelley's novel. In a 2018 interview,[21] Saadawi describes how the inspiration for his monster came to him in a sudden "flash." Working as a journalist for the BBC in 2006 covering the US–UK invasion of Iraq, he found himself interviewing the manager of a morgue in Baghdad. Saadawi recounts: "I saw many dead bodies [...] Not just dead bodies—body parts. Many body parts." While talking with the manager, a man came in requesting his sibling's body, and Saadawi reports the manager blithely replying, "take what you want, and make yourself a body." This traumatic experience served as the crucible that brought the creature to life once again: "in that horrific setting, Frankenstein was born again—two centuries after Mary Shelley's—this time, in Baghdad."

However, at other points, Saadawi has not been so emphatic in linking his creature to the original in Shelley's novel. As Sinéad Murphy notes, it is the global Frankenstein continuum that prompted Saadawi's idea: "Saadawi explains that he was not influenced by Shelley's novel directly so much as 'the vast cultural space that is called 'Frankenstein.'"[22] Consequently, Hadi's recounting of his creation of the Whatsitsname is repeatedly compared to "a Robert De Niro film"[23] by other characters in the novel, displacing, or perhaps better yet overlapping, the issues of acculturation and imperialism from Shelley's text with the notions of global media dominance via Hollywood and the US. Such a vast cultural space calls to mind the sort of "elliptical spaces" that Damrosch highlights world literature as producing.

Yet what makes this notion of world literature so unsatisfying for understanding the globalization of *Frankenstein* and its relationship to *Frankenstein in Baghdad*, as the Warwick Research Collective (WReC) point out, is Damrosch's emphasis on reading and detachment, noting that, for Damrosch, world literature "is to be understood precisely as 'a mode of reading': 'a form of detached engagement with worlds beyond our own place and time.'"[24] Rather than the sort of "elliptical space created between the source and receiving cultures,"[25] WReC propose a notion of world-literature that is connected to the notion of the capitalist world-system of global modernity, what today we might call the political order of global capitalism. While capitalism's globalization necessarily produces unevenness that is experienced "different in every given instance for the simple reason that no two social instances are the same," such unevenness and lived difference "are to be understood as being connected, as being governed by a socio-historical logic of combination, rather than as being contingent and asystematic"—that is global modernity's world-system is "one and unequal."[26] Rather than the notion of purely literary or cultural third spaces of detached readings, they propose a model that bridges our globally differentiated space and time as part of the singular modernity of global capitalism.

To paraphrase Rieder, what is it, then, about *Frankenstein in Baghdad* that speaks to this context? In short, I want to suggest that it is its necropolitical focus on the work with bodies. *Frankenstein in Baghdad* as world-literature butts up against the necropolitical destruction of global south subjects that produces global north subjects and undergirds the contemporary neoliberal-neoimperial moment. For the purposes of this argument, I'm drawing on a few key factors of what Mbembe theorizes as necropolitics. Significantly, necropolitics has its origins in colonial wars "where sovereignty consists fundamentally in the exercise of a power outside the law and where 'peace' is more likely to take on the face of a 'war without end.'"[27] Here, sovereignty entails "*the generalized instrumentalization of human existence and the material destruction of human bodies and populations*,"[28] as opposed to an experience of autonomy through the organization and control of life. In such a necropolitical regime, politics is constituted by "the work of death" and sovereignty is constituted as the indiscriminate "right to kill."[29]

Transferring from the colonial to the current global conjuncture, such neoimperial necropolitical warfare—often accompanied by the soft power of economic sanctions—is typified by surgical strikes and overpowering techno-military might (as in "Shock and Awe"). Rather than the claiming of territory, the point is to eradicate "the enemy's life-support system [...and] to force the enemy into submission regardless of the immediate consequences, side effects, and 'collateral damage' of the military actions."[30]

Anna M. Agathangelou reminds us that the point of such warfare is to secure markets for global capitalism.[31] From the point of view of the neoliberal global north, the dynamics of necropolitics are reversed, such that they are employed in order to maintain and substantiate the "right to liberal life."[32] Moreover, neoliberal subjectivity depends on forgetting the violence to the other that maintains it: "It seems that the New Way Forward, the (un)making and (re)making of (neo) liberal rule of markets, states, subjects, and being requires a forgetting of what is drawn out of our flesh, ecologies, and bodies; this is a necessary condition to participate in a soteriological economy of moribundity."[33] In other words, it's an economy of death in which the salvation of global north subjects is premised on their forgetting their sacrificial murder of those in the global south. We can imagine such a forgetting and disavowal at the end of *Frankenstein* as Walton watches the creature disappear into the distance, his demise (and thus humanity's salvation) promised but never witnessed. Significantly, *Frankenstein in Baghdad* reverses the optics of this final scene and re-centers the monstrous subject in a bid to trouble the rational subject by foregrounding the deathwork upon which the latter is predicated.

In this light, remembering and raising the dead has become a key trope in post-invasion Iraqi art. As Haytham Bahoora writes, "Literary and artistic representations of the body's violent dismemberment and mutilation are a recurring feature of post-2003 Iraqi cultural production, from literature to the visual arts."[34] Critics have likewise noted that the context of a post-invasion Iraq for *Frankenstein in Baghdad* becomes decisively linked to US readers through the unrelenting revelation of bodies and their amputation and dismemberment.[35] This is often presented as both an act of memorial but also ethical confrontation. As Luckhurst notes of the Whatitsname: "The composite formation of Saadawi's monstrous body becomes, then, a gothic emblem for the body that needs to be reconstituted, that needs to count, in an era that abstracts or anonymizes the bodies of the dead."[36] In much contemporary post-invasion Iraqi literature, the emphasis, as Roger Luckhurst and others point out, is on the invisible body of the Iraqi corpse. Such a position drives an ethical response to witness the horrors of neoimperial policy. As Linda Robertson notes, the invasion and occupation of Iraq is politically predicated in the US on the absence of bodies:

> Any attempt to account for the fiasco in Iraq—an opportunistic war of aggression that has cost thousands of American lives and caused hundreds of thousands of Iraqi causalities—must include the American public's capacity to view a sanitized war without either wondering about or protesting the absence of the images of the dead and wounded, both innocents and warriors, particularly during the first three and half years of the war.[37]

However, in *Frankenstein in Baghdad* it's more than just returning bodies to the scene—of reanimating them—that is at stake. In this sense, a metaphorical reanimation of bodies would be to put them in the register of what Margaret Schwartz refers to as iconic martyr corpses that organize an ethical response to the conditions of US neo-imperial policy.[38] As her examples of Emmett Till and Hamza al-Khateeb suggest, such iconic martyr reanimation entails bestowing or restoring subjectivity—a biopolitical process—as figured through the recognition of proper names. But the Whatsitsname resists such iconic subjectivity. At one point, one of his followers attempts to suggest that he is the impossible ideal Iraqi citizen: "the young madman thinks I'm the model citizen that the Iraqi state has filed to produce [. . . b]ecause I'm made up of body parts of people from diverse background—ethnicities, tribes, races, and social classes—I represent the impossible mix that never was achieved in the past."[39] However, because this is attributed to one of his fanatical followers—labeled by the Whatitsname itself as a madman—we should be skeptical of this romanticization.

Instead, *Frankenstein in Baghdad*'s necropolitical production of corpses reveals the global north's subject position as dependent on such actions: the "one and unequal" of world literature. In this sense, *Frankenstein in Baghdad* attaches the Frankensteinian SF tropes of body regeneration to the necropolitical context of the US invasion of Iraq. In so doing, it reveals the design and function of the neoliberal and neoimperial world-system through its emphasis on the work *with* and production *of* corpses that largely resists animation into bodies. This dual emphasis on corpses necessarily takes on a multivalent set of registers, overlapping the production of many thousands of civilian corpses by US-led neoimperial forces and sectarian terror groups, with Hadi's production of the corpse-body of the Whatitsname, as well as the Whatitsname's murder of innocents and terrorists in order to continually regenerate itself.

In *Frankenstein in Baghdad*, then, it's not the in/humanity of the monster—which has been the focus of many western filmic and literary adaptations—that makes it a truly original adaptation. Rather, it's the focus on the bodies, or really the body parts, that comprise the creature. In short, the overdetermined work on corpses is structurally related not only to their otherwise general absence from our picture of the global capitalist world-system, but also the global capitalist world-system's dependence on the production of such corpses that ties the biopolitical construction of populations in the global north to the necropolitical destruction of life in the global south.

In Shelley's novel, scant details accompany the procuring of the bodies—who they were, were they came from, why they were chosen. Somewhat tellingly, in order to remove the scientist from this more macabre and disturbing labor, many popular adaptations have gone to such lengths as to invent the often deformed and/or demented Igor to perform this insalubrious work. In *Frankenstein*, the descriptions of the body procurement and construction is brief. We get a couple of passing references to "dabbl[ing] among the unhallowed damps of the grave [. . .] collect[ing] bones from charnel-houses and disturb[ing], [. . .] the tremendous secrets of the human frame" and the compiling of the creature in his "workshop of filthy creation; [where] eyeballs were starting from their sockets in attending to the details of my employment."[40] But this is largely the extent of it; instead, the focus wavers between the creature's humanity and monstrous visage.

If Shelley's text passes over the matter of the collection and stitching together of body parts somewhat quickly to accentuate other issues, in *Frankenstein in Baghdad*, body part collection is the focus. Yet, it's not the collection of the body parts that is the unsavory labor—in fact, this is initially done out of love (as is giving the monster life). Instead, what is truly monstrous it is the machinations of global political economy that produce the body parts.

As the novel unfolds, we learn that Hadi's inspiration to begin creating the Whatitsname came after the sudden death of his partner, Nahem, via a car bomb. Distraught that he doesn't have a full body to bury—"It had been hard to separate Nahem's flesh from that of [his] horse"[41]—Hadi slowly assembles a substitute corpse out of the various body parts that litter the streets. It is, sadly, not a difficult task. In Saadawi's novel, there is no need to surreptitiously visit charnel houses or slaughter houses, as Baghdad itself is one large open-air morgue due to the US military raids and the near-constant sectarian bombings. Indeed, as Mbembe argues, the point of the sort of necropolitical warfare ravaging Iraq, rather than control, surrender, or assimilation, is simply slaughter: "In the case of massacres in particular, lifeless bodies are quickly reduced to the status of simple skeletons. Their morphology henceforth inscribes them in the register of the undifferentiated generality: simple relics of an unburied pain, empty, meaningless corporealities, strange deposits plunged intro cruel stupor."[42]

It's Hadi's desire to counter this necropolitical proliferation of "meaningless corporealities" that initially drives his work. In direct opposition to Shelley's scientist Victor, animation is an accidental side product, having nothing to do with Hadi's labor to produce a viable corpse for burying. That is, rather than trying to create life, Hadi is trying to create a meaningful corpse. Describing his initial encounter with the corpse that will become the Whatitsname, Hadi tells his friends, "I wanted to hand him over to the forensics department, because it was a complete corpse that had been left in the streets like trash."[43] Yet, when reminded that it wasn't a whole corpse but one that he helped to compose, Hadi simply replies: "I made it complete so it wouldn't be treated as trash, so it would be respected like other dead people and given a proper burial."[44] In other words, *Frankenstein in Baghdad* moves the narrative trope from the production of new life and animation to the production of death, to the creation of corpses that can be known and identified, mapping the move from the biopolitical to the necropolitical.

To whatever extent the Whatitsname serves as metaphor (ideal Iraqi citizen, avenger, criminal/innocent) it also serves as necropolitical synecdoche: the excluded part of the whole of the current neoliberal order imposed through war, austerity, market liberalization and the piling up of bodies that this necessarily entails. In other words, *Frankenstein in Baghdad*'s fantastical, speculative work with bodies serves as an inversion and thus reminder that neoliberalism itself is a work on and production of corpses. Just as countless postcolonial critics (Fanon, Cesaire, and Robinson, to name a few) argued that western Enlightenment modernity is predicated on slavery and imperialism, neoliberal globalization is too grounded on similar actions.

Conclusion: Reversing SF's Colonial Gaze

Turning to *Frankenstein in Baghdad*'s rewriting of *Frankenstein*'s final scene, we can now see how the inexpungable remainder of the monster is less in the form of a general threat (the nameless monstrosity of human hubris or inhuman otherness) that haunts the margins of humanity as popular culture has often received it from Shelley's novel and more a particular reminder of how the ongoing humanly-inhuman horrors in Iraq are a fundamental rather than aberrant aspect of the contemporary global capitalist order. Thus, when *Frankenstein* goes global, it is the monstrousness of necropolitical global modernity looking at us, reaffirming SF's ambivalent, ambiguous relation to the colonial gaze for our contemporary moment. At the very close of the novel, this creature too continues to persist on the margins of the narrative and society, living in an old, dilapidated hotel in an area rendered uninhabitable by the concatenation of a car bomb and a human suicide bomber. Significantly, the ending reverses the optics of Shelley's; now it is the creature peering back at us, the humans: "the specter of an unknown man also lingered there, standing for the past hour at the glassless window of a third floor room, silently watching the people celebrate, smoking and looking every now and then at the dark clouds overhead."[45]

As the Whatsitsname continues to stare out over this life going on in death amidst the destruction of the Bataween neighborhood, its gaze may remind us of Walter Benjamin's Angel of History watching the wreckage of progress accumulate endlessly and stretching the empty homogenous time of modernity onwards. The Whatsitsname compels us to recognize that the wreckage isn't a mere byproduct of global modernity; rather, *Frankenstein in Baghdad*'s reversal of the colonial gaze reveals the necropolitical work and production of corpses as the source of global modernity. Repeating and reversing SF's foundational colonial gaze, *Frankenstein in Baghdad* at once ties the history of SF from 1818 to 2018 in a loop. We're still haunted or, better yet, global modernity is still propped up by, the prodigious monstrous corpses that it produces to justify itself. The looping of this textual relationship merely underscores the monstrous repetitiveness of this logic as the nonsynchronous necropolitical time of the global capital world-system.

Therefore, in this Frankensteinian narrative, the Whatitsname can't be extinguished or promise to extinguish itself as its life in death is necessary for revealing this necropolitical narrative. It is this perspective—from the necropolitical, from the corpse looking back at us—that must be foregrounded, thereby troubling any notion of rational subjectivity, of global north order versus global south disorder. In short, the SF lessons of *Frankenstein*'s globalization aren't the lessons of the past—as the founder and guiding spirit of SF; instead, the novel's circulation of Frankensteinian SF tropes continues to define our present and haunt the shape of our future.

Part Two

Frankensteinia

5

Frankenstein in the Popular Imagination

Sidney E. Berger

Certain figures in literature achieve iconic status, known to many more people than have read the works in which the figures appear. Hamlet, Beowulf, Rhett Butler and Scarlet O'Hara, Julius Caesar, Romeo and Juliet, Doctor Faustus. Their stories transcend their sources. Frankenstein's monster must be added to this brief list. The most enduring character of Mary Shelley's tale has come into the modern consciousness in a variety of ways. It is hard to imagine any other character in literature—and few from real life—so universally recognizable as is Dr. Frankenstein's creature. Depictions of the creature have proliferated over the 200 years of the novel's existence. As recently as April 4, 2020, *The Wall Street Journal* cartoon "Pepper . . . And Salt" had an image of a scientist asking a tall monster figure with a flat-topped head and bolts in his neck, "So, how's that abnormal brain working out?" No need to mention the interlocutor's name. All will recognize Frankenstein's monster figure. The evolution and the extent of the monster imagery is the subject of the present chapter.

The 1818 first edition of the novel was unillustrated, and in some ways that was the most powerful depiction of the characters—especially of the "monster"—for it allows each reader to conjure up its hideousness based on one's own worst fears and nightmares. Depicting the monster—that is, in *pictures*, in a visual manifestation—lets us see him and eventually become familiar with him, which then reduces his scariness. The more familiar we are with something—the more the unknown becomes known—the less afraid we will be. So, the first iteration of the book's characters offers us something that is completely unknown, and the maximum potential for frightfulness.

The second edition of 1824 is merely a resetting, page for page, of the first, with only minimal textual changes; it, too, lacked illustrations. The third edition of 1831 (see Figure 5.1), billed by one bookseller as the first illustrated edition, includes only two images, facing each other: a frontispiece and a vignette on the title page. The title page picture is of Victor Frankenstein's departure from his home, accompanied by his statement, "The day of my departure at length arrived." The frontispiece, however, has a much more provocative caption: "By the glimmer of the half-extinguished light, I saw the dull, yellow eye of the creature open; it breathed hard, and a convulsive motion agitated its limbs. . . . I rushed out of the room." This statement comes at the beginning of Chapter 5. The illustrator has indeed chosen a vibrant moment in the text from

Figure 5.1 *Frankenstein* title page (London: Colburn and R. Bentley, 1823]. Courtesy Smith College Library.

which to create an image; here, Victor's creature comes to life for the first time. Indeed, the many ways and modes in which the creature can come to life presents an intriguing psychological puzzle: why are we so drawn to enacting, even playing, the creature when he clearly experiences pain and humiliation, and is misunderstood even by his own creator? This chapter concerns the multitudinous ways in which modern popular culture, particularly in the West, appropriates and transforms the Frankenstein myth. What is it about Victor Frankenstein's creature that makes people of all ages and identities want to put on the monster head associated with the creature, dress as the creature, play with dolls and other toys made in his image, read novels and comic books about his life and further adventures, play games that invent new ways to enact his experience, and even eat breakfast cereal, snacks and candy promoting his image?

The paraphernalia of popular culture that I have collected under the term "Frankensteiniana" concerns the desire to wear, toy with, and ingest aspects of the creature's appearance and mentality. When we put on a Frankenstein mask for Halloween or some other costume event, do we become the creature even temporarily? There is an opposite question too: in the gaming community, "Frankensteinization" is "the power to turn others into Frankenstein monsters," according to the "Superpowerwiki," a website that tracks powers and capabilities of characters for gaming purposes.[1] We are drawn to becoming, or putting on (as in drag), the creature's visible identity, while at the same time we are horrified at the thought of becoming him—hence the superpower to force others to be trapped in his body, to experience his monstrosity. I take these two responses people have to Mary Shelley's invention, reshaped as he has been by Hollywood movies into a more disfigured and less intelligent creature, to be the guiding principles in the proliferation of Frankensteiniana: a desire to put him on as a kind of dress (the costume allows one to act out as the creature), and a horror of actually becoming him (being singled out as so different that no one understands you, and people flee your presence). The first is what I will call the "drag effect," meaning that dressing as the creature allows a temporary adoption of his personality and mannerisms; the second is the "scapegoat effect," because actually being monstrous is what we all fear—there is no costume to remove because one is actually the thing itself, a thing rather than a person and yet a thing that feels its repulsiveness, rejection, and pain all too keenly.

Another way to think about these two effects is to understand their role semiotically within the code of the Frankenstein myth. That is, all these Frankenstein costumes, comic books, masks, foods, games and toys participate in a code of signs much as do words in a language. Semiotics, the theory of how signs function in a code, has been applied to fashion, advertising, art history, and Disney theme parks.[2] It is possible to consider Frankensteiniana as a code of signs, these being the identifiable markers of the Frankenstein creature as Hollywood has transformed him: the Boris Karloff head and scars, the ungainly body and heavy high-soled boots, the ragged clothing and green-hued skin, and all the other indicators or signs that communicate monstrosity, lethal capacity, and outsized body parts, but also confusion, malevolence, or childish delight. Semiotically studied, Frankensteiniana can be considered a system of signs that, under different configurations such as a scary Halloween mask versus a breakfast cereal, communicate very different aspects of the myth. Some of the signs, such as Frankenstein costumes, allow the wearer to act out (the drag effect) their inner monster in so far as that communicates great strength, physical stature, a frightening masculinity. Other signs offer a more playful engagement with the drag effect, communicating fun, comicalness, wildness. By contrast, those signs that engage the scapegoat effect communicate an experience of isolation, pain, anger, humiliation: these signs belong to interactive games (where the scapegoat does not choose this identity for themselves just as the creature does not), as well as frightening masks that encompass the entire head, and narrative forms such as books and films that heighten the victimhood belonging to the one scapegoated as well as the terror felt by his own victims.

After outlining how Shelley's creature came to be iconically represented in the ways that we recognize him today, I will present a selection of Frankensteinian objects drawn from the popular culture of twentieth- and twenty-first-century America. Concluding the chapter is a table of the extensive array of Frankensteinia I have researched. I will leave it to the readers' imagination to determine whether each object belongs to the scapegoat or drag semiotic systems; in some cases, both code systems will be possible depending on how the object is used. Many of the objects I explore in this chapter are drawn from the Smith College library, which houses a treasure trove of Frankenstein books, comics, spinoffs, and more. In many of the images accompanying this chapter— and in untold numbers of images in the popular depiction of the creature—we see the influence of Boris Karloff.[3] When the *Wall Street Journal* celebrated the 200th anniversary of the novel in its story of December 30, 2017, it chose the Boris Karloff image as the prototypical depiction of the monster. Karloff's representation of the creature shows him as monstrous, when in the prose of the text he was not. His actions are monstrous, however, so perhaps the word "monster" *is* appropriate. Victor Frankenstein himself uses the word *monster*, along with *creature, spectre, fiend, demon, wretch, thing, devil*, and *ogre*. He is speaking as much metaphorically as he is physically, but the use of those words, especially *monster*, to describe him has clearly influenced artists' representations and the popular imagination's depiction of him.

Although there was more than a century of theatrical versions of *Frankenstein* offering a variety of Frankenstein's monsters, and even an earlier film (the short Edison-produced 1910 *Frankenstein*), the Universal film version of 1931 inextricably established Karloff and his image of the monster in the minds of generations to come (see Figures 5.2 and 5.3). The flat-topped head, the prominent features, and most of all, the bolts in the neck are Karloffian, and have become the quintessential elements of the classic Frankenstein image. Alan Brookland explains:

> [C]redit for creating the classic monster look goes largely to the king of monster make-up, Jack Pierce. His monster has all the classic features: square head, brain insertion scar on the forehead and, most importantly, the bolts through the neck (actually electrodes used to conduct the electricity used to bring the monster to life). It is Jack Pierce who puts the pieces together to give us the monster's iconic look.[4]

For a popular audience—one unlikely to have read the original—movie makers needed some logical explanation for the animation of the inanimate monster that could be visually thrilling. Electricity was the answer, and the bolts were born along with the monster. The image of those bizarre and dehumanizing bolts has remained in the popular consciousness, even though, in Shelley's novel, Victor mostly experiments with chemistry and anatomy; electricity only comes into play when he requires the spark of life to animate his creation: "It was on a dreary night of November that I beheld the accomplishment of my toils. With an anxiety that almost amounted to agony, I collected the instruments of life around me, that I might infuse a spark of being into the lifeless thing that lay at my feet."[5] The word "spark" certainly refers to electricity, though readers are not told what scientific tool would impart a spark of electricity. There is no description of the necessary mechanics—flipped switches, attached cables—that the 1931 film presents in high drama. We only read that it opens its eyes and starts to move.

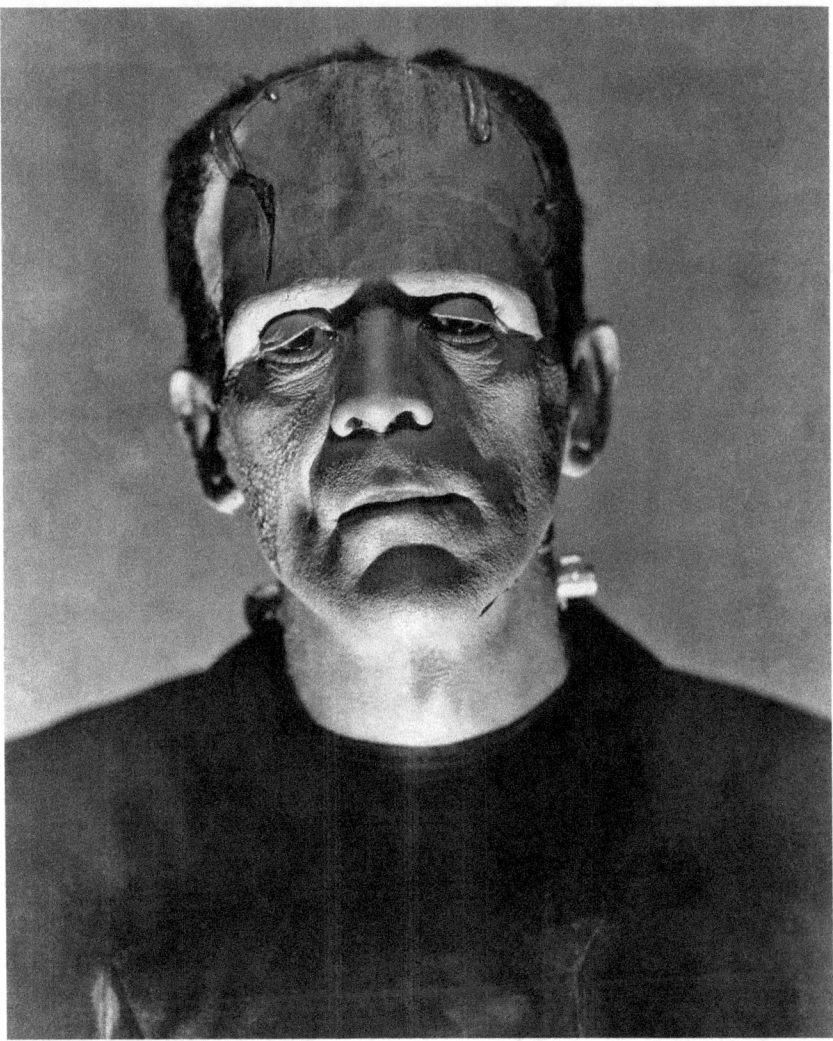

Figure 5.2 Boris Karloff in Bride of Frankenstein, 1935. Everett Collection.

This does not give illustrators as much to go on as do the bolts, and those devices have been reproduced in countless illustrations and objects since 1931.

For the most part, in myriad depictions of the creature that have proliferated in the twentieth and twenty-first centuries, one will see interpretations of the Karloffian monster. And there is a remarkable array of movies (more than 200) and television programs with the Frankenstein theme, including those aimed at teenagers, fans of westerns and science fiction, viewers into comedies, sex, and other monsters. Interestingly, one place where Karloff's image has not dominated the visual presentation of Frankenstein's monster is in new publications of the novel. This makes sense, since

Figure 5.3 Poster for *Frankenstein*, 1931. Everett Collection.

Figure 5.4 Nino Carbe cover for Frankenstein, 1932. More of Carbe's Frankenstein images available at www.ninocarbe.com. Reproduced courtesy of Liza Carbe.

the novel presents Shelley's vision, which precedes that used in the Universal films. And yet, the originally intended image of an appealing-looking creature (Victor says "I had selected his features as beautiful") has taken on increasing ugliness over the decades and centuries, partly occasioned by the horror of the monster's actions, and partly caused by people's imagination. The Nino Carbe illustration for the cover of a 1930s edition of the tale is a case in point (see Figure 5.4). Ugly and shocking sell more than beauty and the mundane. The character has become a commercial commodity, one that can be indexed toward the drag or the scapegoat effect.

Victor Frankenstein's fictional experiments and their results spawned a whole genre of illustration, those in which the scientist is shown with his laboratory, or only body parts or the doctor's tools are shown, hinting at his bringing together limbs and viscera to form the whole person (no matter how unfaithful this is to the original). In some cases, an illustration to prepare a reader for the novel shows practically nothing at all, with the suggestion that the text will speak for itself; or that the story is so gruesome that it would be wrong to depict it; or that the illustration creates a mood rather than showing a picture of something concrete.[6] Artist Maciej Ratajski creatively suggested the monster's origin by designing a cover image that presents fractured lettering, suggesting the disparate parts the illustrator wants us to think about with respect to the "building" of the monster (see Figure 5.5).

Though the original novel is dark and filled with horror, dread, and misery, over the last two centuries, the figure of Frankenstein has transformed into the figure of the

Figure 5.5 Creative cover for *Frankenstein* by Maciej Ratajski. Reproduced courtesy of the artist.

monster, and the monster got less monstrous. We thus find literally thousands of images of the monster in humorous depictions, such as in the 1948 movie *Abbott and Costello Meet Frankenstein*. In the 1960s, the Frankenstein monster was revived in the TV show *The Munsters*, Fred Gwyn portraying the creature, all decked out with the Boris Karloff look, bolts and all (see Figure 5.6). In the happy spirit of a 1960s sitcom, the monster not only has a bride, he has also been blessed with a whole family. By the time the monster has been around for a century and a half, it has lost most of its monstrousness; it has become familiar, ripe for parody and for comic use. A case in point is the movie *Young Frankenstein*, in which the whole story has become a vehicle for humor. Victor Frankenstein is a bumbler, the added character Igor, who appeared in the Boris Karloff version, is played by Marty Feldman, known for his comedic skills, many lines are added for their sheer hilarity, and the monster dances and gets a wife, who appreciates his Schwanzschtücker. The story no longer causes revulsion, so it can be employed for other purposes than to scare or create gloom. There are also tattoos of the monster, who has become friendly enough that people wear permanent

Figure 5.6 Fred Gwynn as Herman Munster on the TV show *The Munsters*, with the prototypical neck bolts.

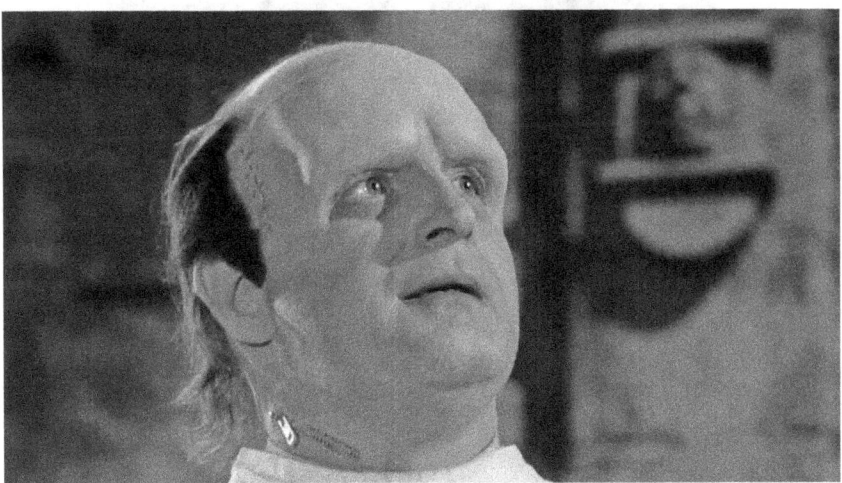

Figure 5.7 *Young Frankenstein*. Peter Boyle as Frankenstein's monster, with a zipper on his neck rather than bolts.

pictures of him on their skin, along with endless comic books where he is front and center.[7]

The Frankenstein monster has become an industry in itself. There seems to be no end to the ways that the images and the deeds the monster perpetrated have been coopted by commercial enterprise for profit, regardless of how hideous he may have appeared and how ugly his acts were. This is popular culture at its most crass, and its most profitable. One collector, Mark Glassy, a University of California, Riverside research scientist, has amassed a collection of more than 100,000 items related to Frankenstein and his monster.[8]

Additional images by the thousands show the character used in humorous ways, including greeting cards (Figure 5.8), artwork (see the cover), and posters (Figure 5.9). In the world of the plastic arts, thousands of objects riff on the monster's image. Audio speakers are a case in point (Figure 5.10). Action figures are another category of

Figure 5.8 Greeting Card from Stufmonsterslike.com.

Figure 5.9 Frankenstein poster.

Figure 5.10 Frankenstein Monster audio speaker.

Figure 5.11 Frankenstein action figure with rattling chains, Telco 1992.

monster items and hundreds of representations of Frankenstein's monster can be found, as in Figure 5.11.

In the world of comestibles, and with science taking liberties with the creation of new forms of food, books have been published about Frankenfoods. Henry I. Miller and Gregory Conko published *The Frankenfood Myth: How Protest and Politics Threaten the Biotech Revolution*,[9] addressing the fear that surrounds genetically modified foods, and riffing on the "Franken" as a prefix. Some of the foods falling under the Frankenstein influence are children's cereals, corn, and tomatoes (see Figures 5.12, 5.13, and 5.14), the last of these shown with no explanation other than the name—it is called a "Frankentomato." Of course, it needs no name. All one needs is the unsubtle reference of the stitching, reminiscent of the way the monster was "built." And one can pay for these products using a Frankenstein bill, a pair of bills in which the artist is plugged into the story and its takeoffs: the woman is called a "runaway bride" and the monster is "love lorn"—a sentimental element in the spinning out of the plot in the original book as well as the film *Bride of Frankenstein*.[10]

Figure 5.12 Frankenberry cereal, Courtesty of the General Mills Archives.

Figure 5.13 Frankenfood image of GMO corn, DDees.com

Figure 5.14 Frankentomato.

In the automotive world there are cars that are put together from disparate parts and labelled Frankencars. And similarly, composed of two types of footwear is the Frankenshoe (see Figure 5.15). This item is sold at TFP /The Fashion Place, and it is billed as "Frankenshoes: Open-Toed Wedge Sneakers with Cut-Outs by DSquared2." Again, its designer knows that the customers will understand the "Franken" part of the name. This blending has been used for untold numbers of objects: toys, beds, clothing, household implements, and more. The monster is part of the fabric of our commercial world—part of the cultural imagination.

For more than a century, Frankenstein's monster has appeared in cartoons, most of them political, as can be seen today by a search of the web, where which one will find thousands of them mocking our political figures. Consistent themes of such cartoons are the uncontrolled figure running rampant through the world, disregarding law, order, and the rights of others; the evil unleashed upon the world by the improper or unbridled use of science; and the silence or helplessness of those around the central figure in the cartoon. Frankenstein's monster is the perfect image to conjure up, partly because he represents these themes, and partly because he need not be named in the cartoons as the figure is so recognizable.

The creature Mary Shelley conjured two centuries ago is still going strong, thanks to our fascination with the scary, the bizarre, the unknown, and the provocative. Modern science has now created test-tube babies and cloned animals, brought people back from death with Automated External Defibrillators, pieced people together after body parts have been severed, transferred body parts from one person (living or dead) to another, helped couples conceive life outside the body, kept all kinds of animals alive in hospital beds and laboratories long after they had technically perished, and performed

Figure 5.15 Frankenshoes: Open-Toes Wedge Sneakers with Cut-Outs by DSquared2. Courtesy DSquared2.

many franken-operations on plants and animals—including people—for decades. As Ed Finn and David H. Guston write in their *Wall Street Journal* article celebrating the 200th anniversary of the publication of Shelley's novel, the story's "durability derives not just from the fact that Frankenstein is a great work of literature, but from the way it encompasses our anxieties about scientific creativity and responsibility."[11] They point out that the novel asks the same questions we must ask today in our highly scientific world: "What is life, what does it mean to be human, and what are our responsibilities as creators?"

We have seen the Frankenstein creature move from the shocking and forbidden to the popularly human, the bathetic, and the humorous—all signaled in the way artists have dealt with this most provocative character and story, and the way the character has been used for untold numbers of products.[12] However, how consumers see themselves in the creature and how they respond to the films, books, costumes, games, and consumables is far more indicative of the creature's importance to the western imagination, popular and artistic. Clearly, he embodies the monstrous outcast, the scapegoat of Shelley's novel, and the monstrosity of scientific experiment, the odd body onto which costuming, masks, and games allow us to project our worst selves or to parody to our hearts' delight.

Appendix

In doing the research for this chapter, I came across an amazing array of objects with a Frankenstein connection. For just one example, see this Frankenstein watch (Figure 5.16). The world of Frankenstein has become so much a part of the popular imagination that almost everyone knows (often incorrectly) who Frankenstein was. An immense number of products use the image. Here is an abbreviated listing of some of those products.

Figure 5.16 Frankenstein watch. Courtesy Smith College Library.

Table 5.1 A Partial List of Frankenstein Products

Action figures	Clothes hangers	Guestbook albums
Aprons	Clothes pins	Hair wraps, clips, and other hair products
Arm covers	Clothing of all kinds (shirts, pants, socks, sweaters, scarves, pajamas, etc.)	
Autograph albums		Halloween lanterns
Backpacks		Halloween ornaments
Badge holders	Clutch bags	Handcuffs
Badge reels	Coasters	Hats
Bags of many kinds	Coffee cozies	Head wraps
Balloons	Coins	Headphone jacks
Banners	Collages	Herb grinders
Bar decor	Collars (for people and dogs)	Hoodies
Bar soap	Coloring books	Hosiery
Baseball caps	Comic books	Incense
Bath salts	Condiment bottles	Inflatable, light-up figures
Beer can holders	Cookie baking pans	Invitation cards
Beer glasses and steins	Cookie cutters	iPad covers
Bells	Cookies	Iron-on monograms
Belt buckles	Coptic-style binding	Jackets
Belts	Costumes	Jar containing Frankenstein's heart
Bibs	Crayons	
Blankets (including baby blankets)	Crocheting kits	Jewelry
Board games	Cufflinks	Jewelry boxes and casks
Body suits	Decals	Key rings, key chains, and key fobs
Bookmarks	Decks of playing cards	
Bookplates	Dishes	Kites
Books (and Pop-up Books)	Dog "jackets"	Labels (see Return-address labels)
Bottle caps	Doggy treats	
Bottle openers	Dolls (see Paper dolls)	Lamp shades
Bowls	Drinking glasses	Lanterns
Boxes of all kinds	Duvet covers	Lapel buttons (including "Frankenstein For President")
Bracelets	Earrings	
Brooches	Elbow patches	
Buttons (for clothing)	Eyeglasses	Lapel pins
CD and DVD cases	Fabrics	Leather bikinis
Candy (see Lollipops)	Face powder holders	Leggings and leg covers
Candy dispensers	Fake cupcakes	Letter openers
Calendars	Figurines of many kinds	License plate holders
Cake toppers and cupcake toppers and other cake decorations	Finger puppets	License plates
	Fingernail art	Light bulbs
Candles and candle holders	Flash drives	Light switch wall plates
Candy	Flasks	Lip balm
Candy bowls	Garden décor	Liquor bottles
Candy corn	Gift bags	Lobby cards
Card holders (business cards; place cards for guests)	Gift cards	Lockets
	Glass gems	Lollipops
Ceramic items (statues, table décor)	Glitter (with tiny Frankenstein-shaped pieces)	Luggage tags
		Magnets
Charm bracelets		Make-up bags
Christmas tree ornaments	Gloves and fingerless gloves	Marshmallows and marshmallow pops
Cigarette lighters	Graphic novels	
Clocks	Greeting cards	

Masks
Mason jars
Maternity shirts
Mirrors
Mobiles
Money clips
Mousepads
Mousetraps
Movie journals
Mugs and steins
Nail decals
Name tags
Napkins
Necklace pendants and other
  necklaces
Nesting dolls
Notepads
Painted gourds
Pajamas
Paper clip holders
Paper dolls
Party favors and party favor
  bags
Patches (iron-on)
Pencil cases
Pencil cups
Pencil toppers
Pencils & pencil sharpeners
Penis covers (knitted)
Penises (sex toys made from
  "sewn-together parts")
Pens
Pet tags
PEZ dispensers
Phone cases
Photo albums
Photo frames

Pillows and pillow cases
Piñatas
Pins (see Lapel pins)
Pipes (for smoking)
Planters
Plates
Plush toys (crocheted)
Popcorn slider (holds a flat bag
  of popcorn)
Pop-up books and cards
Posters and other wall art
Pots (for succulent plants)
Prints
Puppets
Purses
Quilts
Return-address labels
Ribbons and bows
Rings
Rocks (hand-painted)
Rubber ducks
Rubber stamps
Sex toys (see Penises)
Sheets and pillow cases
Shoes and shoelaces
Shower curtains
Skate boards
Sketchbooks
Sleep masks
Slippers and other footwear
Soap holders
Soda bottles (Frankenstein
  Green-Apple Soda)
Speakers
Stationery
Stencils
Stickers

Stockings
Straws
String art
Sunglasses
Table décor and table
  centerpieces
Tape & tape dispensers
Tattoos (temporary)
Teapots
Tee shirts
Telephone cases
Throw pillows
Tic-Tac-Toe games
Tie tacks
Ties
Toothbrush and toothbrush
  holder
Tote bags
Towels
Toys
Vases
Wall hangings
Wallpaper
Wallets
Water bottles
Whiskey bottles
Wigs and headpieces
Wind-up toys
Wine bottles
Wine corks
Wrapping paper
Wreaths
Wrist bands
Wrist watches
Zipper bags
Zipper foam bottle cooler
  holders

6

Frankenstein Masks: Perpetuating the Monster Assemblage

Taylor Hagood

For as much attention as Frankenstein—the novel, the monster, the movies—has received, very little scholarly or even historical attention has been paid to masks and costumes of the monster manufactured and retailed to the general public. Although not an easy history to trace or a simple textual body to analyze in terms of intention and reception, the manufactured envisionings of the monster nevertheless constitute readable phenomena that interweave with the literary and filmic incarnations of the Frankenstein story, image, and idea. This chapter represents a step toward an in-depth delving into the history of these masks and reading of the ways they channel the monster and the images and concepts surrounding him in various contexts to produce a commodity. Particularly interesting are the ways these masks assemble/reassemble aspects of the monster as presented in film, especially the Universal monster films, perpetuating both specific and generic notions of the monster to multiple ends and effects for manufacturers, marketers, collectors, and wearers.

Before turning to the history of the masks, I want to outline the machinery that guides my analysis of them. It is daunting and highly speculative to imagine the many nuances of the affects of the masks themselves for individuals wearing, manufacturing, or encountering them. Such work would seem to necessitate ferreting out comments on masks made in writing or on film over the past nine decades as well as interviewing as many people as possible. I am after something a bit more speculative in that I am considering what "resides" within the objects themselves. Analyzing an inanimate thing such as a mask in such terms requires considering that thing an "actant" in the way Bruno Latour describes nonhuman, nonactive, non-self-evidently-endowed-with-agency items to function in dynamic social situations.[1] I well realize this assertion to be one made on a contested field, but I embrace that contestation and the free-flowing and difficult-to-locate locus of agency and/or source of action that follows when considering such modes of affect when an inanimate thing and an animate human converge. Because that thing, in this case (a mask), so resembles, and in fact influences and can be animated by, and arguably can even animate, a human, an uncanny result follows. Since at least Plato, philosophers and cultural critics have pondered where exactly a mask ends and a "real" person wearing it begins. Because this type of affect is fluid and rooted to the time of the mask's manufacture even as it may be influenced by the moment of a later (which might include a first) encounter, such a discussion must be speculative.

The history of Frankenstein monster masks is inextricably connected with the ways Hollywood films have projected the monster. Although the monster had appeared as a Quasimodo-like hairy Wildman in the 1910 film, *Frankenstein*, unsurprisingly, the story of Frankenstein's monster masks really starts with Universal Studio's *Frankenstein* (1931), starring Boris Karloff in the now iconic make-up design of Jack Pierce. Unlike the articulate monster Mary Shelley imagined in her novel, this monster depended on other modes of communicating, including gesticulation, action, sounds, and subtleties, which together created a very different kind of effect from that of the movie monster that immediately preceded him in Universal's *Dracula*, released earlier in 1931. Frankenstein's monster's persona was far more working-class in comparison to Dracula's aristocratic affect. This working-class identity finds conveyance also in the monster's costume, for as Rafael Jean and Robert I. Lublin write,

> the black clothes that the Monster wears are well-worn and dusty. Practically speaking, this makes no sense. In the movie, Henry Frankenstein is a Baron with a considerable fortune and dresses in clean, expensive, brightly colored clothing. There is no reason he would lack new or at least clean clothing for his creation.[2]

Jean and Lublin go on to explain that, rather than attempting realism, director James Whale was following the diktats of German expressionism, with the clothing invoking "enormous size, physical danger, crudity, uncouthness, and death."[3] The monster's body is big, his gait shambling, the facial expression dull—all designed to convey lack of sophistication and glamour, the opposite of an undead Count.

Jack Pierce's make-up quickly became *the* patented look for the monster. Moviegoers clutched in the grip of the Great Depression saw a dull-faced, hungry, working-class monster in rags. The visible stitches may well have suggested a man coming apart at the seams, while the flat-top cranium implied that Dr. Frankenstein, unaffected by hard times, had a dilettante's carelessness about aesthetics *en route* to creating lesser human life. The intriguing question is: Was the image of the monster meant to represent the elite's view of the working class or the working class's view of itself or both? It is a painful irony that theatergoers who had never read Shelley's novel thought the monster to be Frankenstein, himself. In fact, they could hardly be blamed for thinking the monster's name to be Frankenstein since the name was featured prominently with Karloff's made-up face. Even the film's trailer concluded with the image of the monster and the words "See Karloff in his most terrifying performance … as the fiendish monster … and you'll know why there can never be another … Frankenstein." That appearance and the grunting, stumbling, murderous quasi-undead version of the monster fixed an image in the public imagination that defines what seems to be the distinct experience of *being* the monster when wearing the mask. That character is one of horror, to be sure, but of a big-lug quality that can easily cross the line into comedy. Indeed, the most powerful moments in *Frankenstein*—for example, the moment the monster throws the little girl into the lake—can create in the viewers the impulse of laughter and repulsion simultaneously.

The Karloff-monster face, the body, the costume, ironically became, as it were, thingified parts, isolatable and functioning as identifiers of "Frankenstein." This monster, famously made up of disparate body parts, now existed in the public imagination as instantly iconic parts, whether the flat head, the licks of black hair, the electric bolts coming out of the neck, the almost-closed eyelids, and the stitches. In other words, Universal Studio's "Frankenstein the monster" was a Frankenstein monster of the Frankenstein monster. In this perpetuation of the Frankenstein ethos, manufacturers now had workable parts that could be assembled/reassembled and marketed to the consuming public. As long as designers could bring (most of) these parts into play, a mask could be understood to be the monster, even in the most generic sense. I would highlight the concept of assembly/reassembly especially in light of Latour's identification of constant reassembling of social situations and communities, for Frankenstein masks would seem to bear a complex relationship to reassemblies of the social. It is likely that most mask designers were, either by their own intention or by following the directives of companies, looking primarily to design a compelling mask for the market based on color and shape trends of the moment. At the same time, however, designers and/or companies may have played a prescriptive role in their designs. Meanwhile, there are the questions surrounding the wearers and their intentions in given moments. Navigating these inscrutable waters offers major challenges, of course, and speculation must be brought into play along with more easily discernible markers, testimonies of manufacturers or the wearer's intentions.

The first mask to consider is the over-the-head latex one created by Don Post in 1948, which collector/historian Lee Lambert has called "the most iconic design" of the man who has been called "The Godfather of Halloween."[4] (See Figure 6.1). Post pioneered the over-the-head latex mask in the late 1930s and pursued product licensing. Post capitalized on the iconic monsters of the Universal films and would later create the now-famous Tor Johnson and William Shatner masks; his approach with this mask was to create not a generic monster but the specific face of the monster in the Universal films. Interestingly, the mask copied exactly the features of the monster actor made up not as Karloff but rather as Glenn Strange, the fourth actor to assume the monster's mantle in Universal films at that point. As Donald F. Glut has noted, by the time Glenn Strange played the monster for the first time in 1944's *House of Frankenstein* the marketing and licensing machine was well underway, with Strange's

> familiar, craggy-lined face, usually in the make-up created for him by Bud Westmore's team in Universal-International's comedy-horror classic *Abbott and Costello Meet Frankenstein* (1948), that became the template for a seemingly endless output of masks, dart boards, games, puzzles, model kits, decks of cards, transfers, iron-ons, movie viewers, paint-by-numbers sets, loose-leaf binders, statues, swizzle sticks, candy and yet more paraphernalia.[5]

The aesthetic of this mask depends greatly on verisimilitude, in keeping with the licensing concept, in that the mask does not just represent some idea about Frankenstein's monster but rather recreates *the actual monster* as envisioned in the Universal films. According to Lambert, "the mask of the Frankenstein's Monster used

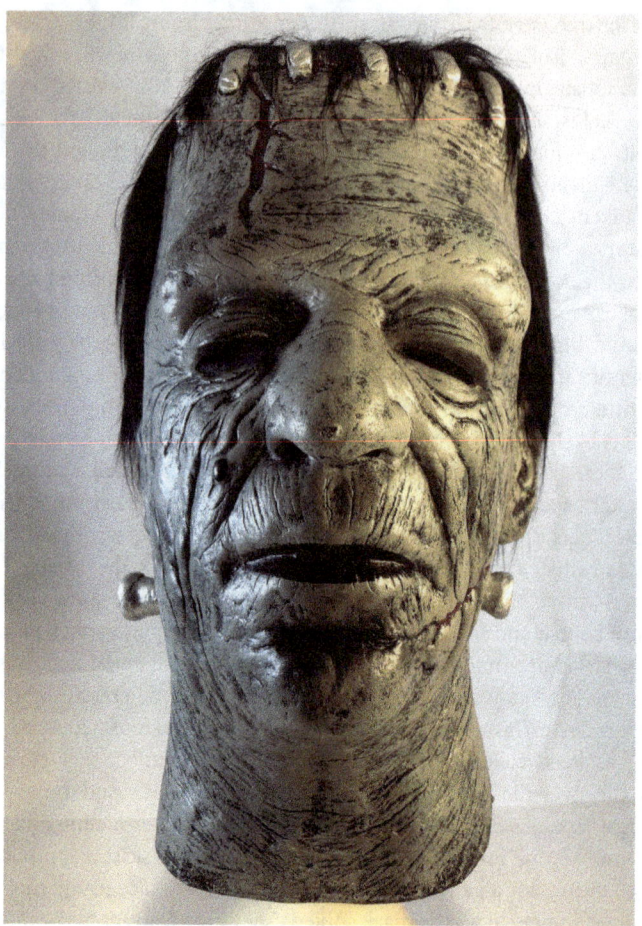

Figure 6.1 Don Post mask, originally created in 1948, featuring the likeness of Glenn Strange (photograph by Taylor Hagood).

the mold for the prop head made for the scene in *Abbott and Costello Meet Frankenstein*, where the monster falls through the pier."[6] In fact, this mask not only functioned to make its wearer look exactly like Strange, its accuracy was put to work in actual filmmaking, for Glut claims that Post made a "silver-gray mask […] for the actor's personal appearances as the character."[7] Anyone who dons (if I may be permitted the pun) this mask was/is keying into the idea of becoming the monster as he exists in the film. The item carries about it the certification of being official: it is the next best thing to the actual make-up, which means that its affect is one-of-a-kind of hyperreal authenticity à la Baudrillard.[8] There results an interesting intentionality that blends both play and seriousness in a way less imaginable with Karloff; in fact, Strange had played the monster both in horror and comic films, and it is easy to imagine wearers playing it for both effects.

Post's 1948 Strange-based mask might be read as carrying a number of revealing implications. The mask is very much of its moment—the idea of creating a Karloff mask might well have seemed passé to Post perhaps because the more prosperous post-the Second World War moment may have found Karloff's Depression-era depiction out of touch. Anyone buying and wearing this mask surely saw him (or perhaps her) self being Glenn Strange being the monster as signified by the assemblage of those Frankenstein parts. The effect of such a mask is based in authenticity, suggesting an association with Strange-as-the-monster as much as the monster himself in a generic sense. That said, in an interesting twist in the context of verisimilitude, it seems that many theatergoers and costume-wearers did not actually realize at the time that the monster was played by Strange instead of Karloff. Ironically, the make-up similarities worked so well, that unintentionally the monster literally existed as a mash-up of two different actors. When Karloff died in 1969, the *New York Times* printed a photo of Strange as the monster instead of Karloff.

And yet Karloff, of course, is better remembered by the general public as the monster in our time, and any play for originality within the Universal universe means recreating his look, which Post did two decades later. According to Lambert, the Karloff mask

> was originally released in 1967; however, this mask was not in constant production. It was produced through to the mid 1970s, then discontinued until it was released again for several years in the mid 1980s. It was released again in the late 1980s to be sold at Universal Studios theme parks, then one more time as part of the 1998 Calendar Reissue series.[9]

The mask lovingly recreated Karloff's face in the monster make-up in a move that seems to take "historical accuracy" to another level (see Figure 6.2). Evidently by this time the veneration of the first wave of monsters had taken root, and creating a mask to represent Karloff seems to key into a different kind of intentionality. Presumably such a wearer could tell the difference between Strange and Karloff and might be making a statement of loyalty to the latter's legacy. This mask's target consumer may have been looking to collect a creation by Post rather than just wear monster memorabilia. The collector aspect of these creations seems to have increased along with the idea of playing a "classic" film version of the monster. Still being produced and sold at the time of this writing, these two masks continue to carry retail power as serious collector's items.

Even as Post was designing these ultra/hyper realistic masks, a very different species of Frankenstein mask was being manufactured and marketed. These masks differed from the latex over-the-head ones; they were made of molded plastic and held in place by elastic bands (see Figure 6.3). As they were much cheaper, they were sold along with costumes for children to go trick-or-treating in, and were packaged in boxes with clear plastic cut-out parts to display the masks, which were the selling points, rather than the costumes themselves. Those accompanying costumes were often made of cheap (and hot) plastic which were silk-screen printed. These mask/costume combos were products of the postwar era as well and were produced by three major costume

Figure 6.2 Don post mask, originally released in 1967, featuring the likeness of Boris Karloff (HalloweenCostumes.com / FUN.com).

companies: Collegeville Flag and Manufacturing Company, H. Halpern Company, and Ben Cooper. Unlike Post's licensed and official approach, these companies may or may not have obtained licenses for their productions, and examining a selection of these products reveals a strategy of (re)assembling and using various labels for the monster to create marketable products.

One product by Halpern, often marketed under the name "Halco," makes the surprising move of presenting the monster's face in Caucasian flesh color, which is a departure from the silver as well as the green typically used in Frankenstein film advertising and masks. The neck bolts and the tell-tale red line of vertically oriented stitches near the right temple evoke the Universal image, but overall the mask represents a more generic take on the monster. The accompanying costume departs even more from the Universal precedent, featuring an image of a completely different kind of monster. Club in hand and exhibiting a distinctly round head, the monster looks like a demented zombie from a horror movie, and under him is written simply "Monster."

Figure 6.3 A reproduction children's over-the-head mask in the style of Ben Cooper, Collegeville, and Halco (photograph by Taylor Hagood).

The image on the costume signals an interesting challenge for the designers and marketers, which is how to produce a commodity for children that traffics in horror of a very specific kind. The mask and costume in a sense seem to work against each other, with the costume apparently designed to trump the mask by selling itself as horrible in an arguably zany way. However, it was the mask that would have been immediately visible to customers, so what did parents and children think when they opened the box and saw the costume itself? A variant costume with the obvious image of Frankenstein in his Universal costume and appropriately labelled "Frankenstein" leaves no doubt as to the specificity of the costume. The variants may simply point to licensing lost or gained, but they may also get at differing strategies in the marketing of monster assemblages.

Ben Cooper's costumes tended to hew more closely to the licensing formula, and in fact the company carried the cheaper line of Don Post masks. While the "H. Halpern

Company was one of the first companies to license the images of fictional characters for their costumes, (think Popeye and Olive Oyl) [it was] Ben Cooper [that was] largely responsible for popularizing the custom of dressing up as pop culture icons."[10] Charles Moss goes into detail about how the idea of licensed costumes exploded in the 1950s and 1960s:

> It wasn't until after the Second World War, however, that Halloween costume manufacturing became big business. With the rise of television in the 1950s and the popularity of TV shows such as *The Adventures of Superman*, *Zorro*, and *Davy Crockett*, Ben Cooper obtained the licenses to many of these live-action shows and began mass producing inexpensive representations of them in costume form for less than $3 each, which amounts to about 12 bucks these days. The company distinguished itself with speed: It would rapidly buy rights, produce costumes and get them onto store shelves, which opened a whole new world of costuming to children. By the 1960s, Ben Cooper owned between 70 and 80 percent of the Halloween costume market, offering pretty much any pop culture reference in costume form. There were Frankenstein costumes. Dennis the Menace costumes. Beatles costumes. Even Magilla costumes.[11]

Like the Halco example, the Ben Cooper costumes were marketed as mask and costume combinations. Different versions of these costumes can be found online, and each could be analyzed in terms of the specific types of "play" they elicit, but I would point to an example rather of how a Frankenstein monster costume was marketed in a 1968 Ben Cooper catalog.[12] Frankenstein is positioned between a clown and the devil. Like the Halco example, Ben Cooper uses the typical mask (although here green) accompanied by a costume featuring a picture of the monster himself in a menacing pose. What is striking in this advertising, however, is the assemblage of costume and child bodies. The idea of "little monsters" plays a large role in the aesthetic of such costume marketing, with the child's body juxtaposed with the horror implications of the mask creating an effect imagined to be, and surely in many cases successfully, one of a kind of innocence. This uncanny effect, somewhat in the line of Kristeva's concept of the powers of horror, walks a fine line between reducing and enhancing horror, giving a twist to children's innocence to create a version of horror cuteness.[13] The result is a transformation of the monster's affect in a reduction and reorienting of his fundamental size and strength, which must necessarily be compromised on a child's body. Arguably, reassembling the monster as cute actually brings out an aspect of the monster of those Universal films.

A Collegeville costume offers a mysterious and intriguing reassemblage sometimes labeled "The Brute."[14] As with Ben Cooper, here the mask is green, and interestingly this mask bears a great deal of resemblance to those Ben Cooper manufactured, perhaps from a mold purchased from him. The mask alters the size and position of the bolts as well as the stitches—instead of vertical-oriented red stitches descending near the right temple as dictated by Universal films, on this mask the stitches run horizontally across the forehead in gray and black. The one-piece costume features the expected image of the monster amid plant-like scrawlings, but he looks more goofy than threatening, the company seeming to want to make the monster more palatable for children. In fact, it is not at all clear that either the mask or the costume are meant to inspire terror in any way, and it may even be the case that the costume designers sought to capitalize on Fred Gwynne's humorous performances of the Frankenstein-like monster, Herman Munster (the look being licensed by Universal) in the 1964–1966 series *The Munsters*.

Humorous versions of Frankenstein masks/costumes have become common. Numerous comic film portrayals of the monster have been released over the past several decades, and the monster may more easily incarnate in comic form than other classic monsters. The Wolfman and Dracula can be used to comic effect, but Frankenstein as a working-class lug represents a distinct kind of joke—a big "dumb" guy might have been and may still be referred to as "Frankenstein." A recent example of a comic costume is the contemporary "Big Frank," an over-the-head mask and costume combo (see Figure 6.4). In the photograph, Big Frank might well be Frank Sinatra, but the catalog description offers one marketer's idea about how exactly this product might strike potential buyers. I quote in full:

Beware, for I am fearless, and therefore powerful.
We all get a little green sometimes. It might be because we are envious. Or because we are not feeling 100%, kind of puke-y really. And sometimes we turn into a giant green rage monster, also known as the Hulk. But that rarely happens.

More often, we turn into the original green guy. No, not the Jolly Green Giant. No we turn into the reanimated monster. We turn into Frankenstein's monster, affectionately called Frank by our friends. Most folks now a days don't chase us down with pitchforks, and torches. They seem to like us now, but maybe that is because we can do all the heavy lifting.

You can let Dr. Frankenstein put you into this Big Frank Costume, or you can just put it on yourself. Either way you are becoming Frank for Halloween this year. Dr. Frankenstein doesn't really ask if he can make someone into a monster. But, you should have it much easier in the 21st century. Hardly anyone has pitchforks, and torches anymore, and that's if they even felt like you were a threat. Just stay the good kind of green in this Frank mask, because turning into a giant green rage monster, like the Hulk, isn't going to be winning you any popularity contests. But being the lovable Frank might. Well, at least no peasants will try to hunt you down! (Hopefully.)[15]

The write-up's humorous tone keys into revealing aspects of what Frankenstein monster masks and costumes are meant to achieve. In this description, the era of Frankenstein's monster being scary or threatening has passed—no longer do villagers hunt him down. Also, the link between the Hulk and "Frank" via the color green gets at the image of a muscle-bound figure who might at any moment explode in rage but otherwise is a nice fellow to have around to lift heavy objects. Anyone wearing this costume to a Halloween party clearly means to get a laugh from the unexpected smile on the mask and the ragged tuxedo. Here, recognizable Frankenstein monster parts combine with incongruent ones to create an effect of audacity—the monster in this guise might almost be taken as sexy, which lends a humorous air to the costume.

Another humorous contemporary reassemblage is Reaganstein. In this case the smile is merely a recognizable aspect of a different kind of icon, Ronald Reagan.

Figure 6.4 "Big Frank" costume (HalloweenCostumes.com / FUN.com).

Figure 6.5 "Reagenstein" mask (photograph by Taylor Hagood).

Likewise, the iconic monster flat-topped cranium has been replaced with Reagan's famous hair, held on with a steel band. And, of course, Reagan's features have been blended with Frankenstein parts to create a new kind of fused monster. It is not easy to tell if this mask was designed for Ronald Reagan fans or Ronald Reagan critics. Is Reagan to be understood as made up of parts of dead bodies? Is the mask supposed to be scary? Or does the fact that "Reagan" rhymes with "Franken" simply lend itself to such a mask? That would seem to be the case, as there is also a "Trill Clinton" zombie mask. Obviously, from a manufacturing standpoint, the joke is the paramount thing but, as is often the case with jokes, it is not always clear who wears it or what kind of effect/affect the wearer seeks to achieve.

Even as Frankenstein as a gag has become commonplace, there have been some efforts to envision the monster in non-Universal assemblage ways to extreme horror effect/affect. "Frankenstein Futura" features a more-or-less normal looking person except that the top of the skull is completely missing and the brain exposed.[16] While there are seams in the skin, the stitches are far less prominent. Another mask, sold by Morris Costumes in the early 2000s, and simply labelled "Frankenstein," also envisions a non-flat head, although the top is sewn on and the stitches are prominent, even under the collar-bone and chest. But instead of several locks of black hair, there are only a few, as if they are somehow left over from the manufacturing process (of either the mask or the character or both). Also, the face is twisted out of shape and the nose is missing, Dr. Frankenstein's workmanship being worse than usual. Most interesting of all, the eyes are a prominent pale blue, a significant departure from the typical approach of either closing the eyes or blackening them, in "Frankenstein Futura." The monster's stare is vacant still, to be sure, but giving him prominent eyes departs from the classic Universal look. Where Big Frank and Reaganstein use smiles, a different cranium, and costumes along with specific features to create comic appearances, these two masks use the cranium and eyes to heighten the effect of horror. Someone wearing these masks runs the risk of not being recognized as the Frankenstein monster at all.

There are many more masks and costumes of the monster than I have discussed, and reassemblage is only one framework by which to approach them. There is also a history of Bride of Frankenstein masks and wigs worthy of analysis. My hope is that this chapter promotes further examination of these commodities within the larger scholarly discussion on the phenomenon of Frankenstein's monster. I know there is much more to discover about the history of these masks and costumes and far more to be learned about what they reveal for the ways the monster exists in the public imagination and its role in consumer tastes.

7

"Machines Within the Machine": Definitions of Humanity in Victor LaValle's and Dietrich Smith's *Destroyer* (2017)

W. Andrew Shephard

In 1818, Mary Shelley introduced us to what would become a familiar stock character over the next two centuries—the mad scientist. This figure, most commonly depicted as white and male, tended to be driven by a combination of hubris and curiosity to attempt scientific feats forbidden by both the laws of his society and common decency. Typically, he is intended as a warning of the dark avenues down which our technological acumen might take us if unchecked by conscience. In 1955, we would be introduced to another similarly ubiquitous figure in the modern media landscape—that of the grieving Black mother. On August 28, 1955, the tortured and mutilated body of fourteen-year-old Emmett Till would be found floating in the Tallahatchie River in Money, Mississippi following his forcible abduction from his uncle's home in the middle of the night for the crime of allegedly whistling at a white woman. While Till's murder was far from the first of such incidents, the decision of his mother, Mamie Till-Mobley, to mourn his loss in the public eye and to hold an open casket funeral for him became a galvanizing event for the then nascent Civil Rights Movement. Sadly, despite the inroads created by this event, the spectacle of the Black mother grieving a child prematurely taken by racially motivated violence would become an all-too-familiar sight in the ensuing decades. The names of the young men and women lost in such a manner have these days become a commonly recited litany at protests: Trayvon Martin, Tamir Rice, Michael Brown, George Floyd, Breonna Taylor, Ahmaud Arbery. In some respects, the greatest horror lies in how inured we've become to this phenomenon.

Victor LaValle's and Dietrich Smith's comic book mini-series *Destroyer* (2017) makes the seemingly counter-intuitive move of combining these two archetypes. The story, a sequel to Mary Shelley's seminal novel, concerns Dr. Josephine Baker, a lineal descendant of the Frankenstein family, who uses nanotechnology to resurrect her twelve-year-old son after he is senselessly murdered by a Chicago P.D. officer. Her efforts attract the attention of The Lab, a Washington D.C.-based scientific thinktank which initially funded Baker's research with an eye towards potential military applications, and Dr. Frankenstein's famous monster himself, who emerges from his centuries long self-imposed exile in the Arctic to rid the Earth of humanity for good once he discovers the continuation of his creator's research.

At first glance, LaValle's and Smith's wedding of contemporary racial injustices to Mary Shelley's gothic masterpiece seems an odd choice. After all, the original novel only briefly touches upon race and the monster himself is typically assumed to be white. His singular hideousness is the most commonly cited explanation for his ostracization. That said, the novel shows itself to be particularly concerned with the metrics and criteria by which we define the term human—a question which is central to our discussions about race and has become considerably more complicated in the 200 years since its original publication. *Destroyer* reframes this debate by putting the conundrum of Frankenstein's monster alongside our contemporary discourses of the posthuman, ongoing concerns regarding the humane treatment of animals, and the ways in which our understanding of race has often framed people of color outside of the boundaries of humanity.

Human beings have always been remarkably inconsistent about the metrics by which we determine which living creatures are worthy of compassion—a tendency which *Destroyer* highlights from the outset. The series starts in contemporary Antarctica, where Victor Frankenstein's monster has sought refuge from humanity for the last two centuries. His sojourn in the wilderness is rudely interrupted by poachers from a Japanese whaling ship, who brutally slaughter a pod of whales in front of him. His horror at this act reignites his long-simmering fury at the human race and he promptly seeks violent reprisal against the whalers for their actions. Before the monster strikes, we are privy to a conversation between the whalers themselves which lends an interesting bit of context to their actions.

Whaler 1   "<They tell me she won't last much longer.>"

Whaler 2   "<That's what they said last year, but she beat all their predictions. Don't lose hope.>"

Whaler 3   "<I went to sea to escape women. Yet here I am stuck with a pair of them.>"

Whaler 1   "<Last year you cried because you lost your staghorn beetle! Who are you to make fun of a man who loves his dog!>"

Whaler 3   "<Whale's up.>"[1]

More than an amusing bit of banter or a "cool down" moment before the horror of the monster's rampage begins, this scene points to a certain hypocrisy among human beings with regard to which animals are considered worthy of sympathy. Many cultures regard dogs as companion animals and thus somewhat sacrosanct; committing an act of violence or cruelty against one is considered verboten in most contexts. Typically, the justification for such protections is the relative intelligence of canid species. Yet, according to many of the metrics by which we measure animal intelligence, cetaceans such as whales, dolphins, and porpoises routinely outperform the canine species.[2] Moreover, the third whaler's dismissal of his coworkers' distress over an ailing pet is then immediately undercut by the reminder of his own earlier grief over the death of his pet stag beetle—an animal more conventionally regarded as a pest than something to shed tears over. This exchange points not only to a fluidity inherent in the concept of which animals are granted sympathy and compassionate treatment, but an arbitrariness as well. There is no rigid and neatly defined hierarchy to such matters, merely human whim.

LaValle and Smith make similarly trenchant observations about the human beings we deem worthy of compassion, through the introduction of two representatives from the fictional scientific thinktank The Lab who have arrived on a ship called the *Robert Walton*, after the fictional explorer who rescues Victor in the framing narrative of the original novel. Upon witnessing the monster's slaughter of the whale poachers, the young woman is not only unfazed by the violence but immediately seeks to recruit him to her cause. Responding to one of her coworkers' objections, she replies: "They killed those whales. Even the calf! Why should I feel anything for them?"[3] This statement reflects a commonly expressed sentiment, namely that the moral failings of certain individuals may be so severe that any number of abuses or mistreatments become morally justified, essentially negating their status as human beings worthy of the protections we typically think of as imperative to a humane society. For example, think of the disregard typically expressed for those who harm children or have committed particularly egregious acts of violence. Yale psychology professor Paul Bloom notes this somewhat paradoxical phenomenon in his book *Against Empathy: The Case for Rational Compassion* (2016). Recounting an incident at the liberation of Germany's Dachau Concentration Camp in 1945 in which American soldiers summarily executed German POWs without trial, he remarks: "The men who murdered the German soldiers were not sadists or psychopaths. They were driven by strong moral feelings."[4] Paraphrasing David Livingston Smith, he adds: "... one type of individual we are prone to dehumanize is the person who does evil. The Nazis dehumanize the Jews; we now dehumanize the Nazis."[5] That such sentiments are given voice by a woman who has shown such passionate regard for the well-being of animals is a telling and significant irony—a reminder of how easily a sense of moral superiority can slide into the justification of the dehumanization of others. Moreover, this young woman quickly becomes a victim of the very same logic herself. Her efforts to recruit the monster to her cause by showing him carefully curated footage of misdeeds that she considers to be worthy of such punishment ultimately ends up radicalizing him against the whole of humanity.

This episode foreshadows an important theme throughout the series, namely the ease and certainty with which we dehumanize other people. Issue 2 opens with a flashback to the monster on the run in Ireland in 1799—desperate, afraid, and alone. He approaches a group of men pleadingly with the words: "Please. I just need hel—."[6] He is immediately met with violence. He is shot in the mouth with a crossbow bolt and pursued by angry (and presumably quite scared) villagers. It's a moment which calls to mind the monster's painful rejection by the French cottagers in Mary Shelley's novel and is an example of the type of treatment which has led him to shun humanity altogether. However, it takes on a peculiar and sad irony when we consider the people turning on him. In late eighteenth-century Ireland, one would find a people subjected to significant, systemic abuse under British imperial law. A colonized people, disinherited in their own land, subject to transportation to the colonies and indentured servitude for offenses such as property crime under the Old English Poor Law, the Irish existed in a subalternized state that was very much outside of the social construct of whiteness as it stood 200 years ago. Their dehumanized status was so widely accepted that it inspired Jonathan Swift's scabrous satire "A Modest Proposal" (1724) as a commentary upon the frequently callous responses from pamphleteers to the ongoing human rights crisis of the Irish famine. Yet the instinctive response of the Irishmen to the monster here is not one of empathy. Moreover, the comic makes it clear that such a response is not unique to them, nor is it uniquely solicited by the monster himself.

Cut to the present day and the monster is trekking across the desert terrain of Mexico, looking to cross over into the U.S. where Josephine Baker's experiments are being conducted. He is identified by a young Mexican boy as "an angel" and is subsequently joined by a group of would-be immigrants looking to cross the border as well. Given the date of publication, one could easily read this scene as a rebuke of the fear-mongering rhetoric about "caravans" of immigrants coming out of the Trump administration at this time. Instead, of the depraved, violent individuals described in such discourse, these migrants have much more in common with the "tired . . . poor . . . huddled masses, yearning to breathe free" of Emma Lazarus' "The New Colossus," the poem famously inscribed on the Statue of Liberty. Encountering the border wall, the monster, blinded by rage and exhausted of empathy, proceeds to tear it down—killing the migrants in the process. The last dialogue we get from the group is the same young boy pleading, "Please! Wait! I just need hel—," an ironic echo of the earlier scene. The monster is met with further resistance in his border crossing from border patrollers, whose dialogue ("Border patrol tipped us off, of course"; "I sure wish they paid us like they loved us"; "A patriot serves his nation, not his bank account") informs us that they are freelancers rather than professional U.S. government agents. Moreover, the slogans on their vehicle make it clear that they are motivated by more than just profit: ("Kill 'Em All." "Proud Again." "Bean count.").[7] The last two statements seem to be deliberately reflective of both the then-nascent ultra nationalist Proud Boys movement as well as a racial slur against Mexicans. The xenophobia these men exhibit seems to deliberately parallel the monster's earlier encounter with the mob in Ireland over 200 years ago. For most readers, it would be hard to think of them as terribly sympathetic victims for the brutality to which they are soon subjected. But considering how callously the monster has just murdered the Mexican immigrants outside of the U.S. border prior to this moment, it is hard to argue that he is much better. Moreover, our own willingness to see such men as subhuman potentially implicates us as well.

These themes come to a head with the stories of Josephine and Akai Baker. We start their story in medias res, with Akai existing as a disembodied artificial intelligence having been murdered by the Chicago P.D. a few years earlier. In issue 4, Akai's father confronts the officer responsible for the shooting, asking: "What could make you decide a child was a threat so quickly?" It is not until issue 5 of the series that we get the entire story. A flashback sequence reveals that Akai was heading back home from a baseball game, bat carelessly slung over his shoulder as he takes a shortcut through a residential neighborhood. The panel shows him in silhouette, in a way which telegraphs the following exchange:

Neighbor "Hello, yes, there's a man with a rifle walking in front of my house."

Dispatcher "Okay. And what is his race?"

Neighbor "He's Black."

Dispatcher "And his age?"

Neighbor "Eighteen? Maybe twenty."

Dispatcher "Officers are on the way."

The hypervigilance of the neighbor in alerting law enforcement calls to mind several high-profile shootings of young Black males in recent years, most notably the murders of Tamir Rice and Trayvon Martin.

The Martin case is probably one of the better-known examples of this phenomenon. On February 26, 2012, seventeen-year-old Trayvon Martin was temporarily staying in the Twin Lakes gated community in Sanford, FL. While headed home, he attracted the attention of then twenty-nine-year-old George Zimmerman, who was the head of the Twin Lakes neighborhood watch. Perceiving Martin to be suspicious and out of place, Zimmerman initially informed the police of the young man, then gave pursuit against the advice of law enforcement when they did not arrive quickly enough for his liking. An altercation between Zimmerman and Martin ensued, during which Zimmerman fired upon and killed Martin, who was unarmed. On July 13, 2013, George Zimmerman was formally acquitted of charges of second-degree murder and manslaughter under Florida's "Stand Your Ground" statute, despite Zimmerman's self-admitted pursuit of a fleeing suspect. Likewise, the assumption of Akai as an adult, and thus a more significant potential threat, echoes the 2015 killing of Tamir Rice in Cleveland, OH. Upon him being gunned down, Rice's case was called in as a "Black male, maybe 20, black revolver, black handgun by him." Rice was later revealed to have been only twelve years old. The weapon in question was a toy that had been traded to him in exchange for a cellphone. The emergency dispatcher who deployed the police officers apparently having failed to relay two vital bits of information from the initial caller: that the gun was "probably fake," and that the wielder was "probably a juvenile."[8]

Both of these cases and that of Michael Brown and many others are reflective of a larger societal trend in terms of how Black male adolescents are perceived. A study from *The Journal of Personality and Social Psychology* determined that "Black boys are seen as older and less innocent and that they prompt a less essential conception of childhood than do their White same-age peers. Further, our findings demonstrate that the Black/ape association predicted actual racial disparities in police violence toward children."[9]

The discourse addressed by this study has informed criminal justice policy, particularly as it affects Black males, in pernicious ways for many years now—often in the form of sentencing policies such as the infamous Rockefeller Drug Laws as well as policies on the type of policing practices deployed in predominantly black and brown neighborhoods. In 1994, then-First Lady Hillary Rodham Clinton would popularize a term which would have dire consequences for inner city minority youth going forward—namely, the "superpredator." The term was deployed in a speech making a case for the necessity of passing a new crime bill which would be signed into law by her husband, President Bill Clinton. However, the term was coined by the University of Pennsylvania-affiliated criminologist and sociologist John J. DiIulio Jr. who hypothesized that there was a small, but steadily growing class of inner-city youth who, due to environmental factors, were more impulsive and naturally predisposed to committing violent crime without remorse. As DiIulio explained in a book jointly authored with William J. Bennett and John P. Walters:

> "America is now home to thickening ranks of juvenile 'superpredators'—radically impulsive, brutally remorseless youngsters, including ever more preteenage boys, who murder, assault, rape, rob, burglarize, deal deadly drugs, join gun toting gangs, and create serious communal disorders. They do not fear the stigma of arrest, the pains of imprisonment, or the pangs of conscience. They perceive hardly any relationship between doing right (and wrong) now and being rewarded (or punished) for it later. For these mean-street youngsters, the words 'right' and 'wrong' have no fixed moral meaning."[10]

Moreover, the findings of who comprised this new class of criminal were certainly not racially neutral. They continue:

> "What, then, is one to make of the widely reported reality that a third of black men in their twenties are under some sort of correctional supervision today (about one-third of them in prison or jail, the rest on probation or parole)? The same, we think, that one should make of the fact that blacks are about 50 times more likely to commit violent crimes against whites than whites are to commit violent crimes against blacks. [...] Blacks have been 'responsible for a disproportionate amount of serious violent crime.'"[11]

These findings were used to support comprehensive reforms such as mandatory minimums for certain types of felonies, the Three Strikes Law, and the sentencing of juvenile offenders as adults. Returning to Pliers' seemingly rhetorical question as to how the officer who murdered his son could assess a child as a threat so quickly, it would seem we have an answer.[12] When one factors in the discourse surrounding young Black males and crime, as well as the carefully cultivated PTSD in law enforcement culture informed by "warrior training" seminars, and access to military grade op-tech, the reasons behind the prolific rate of violent outcomes becomes, sadly, all too clear.[13]

This legacy of violence weighs heavily upon *Destroyer* as a narrative, in ways both explicit and more subtle. In a creative decision which reflects the ubiquity of such shootings, Akai is constructed as something of a composite of several Black male teens and young adults who have been taken by police violence. When asked why he chose the name Akai, series writer Victor LaValle remarks: "[Akai's] a 12-year-old black boy, and the no-brainer would have been to name him Tamir. But in a way, it felt too on the nose, and maybe a little ghoulish. Akai Gurley was another black man killed in New York. I feel like his name and his story has been somewhat missed. This was a small way to at least honor that."[14] Likewise, Akai's visual design is a nod to another shooting victim: Michael Brown. As LaValle explains: "[Dr. Baker] has used nanobots to rebuild the portions of him that were lost. I'm always trying to layer in pieces of truth and history, so when we were coming up with the design, I wrote to the original artist, Dan Mora, and I sent him documents from the Michael Brown shooting in Ferguson. The autopsy includes a figure where they show all the places where the bullets hit. On Akai, the android parts of him match that autopsy image. [...] I want you to be thinking every time you see Akai that this is the proof of how he was murdered. I thought it would be a subtle touch. Most people will look at it and think it's just cool and cyborg-y. But I wanted it to have that underlying layer of something with weight and history."[15]

A central theme within both Mary Shelley's original text and LaValle & Smith's reimagining is the deleterious impact that such treatment can have on one's psyche. Famously, Victor Frankenstein's creation starts out as a *tabula rasa* in keeping with John Locke's theories on cognition and the state of nature. Despite his outward appearance, the creature only truly becomes a monster after his abandonment and subsequent ill-treatment by those with whom he seeks community. In an oft-cited passage from the scene after he has been rejected by the French cottagers, the monster laments: "I, like the arch fiend, bore a hell within me; and, finding myself unsympathized with, wished to tear up the trees, spread havoc and destruction around me, and then to have sat down and enjoyed the ruin."[16] Notably, this is not the only time that LaValle has drawn comparison between the social alienation felt by Frankenstein's creation and the alienation experienced by Black people living under white supremacy. The same passage is quoted verbatim by the eponymous character of LaValle's 2017 novella *The Ballad of Black Tom*, itself a rewriting of H.P. Lovecraft's "The Horror at Red Hook" (1924).[17] In the scene in question, Tom explains to Detective Malone (a white NYPD officer and the protagonist of Lovecraft's original tale) how he has come to align himself with the cult of Cthulhu, the most famous of the Great Old Ones in Lovecraft's invented pantheon of malevolent deities. LaValle's message is clear: if you treat someone like a monster often enough, you shouldn't be surprised if they eventually become one.

LaValle introduces us to the creature on page one of *Destroyer*, where he sits atop an Antarctic glacier on an icy throne, overseeing lands teeming with avian and ocean wildlife but no humans. Visually, the creature exudes death, with an emaciated frame that reveals taut muscles and silver stitches or staples that run all the way down the front of his torso. Additional stitches or staples appear to have been used to attach his limbs to his body, including his right forearm, his left arm at the bicep, and his left foot. Shirtless, the creature wears tattered pants. To create the creature's look, LaValle stated in an interview that he sent the artist two images: Iggy Pop and Moses.[18] These visual influences carry the cultural associations of the individuals. On sight, the creature's long, stringy hair and lanky frame invoke Iggy Pop's rebellious Punk Rock persona as he insouciantly monitors his frozen kingdom. The medium-length, evenly cut beard lends him Moses's religious gravitas. Adding to this image, in the middle of his face, the creature's nose is missing and the bony, cadaverous skull can be descried beneath. The result, visually, is of a rebellious agent of death who may have the moral authority to dole out destruction on a biblical scale.

Such themes come to a head in the character arc of Doctor Josephine "Jo" Baker, the last living descendant of the Frankenstein lineage. In his interview with Anthony Breznican, LaValle describes her as: "Half Storm, half Bride of Frankenstein." In response to Breznican's observation that "[t]he white streak is always a sign of being a little bit crazy," LaValle replies: "That's right. It's like you've seen something. You went past the threshold of the veil and you came back. You have too much knowledge."[19] There is an interesting constellation of references here to unpack. The first is her name itself. While Victor Frankenstein's name is commonly assumed to be a reference to *the Victor*, the epithet by which God is known in John Milton's *Paradise Lost* (1616), the name Josephine Baker can safely be assumed to be a reference to the African American singer, dancer, and actress of the same name. Though she would later expatriate to and become a naturalized citizen of France, Baker was a vocal supporter of the Civil Rights Movement in the United States and vocally protested discrimination against Black peoples—even refusing to play segregated shows at a time when this option was typically not available to Black performers. Storm would be a reference to the character from Marvel Comics' *X-Men* (1963–), a franchise whose characters are commonly read as stand-ins for the Civil Rights struggle as well as those of various other oppressed populations. Notably, Storm is arguably the most iconic Black female character in the comic medium and one who is famous for her steely resolve. Since the character's introduction in 1975, she has been worshipped as a weather goddess on the Serengeti plains, the leader of the X-Men (a position she won by defeating her predecessor in single combat), the Queen Regent of Black Panther's Wakanda, and in recent developments, the Queen of Mars. The white streak evokes Elsa Lancaster's appearance in James Whale's seminal film *The Bride of Frankenstein* (1935), but in a different context. Whereas Whale's Bride earns her streak from having peered beyond the veil of death and returned, one could make the case that Dr. Baker has earned hers by peering beyond the veil spoken of by W.E.B. DuBois in *The Souls of Black Folk* (1904)—an insight into society's failings which has shattered and irrevocably scarred her.

It is a commonly cited truism about Shelley's novel that knowledge is being aware that the monster is not named Frankenstein, but wisdom is being aware that Frankenstein is the true monster. While this interpretation is somewhat reductive, it also seems relevant to LaValle's construction of Jo and overall handling of the mad scientist archetype. However, the series takes great pains to remind us that for all the discussion of hubris and ego as the motivating factors for the mad scientist archetype, Victor's experiments are actually rooted in a much more sympathetic motivation. "Grief," Jo explains to the two agents she has captured from the Lab, "That's what started this whole thing one hundred and thirty years ago. That's what is keeping the story alive now."[20] Indeed, careful readers of Mary Shelley's text will note that Victor Frankenstein's fascination with halting the processes of death begins with the loss of his own mother. As he recounts to Walton during his convalescence: "I need not describe the feelings of those whose dearest ties are rent by that most irreparable evil, the void that presents itself to the soul, and the despair that is exhibited on the countenance. [...] Yet from whom has not that rude hand rent away some dear connexion; and why should I describe a sorrow which all have felt, and must feel?"[21] If *Frankenstein* is a novel driven by a son's grief for the loss of his mother (and arguably the author's own grief for the loss of a mother who died giving birth to her) and the terrible lengths to which it drives him, then it seems fitting that *Destroyer* is a work driven by a mother's grief for a son who was prematurely taken from her.

We see this trauma response surface first in small ways. When two agents from the Lab, amusingly named Percy Shelley and George Gordon, invade her Montana laboratory in order to shut down her experiments, Baker quickly defuses them as a threat. When the two men exhibit an interest in the newly resurrected Akai which borders on the disrespectful, she is equally swift in shutting that down as well:

Gordon They're nanobots.

Shelley I need to get footage of this. Damn, where's my phone?

[...]

Gordon The texture is so interesting.

Baker Stop touching my son. Akai, please let him know... Your hand can be flesh and bone, or just bone. You decide.[22]

While Akai himself seems unbothered in the cited panel, Dr. Baker's decidedly curt response has an important bit of cultural context behind it. The scene, particularly the mention of the "texture" of Akai's nanobot repaired skin, calls to mind the oft-cited complaint about white people's fascination with the texture of black hair (among other physical characteristics) as something alien and unusual as well as the accompanying assumption that this entitles them to touch it. Baker's awareness of the sense of entitlement behind such microaggressions as a precursor to other, more severe, abuses means that she is no longer willing to tolerate such behaviors nor give their perpetrators the benefit of the doubt. Later in the same scene, Baker takes a certain grim satisfaction in having Akai demonstrate the type of pain-compliance techniques utilized by law enforcement upon her recalcitrant guests, while explaining why such techniques often serve to escalate matters. The scene is a mordantly humorous reminder of how the common practices of law enforcement often serve to create the violent outcomes they have been tasked with preventing.

As the series goes on, Dr. Baker's anger escalates further. In a speech which echoes Victor's vision of himself as the progenitor of "a new species" possessed of "many happy and excellent natures [who] would owe their being" to him, Jo imagines Akai as the first of a new posthuman species who will be better equipped to survive the coming apocalypses brought on by humankind's perfidy.[23] As she explains to her son: "You are the start of what will dominate after humanity declines. Global warming, rising tides, none of that will kill you. But we'll be dying by the billions. Some will even blame you for our end. And for creating you, they'll label me mankind's enemy too. The destroyer. And I will welcome the title. If it kept you safe, I would destroy them all."[24] Pointedly, the background to this speech is the image of several early hominid species evolving into modern humankind then evolving into a robot. Beneath this is a statue of Jo seated in a parody of the Lincoln Memorial with the words "Race Traitor" graffitied underneath. The imagery evokes Jo as the Great Emancipator of the species from all the potential threats to its existence, but with the darker implication that such salvation is actually a self-annihilating impulse. The term "race traitor," typically thrown at Black people like Dr. Baker for achieving upward mobility, here takes on a decidedly different valence. At the heart of Jo's "madness" is less ego than concerns over reproductive futurity—the anxiety that she has brought life into a world that is fundamentally inhospitable to it, not just because of racism but also the ravages of the technocratic capitalism that she has herself been serving over her career.

Interestingly, the uncompromising nature of Jo's vision for the future and exhaustion with the moral failings of humankind strongly align her with the worldview of the monster himself. As LaValle explains, his vision of the monster has evolved quite a bit from where we left him at the end of the novel: "[the] funny thing is, there are two different versions of the ending. The one we know is Percy Shelley's ending. Mary Shelley actually had an ending where he pushes away from the shift, but Percy didn't want that because he didn't like that the monster was rejecting civilization. He thought civilization should reject the monster. It's a tiny change, but it makes so much difference ... The other thing that bothers me about the monster in the original novel is the monster is so needy. He needs Victor's approval so profoundly ... But the more modern take on this should be, 'Why should I ask you for your love when you made me and rejected me?' It's the difference between a needy abandoned child and an angry abandoned child."[25] There is something to be said for this as not only a return to the original vision of Mary Shelley, in imagining Victor's creation willingly choosing to isolate himself from humanity, but also as a commentary on the type of alienation that anyone consistently Othered by society might eventually come to feel. John DiIulio's theory of criminality frames antisocial behavior as purely a matter of individual moral failing—that some people, if not necessarily born bad, are unfixably and irredeemably so and should be locked away permanently for the protection of civilized society. Taking his cues from Mary Shelley's vision, LaValle frames the monster's descent into destructive rage as being motivated by the ways in which society has failed him.

Technology is only one of these ways, but for LaValle the technological innovations that have so radicalized the monster have also failed him. In the montage of these innovations it is interesting to note the trajectory: from the positive contributions of Edison's lightbulb and the Wright Brothers' airplane to the destructive power of chemical warfare in World War I and the atomic bombs of the Second World War; from modern-day factory farming practices and the iPhone to a dashcam recording of a police officer callously shooting a Black man in the back. If artificial life is posited as the next step in such a chain, then this trajectory of positive conception to negative implementation doesn't bode well for future technological innovations.

Part of the problem, the series implies, is technological innovation's weddedness to capitalism and the need to be profitable. We see this best reflected through the Lab itself, whose leader is modeled on Ayn Rand—the Russian author and thinker whose philosophy of Objectivism has been touted by many advocates of laissez faire capitalism. On her wall are a photo of disgraced U.S. President Richard Nixon and an early work by the Dutch painter Rembrandt titled "The Anatomy Lesson of Doctor Nicolas Tulip." The painting depicts a criminal being dissected by the eponymous Doctor Tulip in the interest of uncovering the organic causes of his criminal behavior. As she explains: "In his life he did nothing of consequence. In death he's a vital part of Rembrandt's first truly great painting." Her son replies: "Some people are artists. The rest are just material."[26] We can read this scene as emblematic of a larger and more unsettling trend within the history of scientific endeavor—a tendency to view certain human beings as worthy of sacrifice in the service of greater understanding. Unsurprisingly, such treatment has often been reserved for minoritized peoples. The most infamous would be the experiments of the Nazis during the Holocaust on European Jewry, but one could also point to the infamous Tuskegee Syphilis Study (1932–1972) in which the United States Public Health Service and the Center for Disease Control and Prevention allowed a group of nearly 400 African American men with syphilis to go untreated to observe the disease's effects on them, or Alabama physician James Marion Sims' experimental and involuntary gynecological surgeries on enslaved Black women in the 1840s.

At the intersection of Western society's problematic relationship to race and Big Science's lack of regard for the dignity of individual human beings is Pliers, Jo Baker's ex-husband and Akai's father. An ex-soldier and current private military contractor for the Lab, Pliers volunteers to be merged with a mobile combat chassis called "the Bride" in exchange for the opportunity to confront and use the Lab's technology to exact some measure of retribution upon Akai's murderer. Yet, the procedure has some drawbacks—namely that Pliers is permanently "wedded" to the armor in a way that makes it impossible to remove.[27] As Akai points out, in a way this makes Pliers like him—someone who has been radically altered from his organic biological state into a posthuman existence. And, yet, for Pliers this transformation can both literally and figuratively be described as dehumanizing. He no longer has a human face to show his son. Moreover, the body he currently inhabits is prone to having his command of it overridden by the woman who built it, namely Jo, and presumably higher ups at the Lab itself. These factors, coupled with the obvious military applications of this technology, have pretty dire implications going forward. Such a possibility (or at least one notably similar) was anticipated in the early days of cybernetics by Norbert Wiener, who warned against the possibility of interactions between human beings and technology which could be at best described as inhumane and inconsiderate of the well-being of human operators. In his treatise *The Human Use of Human Beings* (1950), Wiener talks about the careful way in which the Second World War-era fighter jets had to be designed to accommodate the physical limitations of the human user:

> If the plane were able to take a perfectly arbitrary evasive action, no amount of skill would permit us to fill in the as yet unknown motion of the plane between the time when the gun was fired and the time when the shell should arrive approximately at its goal. However, under many circumstances the aviator either does not, or cannot, take arbitrary evasive action. He is limited by the fact that if he makes a rapid turn, centrifugal force will render him unconscious; and by the other fact that the control mechanism of his plan and the course of instructions which he has received practically force on him certain regular habits of control which show themselves even in his evasive action.[28]

Weiner concludes the chapter by remarking: "it is interesting to know that the sort of phenomenon which is recorded subjectively as emotion may not be a useless epiphenomenon of nervous action, but may control some essential stage in learning, and in other similar processes."[29] As cultural critic and theorist of transhumanism N. Katherine Hayles explains: "This alien and alienating machine is invested with qualities he wants to purge from cybernetics, including rigidity, oppression, militaristic regulation of thought and action, reduction of humans to antlike elements, manipulation, betrayal and death."[30] It is ironic, then, that these would seem to be essential elements of the machine-human interface commissioned by the Lab, one in which the human operator of such a device is essentially reduced to a servomechanism. Moreover, it is, in many ways, a logical extension of the instrumentalist view of Black bodies and how they have historically been treated by capitalist systems dating back to the days of chattel slavery.

Ultimately, *Destroyer* interrogates how we define the human from a number of angles. It considers how often we define our humanity in relation to other species of animal, in terms of race and ethnicity, in terms of how science and technology might allow us to transcend our human frailties or lead us to even more compromised states of existence than previously dreamed. It also explores what it means to be dehumanized, whether through biological modification or simply systemic sociological abuses, and the devastating effect it can have upon one's psyche. It is notable that, by the series' end, Dr. Baker, Pliers, and the creature himself have all been consumed by their rage and alienation from society. Baker, who reimagines herself as the eponymous Destroyer of the series, has remained biologically human but has been driven to the point of considering species-wide genocide due to her grief and her weariness at society's inability to see people like herself and her son as truly human. In the end, we are left with Akai as the sole survivor, who somehow never loses his sense of optimism or compassion for others despite the fact of his senseless murder and subsequent resurrection. One could chalk this up merely to the naivete of youth and, by implication, question whether it will last. Or, one could make the case that unlike his counterpart from Mary Shelley's novel, Akai has known the love of not just one, but both parents. Either way, the fact that LaValle and Smith choose to leave us on a note of Akai welcoming human society instead of foreswearing it seems significant.

Part Three

Playing Frankenstein

8

Mary Enters: Staging Shelley in Contemporary *Frankenstein* Biodramas

Brittany Reid

Mary Shelley's *Frankenstein* was first dramatized and professionally staged a mere five years after its initial publication and, almost 200 years later, new adaptations continue to haunt the theatre. The novel's long theatrical afterlife began in 1823 with Richard Brinsley Peake's gothic melodrama *Presumption; or, The Fate of Frankenstein*.[1] One of the major changes that *Presumption* introduced to the story was a heightened emphasis on the infamous creation scene, which would soon become a central feature of *Frankenstein* mythology. In adapting *Frankenstein* from page to stage, dramatists since Peake have similarly taken advantage of the creation scene's dramatic potential and, in doing so, placed a greater emphasis on the significance of both creation and creators to *Frankenstein*. Further extending this heightened emphasis on Victor's act of creation within the story, several twenty-first century theatrical adaptations of *Frankenstein* self-reflexively acknowledge the novel's own narrative creation. Contemporary dramatizations of *Frankenstein* often employ Mary Shelley's own literary creation scene, chiefly the famous ghost story competition in 1816, as a double for Victor's infernal act of creation within the novel.[2]

These *Frankenstein* dramatizations prominently feature Shelley herself in the dual role of author-character, thus blurring the line between Romantic lives and writing, highlighting the parallels between both real and fictionalized acts of creation. Shelley's characterization in these adaptations can take many forms, from an excited teenager in love, to a tortured artist in conflict with her burgeoning creation, to mother Mary in a moment of divine inspiration. But in each instance, she appears within the drama to lend a sense of relatability and reality to the artistic creation process, which further nuances the play's featured act of bringing a vision to life. Adaptations that feature Shelley's author avatar first appeared in the late twentieth century and, in recent years, this approach has become exceedingly common for *Frankenstein* plays, resulting in an emerging theatrical tradition.[3] Consequently, these contemporary, theatrical adaptations constitute a new hybrid genre, which I term *Frankenstein* biodramas.

Frankenstein biodramas are creative adaptations that blend elements of fact and fiction to innovatively reimagine Shelley's *Frankenstein* legend for the stage. By drawing from Shelley's life and writing in this way, contemporary dramatists regenerate

Frankenstein through paratextual details and ground this supernatural tale through historical context. Furthermore, through the evocation of the story's creator within these plays, thematic parallels emerge between Shelley's biography and her most famous work. By placing Shelley within the narrative, points of connection can be made between her composition of *Frankenstein*, Victor's animation of the creature, and, subsequently, the theatrical practitioners' own dramatization of the story. These plays-in-performance not only challenge traditional expectations regarding cross-medium adaptation, but also work to recentralize Shelley within modern *Frankenstein* mythology. Consequently, these theatrical adaptations both reflect and contribute to the shared cultural legacies of *Frankenstein* and Shelley by re-establishing the natal link between her and her hideous progeny.[4]

This chapter explores *Frankenstein*'s evolving theatrical legacy through contemporary plays-in-performance that explicitly connect Mary Shelley's life story to that of her most famous novel. Twenty-first-century dramatists have played a key part in the preservation and persistence of *Frankenstein* and Shelley's interconnected cultural afterlives by frequently casting her as an author-character within their plays. *Frankenstein*'s theatrical adaptations have encouraged the book's story and characters to continue regenerating in the popular imagination, and concurrently revitalized Mary Shelley's own biographical and authorial legacies.

Frankenstein Biodramas: An Emerging Theatrical Genre

Five years after *Frankenstein*'s 1818 publication, a frequent and undiminished tradition of dramatizing the novel commenced; by 1826, fifteen dramatizations of the novel had been staged throughout Europe.[5] But while adaptations of *Frankenstein* have become a theatrical fixture, from *Presumption* to Nick Dear's acclaimed 2011 version at London's National Theatre, the role of Mary Shelley as the source text's author was left unacknowledged for many years.[6] As a corrective to that longstanding omission, since the late twentieth-century, scholarly and popular interest in Mary Shelley has fueled a desire for plays that frame *Frankenstein* through the life of its creator.[7]

Following the emergence of plays about Mary Shelley's life in the 1970s and 1980s, the twenty-first century has seen an efflorescence of new plays that focus on Mary and her various roles as creator: chiefly as author of *Frankenstein*, but also as mother, collaborator, editor, and legacy builder. The resulting plays can rightly be termed *Frankenstein* biodramas, since they integrate elements of both *Frankenstein* and Mary Shelley's own life to create new works that collapse the traditional life/writing binary. These plays are framed as biographical treatments of Shelley's life and, although they each refer to *Frankenstein* in some way, they are not positioned or promoted as direct adaptations of the novel. For example, in 2001, Canadian playwright Pauline Carey opened *Don't Talk to Me of Love* in New York City.[8] The play features Shelley as the narrator of her parents' love story, which allows her to address the audience directly as our guide: a role she frequently plays in *Frankenstein* biodramas. By casting Mary as the preserver of her parents' legacies, Carey highlights Shelley's ability to resurrect her loved ones through storytelling. Darrah Teitel's *The Apology* (2011 and 2013) depicts

Shelley's inception of *Frankenstein* in 1816, but then extends the play's setting to the present.[9] In doing so, Teitel not only depicts the historical Mary during *Frankenstein*'s creation, but imaginatively continues her story to allow for the creator to witness the cultural legacy of her creation. This move also lends the character greater agency, which is especially significant in contrast to Mary's anonymous publication of *Frankenstein* in 1818 or lack of compensation over her story's theatrical adaptation in 1823. By depicting her negotiating with her publisher over creative choices or movie rights, Teitel offers a corrective to the historical Shelley's comparative lack of authorial autonomy. In Emily Dendinger's *Hideous Progeny* (2010) and Brittany Reid's *Justified Sinners* (2017), the potential for a biographical link between Percy Shelley and *Frankenstein*'s creature is physically embodied, since Mary is shown resurrecting her husband onstage as her own doppelgänger.[10] In this way, even though neither play is a strict adaptation of *Frankenstein*, they both transfigure the novel's featured act of creation into the literal resurrection of Percy Shelley. Helen Edmundson's *Mary Shelley* (2012) was developed for Shared Experience theatre in England and similarly focuses on the life and creative process of its eponymous character.[11] Although not billed as an adaptation of *Frankenstein*, *Mary Shelley* is a family drama that uses expressionistic elements to offer an expansive look at how Shelley's interpersonal relationships and rich, inner life led to the novel's creation. The popularity of *Mary Shelley*, through both its initial touring production and subsequent remounts, has introduced its titular character to new audiences and tilled new creative ground by focusing on her as an individual, not just as the author of *Frankenstein*.

While many contemporary dramatists have created *Frankenstein* biodramas by integrating elements from *Frankenstein* into Shelley's life story, presently, the more common approach involves staging *Frankenstein* and introducing Mary into cross-medium adaptations of the novel.[12] Most often, this entails three strategies: inserting Shelley into the story as an author-character, using the ghost story competition in 1816 as a frame narrative for the play, or double-casting characters from the novel with figures from Shelley's own life. First, in many adaptations of *Frankenstein*, Shelley appears as a character within the narrative who either interacts with other characters or directly addresses the audience to help elucidate key themes or ideas in the play. The effect of this inclusion is a breaking of the fourth wall that raises the stakes of the story by reminding audiences of the real-world implications of Shelley's own act of creation. For example, Shelley appears as author-character in two distinct operatic productions that were staged in the United States and Scotland: *The Mary Shelley Opera* and *Monster: An Opera in Two Acts*.[13] Both operas opened in 2002 and integrate the story of Mary's life into the plot of *Frankenstein*, allowing for an imaginative interplay between the established documentary record of Shelley's life and the well-known narrative beats and characters of her most famous novel. In another example, Radiohole's *Inflatable Frankenstein* (2013), Shelley appears as a character within the performance, alongside her stepsister Claire Clairmont. In keeping with this postdramatic adaptation's depiction of *Frankenstein*'s creature as a network of organs made from inflated grocery bags, Mary and her sister are shown with ever-growing, inflatable stomachs to represent their pregnancies, which further serves as a metaphor for *Frankenstein*'s own gestation. Second, many *Frankenstein* biodramas use the events at Villa Diodati in 1816 as a frame narrative. This approach allows dramatists to situate the events of *Frankenstein* directly within the context of the novel's creation scene and foregrounds the importance of the novel's own moment of conception. For example, *Mary Shelley's Frankenstein* (2017) by Ensemble for the Romantic Century framed its musical retelling of *Frankenstein* as its author's nightmare, in keeping with Shelley's own famous recollection of the story's genesis (Shelley 1831).[14] In this performance, the choices to begin with Mary waking in terror from a dream, to use the novel and her personal writing as the basis for the play text, and to include Shelley's name in the title as a sign of ownership, explicitly reconnect *Frankenstein* to its author's life and legacy.[15]

The third and final way that dramatists have integrated Mary Shelley into adaptations of *Frankenstein* is through character doubling. Most often, this entails double-casting actors to play characters from *Frankenstein* and figures from Shelley's life, such as her husband Percy and Lord Byron. Speaking to this trend in the talk-back for his own 2011 adaptation of *Frankenstein*, playwright Nick Dear similarly noted that "a lot of adaptations of *Frankenstein* have shoehorned in Mary herself as a substitute for Elizabeth" ("Interview with Danny Boyle and Nick Dear" 2012). The convention of double casting, having the same actor play multiple roles, has been frequently employed to suggest a direct alignment between *Frankenstein*'s fictional characters and their possible historical counterparts. This approach not only realigns Shelley with her literary creation, but also inflects the critical reading of *Frankenstein* as an (auto) biographical work.[16] This tendency to dramatize Mary Shelley, along with her coterie, was seen throughout the late twentieth century, when many theatrical and cinematic adaptations of *Frankenstein* blurred the line between life and writing by doubling members of the Villa Diodati group as characters within the narrative.[17] By having a single actor portray Percy Shelley and Victor Frankenstein, Lord Byron and the creature, or Mary Shelley and Elizabeth, an intrinsic connection is broadcasted onstage between the historical figure and his or her apparent fictional counterpart. An example of this use of character doubling in *Frankenstein* adaptations is Ann Bertram's 2007 play *Frankenstein Incarnate: The Passions of Mary Shelley*.[18] In her play, Bertram juxtaposes the events of the Haunted Summer of 1816 with the events of *Frankenstein* to creatively underscore the story's autobiographical and thematic links with Shelley's life. In the following case studies, I explore two additional examples of *Frankenstein* biodramas that use doubling to underscore the connection between Shelley as creator and her story as creation: *Frankenstein: The Year Without a Summer* (2010) and *Birth of Frankenstein* (2013). Although these are only two case studies, and both received relatively small premiere productions, they represent two distinct approaches to reintegrating Mary Shelley into *Frankenstein* using double casting.

Frankenstein: The Year Without a Summer

The play *Frankenstein: The Year Without a Summer*, was written and directed by Helen Davis, and toured in Autumn 2010. It was originally produced by Dorset Corset, a professional theatre company based in Shaftesbury, England whose "primary focus is period work with a strong musical theme."[19] The play's premiere production bears the distinction of being the first staged in the Shelley Theatre after its partial restoration, more than a century after it was last used.[20] In keeping with Marvin Carlson's conception of "the haunted stage" and physical theatres as "among the most haunted of human cultural structures," the staging of this play at the Shelley theatre explicitly evoked Shelley's memory, which lent a biographical inflection to this adaptation.[21] Looking at how the play is framed, the hybrid-title *Frankenstein: The Year Without a Summer* reflects the dual purposes of a *Frankenstein* biodrama: capturing both the story of *Frankenstein* and the story of Mary Shelley. While the play's title announces itself as an adaptation of *Frankenstein*, its second part, "The Year Without a Summer" recalls the summer of 1816 and the setting of *Frankenstein*'s origin story at Villa Diodati.[22] This sense of narrative hybridity, one story sutured onto another, begins with this title and extends to the performance's play-within-a-play structure. In *Frankenstein: The Year Without a Summer*, Davis nests *Frankenstein* within its own creation myth by showing members of the Villa Diodati group acting out the story during their stormy stay beside Lake Geneva.[23] Consequently, rather than simply re-telling the story of *Frankenstein* to the audience, Davis instead uses Mary Shelley and her companions to act out the drama themselves, all the while highlighting the similarities between members of the group and their respective fictional counterparts. This begins in the play's opening scene featuring Mary bashfully refusing to read *Frankenstein*, which she refers to as her "feeble attempt," out loud and instead suggesting that they stage her story as a "home theatrical."[24] In choosing to double-cast Mary, Percy, and Byron within the play and having them act out the novel onstage, Davis uses her theatrical adaptation to explicitly broadcast the biographical connection between Mary's life and writing in *Frankenstein*. Moreover, this meta-theatrical gesture not only re-figures the group as stand-ins for *Frankenstein*'s characters, but also allows them to self-reflexively critique and comment on their own domestic drama as they perform for each other and, by extension, for the audience.

In *Frankenstein: The Year Without a Summer*, the actors playing these three characters from Shelley's life are then tasked with taking on many roles from *Frankenstein*. In total, eighteen characters are directly lifted from *Frankenstein* itself and these parts are split among the actors playing Mary, Percy, and Lord Byron during their play-within-a-play. Specifically, the actor playing Lord Byron takes on eight total roles, including Clerval, Robert Walton, and Byron's most frequent role in *Frankenstein* biodramas, the creature. The actor playing Mary Shelley is also charged with playing eight characters, primarily adopting the novel's female characters, including Mary's most common counterpart, Elizabeth. Finally, the actor playing Percy Shelley plays De Lacey and Victor Frankenstein, a character that has commonly been read, and re-staged, as Percy's fictional alter-ego. This sense of doubling upon doubling, where double-casted actors are playing the role of double-casted actors, creates a sense of uncertainty at times; despite visual cues or shifts in acting style, it is often intentionally unclear which character is seen onstage or which layer of the performance the audience is witnessing.

In *Frankenstein: The Year Without a Summer*, Davis does not merely suggest a possible likeness between the Villa Diodati group and the characters they play within this meta-drama with double casting. Instead, she has the group periodically break from their staging of *Frankenstein* so that the audience can see a direct correlation between Mary's story and the lives that may have inspired it, thus further encouraging an (auto)biographical reading of the novel. At one point in the play, Percy breaks character to inquire "What happens to Victor?" while Byron asks, "And the monster?"[25] In both cases, Percy and Byron express allegiance to their own key roles and imagine their fates as tied up in those of their characters, which underscores the shared likeness between them and their fictional counterparts. Instances like this showcase how double-casting works to create a sense of slippage between characters from Mary Shelley's life and fiction, causing the audience to question, in many cases, where each ends and the other begins.

In another of these exchanges that breaks the fourth wall, Byron lashes out at Percy, saying "You are infuriating. It's the same as the monster's need for a patriarchal figure and to be respected and loved. Don't you see? ... You are more of a monster than I am."[26] Here, Byron directly employs the moral meaning of *Frankenstein* to chide Percy's behavior and, in so doing, underscores the link between Shelley's life and her writing. By associating Percy's neglect of Mary with Victor's abandonment of the creature, Byron articulates the significance of Percy's casting as Victor within the play. In response to this comparison, Percy continues to justify his own actions in relation to Victor's. The directions indicate that he "*takes up Victor's coat*," again taking refuge under the guise of his fictional alter-ego, and claims that both he and Victor are "impelled by the purest and the truest motives to the best and noblest ends."[27] In both cases, Byron's explicit evocation of the novel to explain their circumstances, and Percy's justification of his own behavior through Victor's, allows for the possibility of interpreting *Frankenstein* as a *roman à clef* based on Mary's own life.

Finally, after the play-within-a-play concludes, the group reflects on the moral meaning of the story they have staged, relating the circumstances of the narrative back to their relationships and treatment of one another. In a particularly poignant moment, Percy reflects upon his earlier conversation with Byron about Victor's neglect of the creature, remarking that "I can't help thinking Victor Frankenstein was a fool ... Kindness, consideration, love. It was all the creature asked for."[28] The stage direction indicates that "*Byron and Mary look at Shelley*" in silent acknowledgement before Byron responds with a quote from Victor Frankenstein: "How dangerous is the acquirement of knowledge."[29] Percy completes the quote from the novel, stating: "How much happier is that man who believes his native town to be the world, than he who aspires to become greater than his nature will allow."[30] Although Byron and Percy are here speaking lines from *Frankenstein*, they apply these sentiments to their own situation, having seen the truth behind Mary's fiction, and make this connection salient for the audience.

The decision to introduce the story through its compositional context, rather than its original framework, effectively repositions the subsequent narrative through Mary Shelley's life. Instead of highlighting the similarities between Robert Walton and Victor Frankenstein, two overreaching explorers, this juxtaposition invites audiences to read similarities between Mary, her coterie, and her characters. In the case of *Frankenstein: The Year Without a Summer*, this sense of doubling is further underscored by the interstitial scenes, which allow the group to temporarily 'break character' and permit us to see behind the curtain of their complex relationships. Consequently, in Helen Davis' *Frankenstein: The Year Without a Summer*, the play-within-a-play structure and use of doubling compels Shelley's companions to re-live their own domestic drama and re-evaluate it according to the novel's moral compass.

Significantly, *Frankenstein: The Year Without a Summer* is not the first retelling of *Frankenstein* to use this same device of having the Villa Diodati group acting out the novel's events. In the 1935 film *Bride of Frankenstein*, the novel's frame narrative, involving Robert Walton and his search for the Northwest Passage, was replaced by Mary narrating the story to Byron and Percy in 1816. Since this formative film adaptation, many dramatists have followed suit by replacing the novel's framing with the backstory outlined by Mary in the introduction to the novel's 1831 re-edition. Read in this way, Davis' choice to use the Villa Diodati as the story's frame narrative honors *Frankenstein*'s adaptation history, rather than reflecting the novel's innate structure. From the staging of the creation scene to the addition of an assistant for Victor, the history of *Frankenstein* biodramas often features recurring elements that are not derived from Shelley's novel itself. The depiction of the ghost story competition that inspired *Frankenstein*'s conception is another of these elements, which have come to define contemporary *Frankenstein* biodramas without ever appearing in the source text. By using Mary, Percy, and Byron to act out the story of *Frankenstein* onstage, Davis and Dorset Corset both honored the novel's compositional history, while also building on its long tradition of adaptation.

Birth of Frankenstein

Litmus Theatre is an emerging performance ensemble in Toronto, Canada with a mandate to reimagine classic stories in inventive ways for urban audiences. Their 2013 play, *Birth of Frankenstein*, debuted as a site-specific performance, set in the Parlor Room of St. Luke's, a nineteenth-century United Church in Toronto.[31] Much like my first performance case study, *Birth of Frankenstein* employs the theatrical convention of double casting to suggest direct parallels between the characters of *Frankenstein* and members of Mary Shelley's circle. But while *Frankenstein: The Year Without a Summer* saw the Villa Diodati group acting out *Frankenstein* to dramatize this connection, *Birth of Frankenstein* literalizes this auto-biographical dimension by having the characters of Shelley's novel and important individuals from her life literally transform into one another onstage. Elements of Shelley's life and writing are freely intertwined, producing a biofictional gothic fantasia in keeping with *Frankenstein*'s theatrical legacy. While *Frankenstein: The Year Without a Summer* featured eighteen characters played by only three actors, *Birth of Frankenstein* includes nine characters performed by four actors. The first actor plays Percy and Victor Frankenstein, in addition to other, minor characters from *Frankenstein*. The second actor portrays Byron, who returns to his role of the creature and begins the drama as Mary's father, William Godwin. Claire Clairmont is added to the story as a fourth member of the Villa Diodati group; she assumes Mary's usual role of Elizabeth, while also beginning the play as Mary Wollstonecraft. Notably, only the actor playing Mary Shelley is not double cast, which allows her to exist as a character within both stories: the story of *Frankenstein* and the novel's origin story. Additionally, because Mary is not double cast, she can transcend time and place, stepping outside of the events of the play to address the audience directly and serve as our guiding narrator throughout.

To complete these character transitions onstage, Litmus Theatre developed an innovative approach that highlighted the connection between Shelley's life and writing: a séance. By staging a resurrection of Mary Shelley, her friends and family, and her characters from *Frankenstein*, Litmus Theatre literalizes the themes of creation and reanimation that pervade *Frankenstein* biodramas. Whereas *Frankenstein: The Year Without a Summer* showed members of the Villa Diodati group playing the characters of *Frankenstein* in a game of pretend, *Birth of Frankenstein* introduces a supernatural element to the performance by depicting characters transfiguring onstage. Accordingly, an actor playing Lord Byron can suddenly transform into *Frankenstein*'s creature without comment. Here, character parallels and the fluid relationship between Mary's life and fiction are embodied by showing figures from her circle physically transform into her fictional characters. The first of these character transitions occurs before the play itself begins and involves the actors, appearing onstage and out of character, evoking the "spirit" of Mary Shelley. This staged resurrection of her "spirit" commences in the prologue, entitled "A Wakening," and shows the ensemble conjuring Mary Shelley and inviting her to possess one of the actors. In this excerpt from the play's opening stage directions, this invocation of Mary Shelley "for the first time in 150 years" is described as a physical and spiritual transformation:

> The four actors move to four points around a shroud laying downstage. One actor offers her body to the circle, laying flat on her back. The others sit around her and join hands. They create a drone that is in dissonance with the music. Something is being conjured. Flickers of lightning. The Actor who has offered her body begins to convulse and shake. She gasps for breath as if for the first time in 150 years. MARY shudders and takes in her surroundings.[32]

This depiction of the actors coming together and calling forward the spirit of Mary Shelley represents an immediate and literal form of re-embodiment and reincarnation. Through the ritualistic execution and the sense that "something is being conjured," the actors are positioned as willing, corporeal vessels for the spirits of Mary Shelley, members of her coterie, and her characters from *Frankenstein*. Furthermore, the direction that the actor possessed by the spirit of Mary Shelley "gasps for breath as if for the first time in 150 years" underscores the fact that it is the historical figure of Shelley herself that is supposedly conjured onstage. This process transcends the limits of representation, suggesting that *Frankenstein* biodramas have the potential to go beyond merely reenacting the imagined resurrection at the center of Shelley's novel. By beginning their performance with the reanimation of Mary Shelley, Litmus Theatre transcend the limits of "*surrogation*," which Joseph Roach suggests occurs when "survivors attempt to fit satisfactory alternates" into "the cavities created by loss through death or other forms of departure."[33] Framed as the resurrection of Mary Shelley, along with her characters and loved ones, *Birth of Frankenstein* exemplifies how *Frankenstein* biodramas continue to push the limits of creative adaptation and find new ways to vivify Shelley's story.

Litmus Theatre's decision to frame their adaptation of the novel in terms of resurrection, rather than re-creation or representation, further reflects the fluid relationship between fact and fiction that defines *Frankenstein* and its afterlives. In "The Politics of Autobiography in Mary Wollstonecraft and Mary Shelley" (2001), Gary Kelly argues that Mary Shelley's writing is defined by both the "presence of the 'author' and the disclosures of autobiographical reference in the text, whether fictional or non-fictional."[34] This observation highlights the heightened role of performativity and identity in Shelley's writing, including *Frankenstein*. By creating a sense of intimacy with her readers, whether authentic or illusory, Shelley encourages readers to project her into her stories and imagine her authorial presence. In *Frankenstein* biodramas, such as *Birth of Frankenstein*, this interplay between fact and fiction permits playwrights to reanimate her onstage through the retelling of her story. Viewed in this way, Litmus Theatre's frame narrative, a dramatized séance of Mary Shelley, literalizes the impulse behind all *Frankenstein* biodramas by manifesting her onstage to tell her story.

This sense of spiritual possession is a recurring theme in *Birth of Frankenstein*, as seen through Mary's "waking dreams" where she envisions her companions transforming into the characters of *Frankenstein*. For example, in a waking dream entitled "Victor Appears," Mary encounters Victor for the first time as he "begins to dig up body parts in the graveyard."[35] When Mary asks Victor who he is, he responds "you will give me life." Victor then "*wraps the book MARY was reading into the shroud, shaping it into a bundle*" and explains that he is "gathering materials for [his] creation."[36] When Mary asks, "How will you do it?" Victor responds, "Same way you will create me."[37] In this way, Victor is not only derived from Mary's husband, Percy, but also appears to her as a corporeal being before she brings him to life through the composition of *Frankenstein*. By imagining Victor as a transformed version of Percy and showing Mary encountering the character onstage, *Birth of Frankenstein* depicts *Frankenstein*'s creation as an act of discovery within Shelley's own imagined life. Throughout the performance, these waking dreams play out alongside scenes from both *Frankenstein* and Mary's life story. The overall effect of this chaotic shifting between the events and characters of *Frankenstein* and the documentary record of Shelley's life destabilizes the traditional life/writing binary. In the process, Litmus Theatre's *Frankenstein* biodrama uses character doubling, the blending of events from literature and literary history, and the evocation of Shelley's "spirit" onstage to suggest a natal link between *Frankenstein* and its creator. *Birth of Frankenstein* not only depicts the events of *Frankenstein*, but it also uses the theatrical medium in new ways to capture the novel's theme of resurrection while continuing to revitalize the story for contemporary audiences.

Conclusion: *Frankenstein* Biodramas' Next Stages

Since 1823, *Frankenstein* has been adapted innumerable times from page to stage. 200 years later, many audiences throughout the transatlantic world have been introduced to the story through its many theatrical afterlives. Through their own reworking of the *Frankenstein* mythology, playwrights have the unique potential to reframe, reimagine, and ultimately rewrite Shelley's most famous story for their contemporary contexts. A consequence of this ubiquity is that these plays have directly informed individual and collective recollections of Shelley's novel. Through nearly two centuries of theatrical adaptations, playwrights' many additions or omissions have influenced the cultural memory of *Frankenstein*. By changing the plot, characters, or other narrative elements of the original novel, dramatists have the power to alter perceptions of this literary classic and re-form it in their own image. In a process that reflects Victor Frankenstein's own act of creation, *Frankenstein*'s theatrical legacy is itself rendered a monstrous palimpsest: a piecemeal textual creation that bears the surgical scars left by the hands of many makers. But, ironically, although *Frankenstein*'s theatrical afterlife is both heterogenous and polyvocal in nature, it has been sustained by the privileged position granted to the story's primal author: Mary Shelley. While the popularity and sheer number of plays based on the novel has helped to maintain the story's place in the broader cultural consciousness, these dramas have also extended beyond their literary source text by drawing from the biography of its famous author. As the constellation of recent performances and exemplary case studies covered in this study has helped demonstrate, contemporary *Frankenstein* plays frequently extend beyond direct adaptations of their literary source text to accomplish a larger legacy-building project, for both Shelley and her novel. In doing so, these performances have led to the creation of a new hybrid genre of performances, which I termed *Frankenstein* biodramas, that suture together elements of biographical theatre, literary adaptation, and *Frankenstein*'s evolving cultural legacy to reanimate the story for contemporary audiences. Whether these performances are billed as biographical plays about Mary Shelley or theatrical adaptations of *Frankenstein*, *Frankenstein* biodramas reinforce the innate connection between creator and creation that has come to define this novel's theatrical afterlife by depicting Mary's author avatar, dramatizing the novel's own creation, or double casting Shelley's coterie and characters. At the same time, by reuniting Shelley with her monster, these dramatists position themselves as collaborators in the continuing retelling of *Frankenstein*. As these cross-medium adaptations continue to be staged, dramatists will reimagine *Frankenstein* through innovative staging choices that bring new immediacy and poignancy to three forms of creation: Victor Frankenstein's experimentation, Mary Shelley's narrative conception, and the playwright's dramatization. Thanks to the persisting popularity of these *Frankenstein* biodramas, the theatrical legacies of both *Frankenstein* and Mary Shelley remain alive and well today.

9

The Frankenstein Myth in Twenty-First-Century Film

Robert I. Lublin

> "You know this story. Crack of lightning.
> A mad genius. An unholy creation."
>
> Victor Frankenstein (2015)

In the years 2000 to 2020, more than twenty-three new full-length "Frankenstein" films were produced. That averages more than one new film per year being directly indebted to *Frankenstein* for its title and motivating myth, and if we count films that are merely indebted to Shelley's novel but do not appeal to it for their title, the number would be considerably higher. These new "Frankenstein" films represent an extraordinarily diverse range of movies that take a variety of creative approaches. Studied collectively, however, they lend themselves to meaningful generalizations. To start, twenty-first-century "Frankenstein" films first reengaged with and then purposefully broke their connection to Mary Shelley's novel. Additionally, these recent movies almost uniformly find Victor to be more monstrous than his creation. Also, and excitingly, women feature more prominently in modern film adaptations, providing meaningful alternatives to the parthenogenetic fantasy that motivates the novel *Frankenstein*. In sum, "Frankenstein" films produced in the first two decades of the twenty-first century show the continuing significance of the Frankenstein myth to how we view ourselves today.

A proper study of twenty-first-century "Frankenstein" films begins a bit earlier, in 1994, with the release of Kenneth Branagh's *Mary Shelley's Frankenstein*.[1] The movie stars famous actors, employs lavish sets and costumes, and worldwide marketing was engaged to establish the film as a definitive adaptation of the novel.[2] Although the movie received mixed reviews, its $45 million budget yielded a total box office return of $112 million, drew worldwide attention, and fashioned the cinematic shape of the Frankenstein myth in the years immediately preceding the turn of the century.[3]

Branagh's adaptation was so influential that it was another decade before Victor and his creation appeared again on screen in a major adaptation.[4] Branagh's film cast a long shadow and established the backdrop against which more recent films can be understood in their historic and cinematic moment. *Mary Shelley's Frankenstein*, despite announcing its indebtedness to Shelley's novel in the title, exercised considerable creative license.[5] At the heart of Branagh's film is a concrete explanation for Victor Frankenstein's determination to create life. As Esther Schor notes, "the sight of his mother dying in childbed, smeared with afterbirth and blood, sets a bereft Victor (Branagh) on his quest to defy the limits of life."[6] This differs from the novel, in which Victor's mother dies of scarlet fever; the violence of death during childbirth is a significant departure from the novel. Caroline Picart explains, "the film gives the parthenogenetic myth an idealistic motive: the desire to enable love to endure forever through immortal physical union."[7] In Branagh's film, Victor Frankenstein appears a much more sympathetic character than Shelley presents in her novel.[8]

The pervasive influence of Branagh's production deterred filmmakers from creating new "Frankenstein" movies for ten long years but when they resumed, they did so with energy and creativity. The twenty-first century has seen a virtual explosion of new "Frankenstein" films. 2014 was a banner year for cinematic "Frankensteins," which saw the release of four new films: *I, Frankenstein*, *Frankenstein's Monster*, *Frankenstein vs. The Mummy*, and *Scooby Doo! Frankencreepy*.[9] It even managed to surpass 2013, which introduced three new movies: *The Frankenstein Theory*, *Frankenstein's Army*, and *Army of Frankensteins*.[10] As the titles suggest and the plots corroborate, these films take significant liberties with Shelley's novel. In fact, they change the story so much that some may find it a stretch to label these films inheritors of the "Frankenstein" moniker. But their undeniable connection to the Frankenstein myth is announced in their titles and carries with it numerous associations that inevitably append to the appellation. Furthermore, even a short survey of the history of "Frankenstein" in film demonstrates that it is quite common for movies to take extensive liberties with the story.[11] In the twenty-first century, these liberties have been taken to new heights, with films changing the time, location, premise, plot, characters, and more. But all these films appeal directly to *Frankenstein* with their titles and lay claim to its heritage.

Among the new films, only two attempt to follow the basic storyline of the novel. The 2004 made-for-television film *Frankenstein*, directed by Kevin Connor, offers a three-hour adaptation of the novel that was professionally produced and includes some highly respected actors in minor roles.[12] Following Branagh's production, which announced its indebtedness to Shelley's work in its title, Connor managed to distinguish his film by adhering to the novel far more faithfully. Kim Newman praises the film, saying that it "fulfils the promise many [adaptations]—including *Frankenstein: The True Story* (1973) and *Mary Shelley's Frankenstein*—failed to keep, and is a faithful, respectable, slightly stiff adaptation of the novel."[13] So faithful is Connor's adaptation that Brian Lowry "commends" the film by remarking that it "should become the official home-study alternative for kids too lazy to read the book."[14] The film was made by the Hallmark channel and, as a result, focuses its efforts more on accurately establishing the drama of Shelley's story than in provoking any actual sense of horror.

Connor's Victor (Alex Newman) differs substantially from Branagh's. In the earlier movie, as James Heffernan has noted, Victor radiates "a robust vitality that scarcely recalls the wasted, emaciated figure we meet in the novel."[15] Newman more accurately presents the frail, overextended scientist Shelley describes. Additionally, when the creature is brought to life, Newman's Victor flees in horror before his own creation. Branagh's Victor, on the other hand, sought to help his creation (Robert De Niro) and only abandoned him when, through an accident, he thought the creature had been killed. By having Victor flee in fear and disgust, Connor more accurately follows the novel and presents the eponymous scientist as a less respectable figure.

The creature in Connor's film (Luke Goss) primarily inspires pity as he longs for companionship after being abandoned by his creator and spurned by others. He instills minimal fear, which is to be expected in a movie intended to be family friendly. Even when the monster kills Elizabeth, the scene is quite tame, particularly when compared with the gruesome demise Elizabeth meets in Branagh's film. Connor's monster calmly walks up to Elizabeth and almost gently puts his hand around her neck before the scene abruptly shifts. When we see Elizabeth next, she is dead, bearing a slight mark on her neck but no other signs of trauma. In Branagh's movie, Elizabeth's death is extraordinarily violent, even by Hollywood horror standards: the creature plunges his hand into Elizabeth's chest, tearing out her still-beating heart, and she falls off the bed, smashing her face into an oil lamp which sets her hair on fire.[16]

And yet, it is what happens after the death of Elizabeth that separates the two films most significantly. In Branagh's movie, the plot breaks entirely with the novel as Victor pieces together the newly killed Elizabeth with Justine's corpse to bring his beloved back to life. Newly resurrected, this Bride of Frankenstein must then choose between Victor and the creature. She instead chooses suicide, setting herself on fire and burning down Frankenstein's house around her. Connor's Victor, following the novel, has learned his parthenogenetic lesson and accepts the finality of Elizabeth's death. He sets out in search of his creation, pursuing him to the icy north with hopes of exacting revenge. The final moments of these two movies again differ in a significant way. Branagh's creature holds aloft a burning torch and sets himself and Victor ablaze as Captain Walton watches from his ship. Connor's Captain Walton watches the creature carry the dead Victor into the icy tundra and the film ends as the two disappear. The movie, as the novel, suggests that the creature goes off to die, but we are left with no certainty that he does so.

The second and final "Frankenstein" film in the twenty-first century to follow the basic story of Shelley's novel was released ten years later and was a low-budget affair that was not widely seen. *Frankenstein's Monster* (2014), directed by Syd Lance, is a cheaply produced, steampunk version of Frankenstein. The story is rushed and requires that the viewer be familiar with the novel to follow the plot. The monster (Matt Risoldi) does not look threatening or even scary—he merely wears a red beard along with a small, metal apparatus on his neck that releases steam, yet people respond as though he were terrifying to behold.

One detail of *Frankenstein's Monster* that deserves note is how the body used to create the monster was procured. Victor's Professor, impressed with the progression of the young pupil's research, offers to provide Victor with a human body on which he could continue his experiments. Consequently, Victor does not so much create life as reanimate or resurrect it (although the monster does not demonstrate any memory of or connection to his body's previous experiences). In the novel, Victor's creation is made with material drawn from charnel houses and slaughterhouses, but he ultimately creates an entirely new life. Connor's *Frankenstein*, not surprisingly, follows the novel and has Victor create a new life that evinces no connection to the pieces that were used to construct it. Branagh took a different approach. In his film, Victor drew pieces from multiple bodies, but then the film notes that the limbs were taken from criminals whose sins carry over to the composite body: "bits of thieves, bits of murderers, evil stitched to evil stitched to evil" (1:11:56). By considering the life that previously inhabited the body parts of the creature, Branagh's film follows the example originally set by the 1931 Universal film, whose monster was not a blank slate when he was created but a consequence of using an abnormal brain (which Mel Brooks brilliantly parodied in his 1974 *Young Frankenstein*). In twenty-first-century "Frankenstein" films, Victor interchangeably creates new life, reanimates the dead, and builds beings that walk unsteadily between the two.

Among the many new "Frankenstein" films appearing in the twenty-first century, the most surprising thing to note is the almost dizzying range of creative approaches the Frankenstein myth has inspired. The film industry broke completely free of Branagh's influence and expanded the scope of possibilities the Frankenstein myth could inspire. In 2004, in addition to Connor's film, another movie, simply titled *Frankenstein*, appeared. Also made for television and intended to be the pilot for a series, this film, directed by Marcus Nispel, is essentially a contemporary crime drama that highlights the efforts of police detectives to make sense of a Frankensteinian creation who desperately wants to die and has turned into a serial killer since it has been rendered incapable of suicide. The police are aided in their search for the monster-cum-criminal by the original Victor's creature who inconspicuously and heroically fights for justice.

The Frankenstein Syndrome (2010), directed by Sean Tretta, locates the action in a secret hospital in which scientists work collaboratively to defeat death in the service of a rich, immoral financier seeking a cure for his own cancer.[17] Their risky experiments on unwilling participants ultimately produce a monster that seeks revenge. *Frankenstein's Army* (2013) is set during the Second World War and is presented as the efforts of a Soviet film crew to document an army platoon as it fights in Germany. The soldiers happen upon the work of a mad Nazi scientist who has been developing monstrous cyborgs that blindly follow their creator's orders and are nearly impossible to kill. *I, Frankenstein* presents Frankenstein's creation as a troubled modern superhero who reluctantly joins the forces of good in a battle against infernal demons.

And yet, trends can be identified among the wildly disparate "Frankenstein" movies produced in the recent past. Many of the new films share the opinion that between the scientist and his creation, the former is the true monster. The extended quote from the 2015 *Victor Frankenstein* that begins this chapter draws explicit attention to man's monstrousness: "You know this story. Crack of lightning. A mad genius. An unholy creation. The world, of course, remembers the monster, not the man. But sometimes, when you look closely, there's more to a tale. Sometimes the monster is the man" (0:00:34–0:01:13). Despite starting with a damning assessment of Victor Frankenstein, this film, directed by Paul McGuigan, presents a relatively benevolent mad scientist when compared with other recent "Frankenstein" movies. Victor (James McAvoy) may appear overexcited and even a bit loony in his mannerisms and determination to create life, but the character has a clear dramatic motivation for his experiments: he seeks to atone for his role as a child in the death of his older brother, a transgression that lost him the love and respect of his father.[18] Wishing to create a life to make amends for the one he lost, Victor earns audience sympathy. McAvoy has played a monster on film before in *Split* (2016), and he was truly scary in the role. In *Victor Frankenstein*, he plays an erratic, eccentric scientist who uses his genius to rectify the mistakes of his past. If we are to accept the movie's premise that the man is the monster, then he would appear to be fairly tame.

Other twenty-first-century "Frankenstein" films, however, present the scientist as a true monster who pursues wicked designs without any clear motivation that might explain the man's choices or his cruelty. One notable subset of films links the scientist's immorality to sexual violence. The 2004 crime drama *Frankenstein* features a thoroughly corrupt Frankenstein, now calling himself Victor Helios (Thomas Kretschmann), who is an attractive, wealthy, powerful man who has lived for 200 years and bears the medical marks on his body that evince his efforts to prolong his lifespan. Helios's physical imperfection serves visually to signify his immorality. As Heffernan notes, "few ideas are more enduring or more deductively plausible than the assumption that deformity signifies depravity."[19] Heffernan is referring to Frankenstein's creation when he makes this observation, but, in this film, it holds true for the scientist as well. Victor has created life numerous times and shows no signs of a conscience when one of his creations goes on a killing spree.

A significant dimension of Victor's cruelty is how he engages with his wife Erika (Ivana Milicevic), who is also a product of his scientific experiments, created to live up to his ideals of perfection. When the two have sex on screen, Victor is overly aggressive, demonstrating dominance more than passion in an act that gives neither any pleasure. Later, when Erika asks Victor to allow her to die, he accommodates her request but does so by putting his hand on her chest and physically holding her under water so that she drowns in an unnecessarily painful, personal, and sexualized murder. As a scientist, Victor Helios is dually defined by his genius and his callous immorality. This interpretation of Victor Frankenstein follows directly in the tradition of the Hammer Frankenstein films (1957–1974), which starred Peter Cushing as a "magnificently arrogant aristocratic rebel . . . who never relinquishes his exploration for one moment."[20] Kretschmann's Victor Helios similarly wears fine apparel, enjoys good food, engages in sex, and is utterly merciless in his pursuit of scientific achievement.[21]

The next "Frankenstein" film released, *Frankenstein Reborn* (2005), similarly introduces a monstrous scientist who exhibits brilliance coupled with gratuitous cruelty and wanton, sexual immorality. Like the 2004 film, *Frankenstein Reborn* also presents its scientist's depravity through his sexual activity. Dr. Victor Franks (Rhett Giles) initially introduces his pioneering nanotechnology to help a patient who has lost the use of his legs in a motorcycle accident. The treatment restores function to the man's legs, but it also gives him homicidal dreams that won't relent. Driven mad, the patient comes to Victor's apartment with a gun, demanding that he be cured of his violent dreams. Victor convinces him to relinquish the gun, but the scientist then shoots his patient without hesitation or regret. Now he has a body to experiment on, and Dr. Franks creates his creature. For no clear dramatic purpose, Victor takes a break from his medical experiments, does heroin, and has a drug-fueled sexual threesome with his girlfriend and a young female lab assistant. The sex and drug use are unrelated to the action of the film and serve merely to establish more pervasively Victor's depravity. The doctor ultimately dies along with his monster, but the film suggests that his evil experiments will live on. In a related manner, Larry Fessenden's *Depraved* (2019), which does not have "Frankenstein" in its title but was so widely advertised as a *Frankenstein* remake that it deserves consideration here, also casts the human as depraved. In this film, the brilliant scientist Henry has a close associate and financial supporter John, who inexplicably takes the resurrected creature Adam to a topless bar and has him try cocaine. As with the former films, those responsible for overseeing the creation of life establish their identity with their sexual immorality.

Beyond these three films, other "Frankenstein" movies from the twenty-first century do not directly link the scientist's iniquity with deviant sexuality, but are creative in their depiction of both the scientist's superlative intelligence and immorality. *The Frankenstein Syndrome*, also called *The Prometheus Project* (2010), takes a particularly exciting approach. The film introduces a principled scientist, Dr. Elizabeth Barnes (Tiffany Shepis), who is invited to join the Prometheus Project, a private laboratory pursuing cutting-edge experiments funded by the rich, mysterious Dr. Walton (Ed Lauter). The film demonstrates how she is corrupted by pride after witnessing the growing success and future promise of her experiments. (With the names "Elizabeth" and "Walton," the movie recalls Victor Frankenstein's wife and Captain Walton in Shelley's novel—many "Frankenstein" films pay quiet homage to Mary Shelley by indiscriminately using names drawn from her novel.) Barnes has a sick mother and Walton assumes the debt for her medical care. In this manner, Barnes's decision to work for Walton is presented in a positive light, as it stems from her medical desire to save lives coupled with her need to help her vulnerable mother.

As the film proceeds and Barnes's research achieves the fantastic result of restoring life to a dead heart, she makes hubristic decisions that seem reasonable at the time but ultimately prove disastrous. When a young woman in the scientific compound commits suicide, Barnes sees an opportunity to try to resurrect her. She accomplishes this by administering a large dose of her new, highly experimental, formula. The woman returns from the dead, but she is in agony, writhing blindly, and spitting up black, acidic bile. She attacks and kills a guard before being shot and killed. Barnes had good intentions when she started her research, like Victor in Shelley's novel, but the possibility of creating life becomes intoxicating and results in disaster. Barnes does not bear the mantle of Victor Frankenstein alone in this film. All the scientists and even the guards that support the practice of highly immoral scientific experiments are jointly culpable for the monster they create in the name of scientific discovery. This monster (Scott Anthony Leet), drawn from a murdered guard resurrected by Barnes's formula, exhibits superior physical strength but also ever-increasing intelligence and even psychic capabilities. The monster ultimately kills all the people at the facility except for Barnes, but he severs her spine and removes the skin from her face so that she can tell her story bearing the terrible physical marks of her moral transgression.

Frankenstein's Army (2013) introduces the most categorically evil Dr. Frankenstein of twenty-first-century film as a mad Nazi scientist who builds monstrous cybernetic machines to fight in the Second World War. These destructive creations kill indiscriminately, even massacring a group of nuns. When confronted, the scientist proudly announces he is the Grandson of Victor Frankenstein and explains that whereas his predecessor needed storms to provide electricity to create life, he has a generator. This Dr. Frankenstein does not actually create life, but his experiments are more (and more horrible) than simply resurrecting the dead. He explains that he wants to take half of the brain of a Nazi and connect it to half of the brain of a Communist, thereby creating a mind and a being that can pursue peace. He is clearly mad but, as he explains, "A man of vision is always misunderstood." So misunderstood was this Dr. Frankenstein that his own father tried to have him incarcerated. In retaliation, Dr. Frankenstein injected his father with a formula that paralyzed him but allowed him to see and experience pain. Dr. Frankenstein's murder of his own father echoes the novel in which the monster ultimately leads his own creator, Victor, to his death. The film reaches its satisfying dénouement when the fiendish Dr. Frankenstein is killed and beheaded, and his laboratory is destroyed by Soviet artillery. *Frankenstein's Army* provides the most horrific and extreme mad genius in recent "Frankenstein" films, but he is more emblematic of, than an exception to, the twenty-first-century tendency to present the man as the true monster.[22]

Victor's creature, on the other hand, has taken an extraordinarily wide variety of forms in the recent past. Xavier Reyes observes that, following Branagh's film and in the wake of recent Hollywood superhero productions, modern Frankenstein monsters have been presented as tragic heroes.[23] This proves true for three twenty-first-century "Frankenstein" films. The monster in Nispel's 2004 *Frankenstein* is a relatively minor figure in the film, but he works quietly and effectively from the shadows just beyond the reach of the law, striving to fight for good. Rather than remain nameless, the figure calls himself Deucalion, taking the name of the son of Prometheus from Greek mythology. The film opens on a ship with a young boy bringing him food. When a man finds the boy and threatens to hurt him, Deucalion quickly and violently dispatches him, simultaneously demonstrating his physical superiority, potential for violence, and virtuous moral compass. Throughout the film, Deucalion is quiet, sad, and alone, but he does what is right and, by the end, he destroys the Frankensteinian creation/serial killer and expresses his willingness to collaborate with the police detectives in the future.

I, Frankenstein (2014) works from the start to establish its monster, given the name Adam, as a tragic hero. The movie opens with Adam (Aaron Eckhart) providing a spoken narrative of his origin: "I was cast into being in winter of 1795, a living corpse without a soul, stitched, jolted, bludgeoned back to life by a madman. Horrified by his creation, he tried to destroy me, but I survived" (0:01:42–0:02:01). The monster continues to summarize the novel, saying that Victor promised him a mate and reneged on his obligation, so he killed Victor's wife. The film's action begins with the end of the novel as the monster is shown enduring 200 years of loneliness, ruminating on the tragic choices he has made. Beyond this beginning, the film is essentially a modern superhero movie. As Jancovich has noted, "the film's debts are not to Shelley's novel but to other texts: the film is not only 'the brainchild of Kevin Grevioux,' a comic book artist, but is produced by the makers of the Underworld franchise, which it clearly hopes to emulate."[24] The tragic aspects of this hero echo those of many other superheroes, cursed by their gifts to lead a lonely life.

The notion that Frankenstein's monster is a tragic hero plays a more poignant role in *Army of Frankensteins* (2013). Summarizing the convoluted and entirely implausible plot of this low budget B movie is no easy feat. The writer/director, Ryan Bellgardt, tries:

> After a failed attempt to propose to his girlfriend, Alan Jones is beaten to within an inch of his life by a street gang and taken to a mysterious lab where Dr. Tanner Finski and his kid genius assistant perform horrible experiments on him hoping to re-animate a Frankenstein. The experiments lead to a hole being ripped in space and time, manifesting an Army of Frankensteins from hundreds of parallel universes and sending them all back to the 19th century, directly into the heart of a bloody battle between the North and South. History will never be the same.[25]

The Frankensteins (as the monsters are called) follow the model set by Boris Karloff with their flat-headed outward appearance, unsteady walk, and inability to articulate more than groans and grunts. The movie ultimately becomes a Civil War struggle between the North and the South with the Confederacy on track to win. The tide turns when an ex-slave turned nurse manages to connect with the main Frankenstein and convince him to fight for the North by appealing to their shared sense of alienation from a society that does not appreciate or respect them. What is most interesting about their interaction is that the movie provides no backstory for its monsters. The film appeals entirely to the Frankenstein myth for the notion that, although the monster is violent, he is essentially lonesome, misunderstood, and good at heart. The film only continues to make sense if the audience accepts, de facto, this aspect of a Frankenstein creature.

An additional, important trend which can be noted in recent Frankenstein films is their tendency to include strong female characters. This practice actually begins with Branagh's film, which presents the character Elizabeth as having far more strength and initiative than the novel ascribes to her.[26] Branagh's Elizabeth is Victor's equal, standing up to him when necessary and nursing him back to health when he falls ill. Her true strength becomes most evident in Branagh's film when, at the end, she is forced to choose between two men, the creature and Victor, but boldly chooses suicide in a final act of feminist agency that rejects the patriarchal options she has been given.

The majority of twenty-first-century Frankenstein films follow Branagh's lead and include significant female characters that demonstrate agency and self-determination, but not all of them. When Connor directed his faithful adaptation of the novel in 2004, he went back to the older tradition of presenting Elizabeth as little more than a romantic partner to Victor and ultimately a victim killed by the monster in an act of revenge against his creator. On the other hand, Nispel's crime drama, which came out the same year, introduces a strong female protagonist. Parker Posey plays Carson O'Conner, a hardnosed detective who fearlessly pursues the criminal responsible for a string of grisly murders. One can only imagine how her story would have developed if the intended sequels had been made. In her pursuit of justice, O'Conner proves too busy to have a personal life, and the only non-professional relationship she has is with her autistic brother whom she helps to raise. The fact that she devotes her only free time to raising her brother has the result of making O'Conner rather one dimensional, but it is a more innovative choice than defining her character primarily in relation to a romantic interest. In *The Frankenstein Syndrome*, Dr. Elizabeth Barnes is another strong female protagonist driven by her professional pursuits to the exclusion of romantic relationships in the film. The complexity of her character derives from the arc it follows as she becomes more successful in her experiments and bolder in her scientific ventures. Taken together, these two leading female characters mark a noteworthy evolution of "Frankenstein" films in the twenty-first century.

More exciting are the two twenty-first century "Frankenstein" films which present female scientists who take lead roles in the creation of life. *Frankenstein* (2007), directed by Jed Mercurio, and FRANK3N5T31N (2015), directed by Bernard Rose, both include women who play "feminine" roles while pursuing scientific work that puts them at the forefront of their professional fields.[27] In their fascinating study of female scientists in *Frankenstein* films over seven decades, Lissette Szwydky and Michelle Pribbernow note that "female Frankensteins (or laboratory assistants who might one day aspire to this role) are typically abject figures, mocked or made monstrous through some combination of embodiment, intelligence or ambition."[28] Not so with these two films.

Mercurio's made-for-television film presents Victoria Frankenstein as a scientist pursuing stem cell research to create organs she can use to save the life of her son who needs multiple transplants. By linking the life of Victoria's son to her work as a scientist, the film proves quite original. Gone is the parthenogenetic fantasy of men creating life without women, and in its place is a brilliant woman's desire to save her child. The movie includes Victoria's ex-husband who plays a major role in the film and rekindles his romantic relationship with her, but he never diminishes the significance of her character or the role she plays as a mother and a scientist. Victoria's determination to cure her son includes surreptitiously introducing a sample of his blood into the stem cell experiment in the hope of creating a perfect match. Her experiment does not create viable organs and Victoria's son dies. Furthermore, her experiment actually creates a monster which breaks free when the electricity in the laboratory goes down in a storm. Unlike the monster in most other Frankenstein films, this one, called UX (for Universal Xenograft Project), hardly looks human at all. Scared, taunted, and tortured by several people, the UX begins to kill and is cruelly imprisoned by security personnel. Victoria feels connected to this new creation made with the blood of her son. She frees the UX and attempts to lead it to safety but the two are captured and confined with the likelihood that they will never be allowed to be free. The final scene of the movie shows Victoria patiently teaching the UX in a laboratory facility as she assumes a maternal role that sharply contrasts with earlier Frankenstein films and even the novel, which demonstrate the scientist's failure to love or care for the life that has been created.[29]

FRANK3N5T31N similarly highlights a female scientist, Elizabeth (Carrie-Ann Moss), actively engaged in cutting-edge research but, in this film, she works in tandem with her husband Victor (Danny Huston) to create life. At the time of its writing, the movie was unique among Frankenstein films in that it is told from the point of the creature, called Adam, who is born with the body of an adult and the mind of a child. Unlike the monster in Shelley's novel and most Frankenstein films, Adam receives a great deal of love and attention from the team of scientists, particularly Elizabeth who assumes a maternal role in caring for the new life.[30]

The science team's devotion to Adam changes, however, when he develops a skin disease that shows flaws in the research design. They decide to terminate Adam and start fresh. Their efforts to kill him, however, are unsuccessful and Adam awakens to find scientists attempting to cut into his skull with a bone saw. He fights back, brutally killing the scientists, and flees the laboratory instillation. In his naiveté and simple effort to survive, Adam ends up killing again, and he is picked up by the police, who find Elizabeth's laboratory name tag among his possessions. They call her in, but Elizabeth rejects her creation, telling the officer that she has never seen Adam before. The scene is one of the most poignant in the film as Elizabeth abrogates her maternal connection to Adam in favor of her professional reputation and the security of her scientific laboratory.[31] At the close of the film, however, Elizabeth resumes her maternal relationship to Adam. He has freed himself from police custody and found his way back to his "parents." Victor takes the opportunity to give Adam an injection and attack him with a surgical saw, but Elizabeth intervenes. Stepping between the two, she is fatally struck by the saw, but she saves Adam who then kills Victor. Affirming the mother-child relationship between the two and connecting the end of the film to the conclusion of the novel, Adam takes Elizabeth into the woods and sets a fire in which he burns himself and his "mother."

The trend among twenty-first-century Frankenstein films to present strong female characters at the center of the story found new articulation in *A Nightmare Wakes: The Birth of Frankenstein* (2020).[32] This film focuses on the life of Mary Shelley and the events surrounding the authoring of *Frankenstein* as it cinematically connects her efforts to write the novel to her efforts to give birth to a baby that survives childhood. With striking images of blood and ink simultaneously flowing from Mary's pelvis and soaking her clothes, the film stresses her dual efforts of creation. At the close of the film, Mary has completed her novel and given birth to her son who survives, achieving success on both fronts but at the cost of losing her husband Percy Shelley, who is shown walking away from her to his death in a lake.

"Frankenstein" films have seen an extraordinary resurgence in the twenty-first century, but they have not been received with the enthusiasm with which they have been produced. Reyes has noted that, starting with Branagh's film, which was far less successful than expected, mainstream cinematic adaptations of *Frankenstein* have, on the whole, met with little critical or financial success. He goes on to suggests that adaptations that directly link to *Frankenstein*, especially by name, "show clear signs of creative exhaustion."[33] And yet, in the twenty-first century, we have seen an average of more than one new "Frankenstein" movie released each year, and at the writing of this chapter, IMDB lists many new "Frankenstein" films at various points of production which, when released, will generate a whole new cadre of Frankenstein films for enjoyment and analysis. Whatever the success or failure of recent Frankenstein movies, there is no denying that film studios, screenwriters, and actors are financially and creatively invested in making more. Picart succinctly summarizes a myth as "a recurring and ever-malleable narrative that both reveals and conceals primordial sites of fascination and repulsion."[34] Throughout the twenty-first century to date and into the foreseeable future, "Frankenstein" films provide an illuminating window into our collective sites of fascination and repulsion.

10

The Water and the Corpse: Exploring Nature, Shelley's Echoes, and Twenty-first-Century Cultural Anxieties in *The Frankenstein Chronicles*

Lorna Piatti-Farnell

The Frankenstein Chronicles (2015–2017) is a television series that develops against the backdrop of *Frankenstein*'s historical narrative, interlacing itself with the imaginations of both the creature and its science-driven monstrosity. Set in London in 1827, the series is marked by dismembered bodies, tortured experimentations, and horrific cultural disquiets. In the midst of it all, flows the river Thames, an entity that within the narrative acts both a physical placing and a symbolic channel. As part of the gothic cartographies of place, water often indicates a liminal area, taking on complex meanings as a cultural and representational conduit. Considered as an allegorical entity, a river can be seen as more than a simple material body of flowing water: indeed, it can be taken instead to be an iconographic presence signifying otherworldliness, secrecy, and a metaphor for the cyclical intangibility of human life. Justin Edwards contends that the river is a "haunting" feature in the gothic landscape: "imbued with gothic import," the river allows us to explore the ways in which society is "corrupted, afflicted, and decayed."[1] Taking this idea as a point of departure, I explore the representational connection between the river, monstrous liminalities, and contemporary cultural anxieties in *The Frankenstein Chronicles*. As it flows, the river brings to the surface a critical focus on preoccupations connected to ecological concerns and the continuous perils of experimental science. Evoking abject imagery and materialities, the river embodies a haunting blend of natural geography, spectrality, corporeality, and decay. In *The Frankenstein Chronicles*, the Thames is a river of corpses, and of barely concealed unthinkable secrets. It is a locus of horror, ghostly memory, and fear, as its waters fail to hide the cultural repulsions and anxieties that are deeply rooted in the gothicized fringes of the urban collectivity. The shadow of Shelley's creature haunts the water, a narrative evocation of *Frankenstein* that provides the metaphorical framework for exploring a number of concerns connected to science, ethics, and the place of the human in the twenty-first century.

Neither a direct adaptation nor a re-thinking of Mary Shelley's famous tale, the television series uses the historical framework of the early nineteenth century as a representational context. It follows a river police inspector, John Marlott (Sean Bean), as he finds a strange "corpse" on the riverbanks. After this gruesome discovery, Marlott then sets out to determine the identity of the corpse, and where it came from. During his investigation, Marlott becomes entangled with a number of social, cultural, and political issues from child abductions and prostitution to body snatching, scientific pursuits (including Galvanism) and social unrest caused by the impending passage of the Anatomy Act. This particular legislation gave freer licence to medical practitioners to dissect donated bodies, and essentially put an end to the illegal trade of corpses by the so-called resurrectionists. Despite the obvious resonances between the two narratives, the series does not re-imagine Shelley's tale: none of the characters from the novel appear as such, and there are no plot connections. *The Frankenstein Chronicles* is set about ten years or so after the publication of Shelley's famous novel. She, however, does appear as a character (played by Anna Maxwell Martin); throughout the series, several other peripheral characters also comment on *Frankenstein's* lurid frivolity. What the series does share with *Frankenstein* is a general preoccupation with science, with the place of the human being in the larger order, and the overarching shadows of suffering and death. A specific aspect in which *The Frankenstein Chronicles* recalls Frankenstein can be found in its ability to render cultural anxieties through horror, the grotesque, and the monstrous, so that its narrative can propose critical ruminations with a "global impact."[2] It comes as no surprise to find that, as the series progresses, it becomes increasingly marked by a growing number of corpses, and a pervasive sense of fear for the strange and the unknown. In this, the river Thames plays a special part in channeling the horror, as body politics mix and mingle with medical perceptions and understandings of both the natural and the unnatural. Continuing to be mindful of the debt that *The Frankenstein Chronicles* owes to Shelley's novel, this chapter contextualizes "*Frankenstein's* traces in modern discourses."[3] Focusing primarily on the first season of the show, I first analyze the multilayers of interpretations for what is considered "natural," and then uncover the river as a metaphorical rendition of cultural anxieties that lie at the heart of the series itself.[4] These are profoundly entangled with twenty-first-century preoccupations connected to scientific experimentation, environmental concerns, and the fear of ecological disaster.

Water Echoes

Far removed from notions of the sublime, or any Romantic ideas of nature—from which, to some extent, the gothic originally stemmed—the river in *The Frankenstein Chronicles* is a locus of horror and displacement. Andrew Smith and William Hughes contend that, as far as the gothic framework is concerned, the very notion of "nature" is complicated. A contested term, nature in gothic works often "appears to participate in a language of estrangement rather than belonging," and water lies at the center of this conceptualization.[5] Natural bodies of water provide a representation of both the physical and the metaphysical world that challenge the human by acting as liminal entities, making them useful in rendering difficult human interactions and emotions, as well as the socio-cultural repercussions inevitable to human interactions with nature in terms of exchange, travel, and identity.

The significance of water in *The Frankenstein Chronicles* is something that the series appears to have inherited from Shelley's novel itself. Water is at the center of *Frankenstein* as a symbolic presence that constantly reminds the reader of the fluidity of existence; as a trope, however, it also has more multifaceted uses. On the one hand, water in the novel is often associated with notions of calmness and peace. For instance, on his voyage to the northern seas Victor takes solace in knowing that water surrounds the vessel. He claims to find a "sense of security" and "a feeling of truce" in being embraced by water, where he relishes "a kind of calm forgetfulness."[6] Water often stands as not only a physical but also a conceptual divider between Victor's "awful" actions and the guilt derived from them, and the sense of solace that comes from his attempts to forget. That watery separation is also repeated during Elizabeth and Victor's honeymoon on the shores of Lake Geneva as he muses over the healing power of the water. This is confirmed by his feelings of dread, as he must abandon its calmness: "as I touched the shore, I felt those cares and fears revive."[7]

Water, however, is also often associated with metaphors of death, and Victor equally experiences a sense of disruption and disengagement from the natural world when afloat, which reflects his troubled state of mind. On his voyage to Ireland, Victor describes the seas as tumultuous, with waves that "continually threatened" their passage.[8] Even on the seemingly peaceful journey on the lake, Victor and Elizabeth perceive the waters in different terms. Elizabeth describes them as "transparent," while Victor often mentions how unclear and opaque they are, able to hide and conceal. This dichotomous view of the water in *Frankenstein* is significant, aiding in the creation of that sense of dissonance proper to its evocation of both the natural and unnatural world. Nicholas Marsh suggests that *Frankenstein*'s discordant treatment of water is reflective of Victor's own "disharmony with nature," as his actions seemingly caused some imbalance.[9] At the heart of the novel lies the question of what it means to challenge "nature" and where men and science fit in the conception of what is "natural." The dichotomous representation of water is at the heart of that negotiation, as water's own liminality suggests metaphorical renditions of both life and death, and provides fluid interpretations—both physically and conceptually—over notions of suffering and wrong doing. This sentiment and use of water as a dichotomous and reflective entity is echoed throughout *The Frankenstein Chronicles*, and it all begins with the river as a site of abject discovery. Both geographically and metaphorically, rivers can function as boundaries, and as seemingly natural systems of division: the River Thames, for instance, splits the city of London into northern and southern sections. Suggestively, this metaphor of splitting human geography goes much further than the city itself. Through metaphors of disquiet, disagreement, and horror, the Thames splits opinions, and functions as a critical conduit for the exploration of post-millennial concerns.

Slimy Entities

In *The Frankenstein Chronicles*, the Thames is portrayed as a murky entity. Its waters are perennially cloudy, and its banks are a distinct mixture of debris and sliminess. When Marlott finds the body, it is shown as almost embedded in the slime of the riverbanks, as if the corpse is part of the river itself. Part of the horror here comes from not actually knowing where the human ends and the river begins, almost as if what it means to be human actually ceases to be, and the body becomes part of an ever-growing mass of the river's decay and excess. Of course, the presence of dead flesh amid all matters of waste in the river cements its status as an abject entity in the series. Julia Kristeva famously deems the corpse, like bodily waste, a vehicle of abjection, and the Thames of 1827 was seemingly full of both. The corpse, Kristeva argues, "[i]s the utmost of abjection": it is "death infecting life."[10]

The narrative of Otherness here is strong and unavoidable, recalling that which is not fully human, but which exists in conjunction with the human, challenging its fragile sense of being. The corpse found by Marlott is presented as part of the river's sliminess, and inseparable from its dark waters as much as it is indivisible from its decaying landscape. Jean-Paul Sartre suggests that the slimy is "a cross-section in a process of change." It stands for liminality and recalls in-between states of existence that challenge our psychological and cultural certainties. The slimy is "without stability"; "to touch the slimy is to risk being dissolved" into nothingness, as a reminder of our mortality.[11] This notion of dissolving is made tangible in *The Frankenstein Chronicles* as the corpse ceases to be its own entity and is presented instead as part of the river's viscosity, as the slime literally dispenses the human and consumes it. What is left of the body is a gelatinous, decomposing mass with a coloring that is akin to the murkiness of the river's waters. One can see here a return to nature which is anything but reassuring, with even the notion of burial denied. The body floats in a liminal state belonging to neither the living nor the dead.

The suggestive "loss of being" represented by the disintegrating corpse is a primordial return to a state of sliminess before knowledge and culture can negotiate the body's boundaries or its place in the social order, echoing the earliest stages of the foetus as it floats in a fluid and liminal state. This notion of losing being to the river becomes even more evocative later when the river body is actually revealed to have been assembled using parts from eight different bodies, all children. Denied the privilege of being called a "corpse," the identity-loss of this dead human flesh intensifies, reinforcing Sartre's idea that encountering the slimy exposes the possibility of shapeless existence, and within this lies its conceptualization as horrific, an inescapable fluidity of matter that "holds" and "compromises" existence.[12] The metaphorical rendition of watery sliminess and decay in *The Frankenstein Chronicles* suggests that the river represents a limbo state of non-being: once human flesh is given to the river, it becomes something else, something strange, polluting, and ungraspable.

The narrative staging of *The Frankenstein Chronicles* encourages viewers to see the overpowering naturality of the river as contrasting with the urban confines of the city of London. This is not necessarily a new turn of events for the gothic, where the uncanny usually manifests right at the cusp of the two worlds of nature and city. However, what becomes very clear, very quickly is that the uncontrollable river is a symbolic reflection of the out-of-bounds city, especially its politics, its cultural decadence and, of course, its science. *The Frankenstein Chronicles* uses the river as the conduit for channeling a number of illicit desires that, unsurprisingly, have a lot to do with the idea of conquering death. This, of course, is not only a debt to the narrative of creation and resurrection from which the series takes its name, but it is also a contemporary re-thinking of the relationship between natural, unnatural, and the place occupied by the human therein. In this, the series echoes a well-known contention for the gothic. The natural world is often seen as a link to the past, with embedded historical memory. Uncovering secrets, with the return of long-forgotten memories, is one of the definitive characteristics of the gothic narrative.

Contested Science

While the narrative ostensibly recalls issues of scientific manipulation that belong in the early nineteenth century, the overarching preoccupations of the series are contemporary. In a nod to both traditional and contemporary gothic and horror narratives, *The Frankenstein Chronicles* utilizes the river and its banks as an "uncanny and Othered geographical locale" in order to examine displacements and anxieties that lie at the core of our twenty-first-century experience.[13] There are a number of clues that are entangled and interlaced with the narrative of water, bodies, and science. Firstly, attention is placed on the "non-corpse," as it is referred to in the series, made up of child body parts. Secondly, the narrative continuously returns to the river's significance as a constantly flowing physical entity made abject by its association with sliminess and dead matter, and a focus on its tides as "cycles." In conjunction with this, a particular focus on pregnancy runs throughout the show: Flora (Eloise Smyth), one of the child prostitutes who becomes an ally in Marlott's investigation, is pregnant; she later asks surgeon Lord Hervey (Ed Stoppard)—a mysterious figure whose activities catch Marlott's eye—to abort her baby. Lord Hervey, who is himself a scientist with a secret interest in revivifying dead bodies, is estranged from the medical community as it fights to have the Anatomy Act approved. Later, he admits that he had "kept" Flora's aborted baby for some form of experimentation. When it is finally revealed that Lord Hervey was indeed the culprit who created the assembled non-corpse, he declares that the answer to curing disease and bringing dead matter back to life is "within us" from birth. At the end of Season One, and after a series of failures, Lord Hervey successfully brings someone back from the dead: Marlott himself, who had been previously executed for treason and murder.

The narrative trajectory of the series, together with its metaphorical renditions of both actions and ideas, would appear to point us in the direction of a critique of scientific experimentation that involves pregnancy and foetuses, and the search for a cure-all for disease. It is possible to suggest that the science in question may surround stem cells, in particular the use of embryonic stem cells as part of regenerative medicine. These are particular sets of cells that are found in the developing foetuses, and which provide a blueprint for cellular generation and regeneration. Stem cells are "cells that can both renew themselves in the undifferentiated state as well as differentiate into descendant cells that have a specific function."[14] They come in a variety of shapes and sizes, but the embryonic cells are known as pluripotent; theoretically they can be used to regenerate cells in the human body, child or adult, and are often thought by some to be a way to preserve life. Nonetheless, there is a lot of debate on the use of embryonic stem cells, as they need to be harvested from the placenta, the umbilical cord, or even the foetus itself. A great number of ethical issues accompanies the discussion of this alleged miracle solution. These are particularly connected to what is known as "boundary-work," a group of scientific practices that are closely connected "choice[s] over how to conduct oneself in a complicated political, moral and scientific context."[15] The use of stem cells is seen by some as exceeding the boundary of cultural, social, moral, and scientific propriety, connected as it is to the death of a foetus and the uses of its physical remains.

The Frankenstein Chronicles uses the abject representation of the river as a starting point to critique the very notion of regenerating and preserving life in the scientific twenty-first century. The failed experiment of Lord Hervey, constructed of dead children's bodies, is discarded, forcefully dispatched into the liminal wateriness of the womb-like river; this acts as a twisted representation of a failed birth, and forcefully recalls the abortion of a dead foetus. When Lord Hervey is successful in his foetus-based corpse experiment, his creation is seen as abhorrent, as unnatural, and as disrespectful to life itself. Through this, *The Frankenstein Chronicles* provides a bleak overview and critique of embryonic stem cell medicine and experimentation. Although "rejected," the foetus lingers as an othered scientific creation: in its "imaginary uncanniness" it becomes a "real threat."[16] The river, within this narrative, is exploited as a warped geographical metaphor for the simultaneous interruption and unstoppability of both life and death. Just like the promise of stem cell science, the river is transformative. The outcome, however, is something distorted, repulsive, and abject. The river's natural status is figuratively disturbed by the conjunction with the non-corpse, an entity that does not belong in either the natural or unnatural world.

Recycled Bodies and the EcoGothic

In its engagement with debates over matters related to nature, and how these fit into our cultural psyche, *The Frankenstein Chronicles* also provides a subtle critique of environmental concerns. Specifically, the series uses mixed metaphors of dead, discarded bodies and polluted nature to point us toward a critical exploration of what can be described as a "throw-away society." The bodies used for the experiments in the series are recycled bodies, easily discarded when no longer needed. The very notion of stem cells science also introduces the idea that the series may be proposing an even more in-depth critique over issues that are not just moral and scientific, but also environmental and ecological in quality. In Lord Hervey's experiments, selected deceased individuals can only be brought back to life by using the cells from an aborted foetus. The foetus itself is a recycled entity, but that re-use of the body carries with it abominable consequences. These are uncovered by interactions with the Thames, which metaphorically becomes the liminal entity between moral and immoral, natural and unnatural, life and death. Taking on the qualities of the discarded foetus, the un/natural re-amalgamated body, as well as the culturally abominable, the river becomes abject by rendering, in a physical way, "the in-between, the ambiguous, the composite."[17] The river tells a tale of destruction as much as it channels acts of horrific creation.

In its approach to the river as a liminal, and horror-imbued entity, *The Frankenstein Chronicles* provides a representational framework that carries touches of the EcoGothic.

This term refers to a set of textual, cultural and, theoretical concerns that connect nature and the human through a number of overarching preoccupations. Still in its nascent stages, EcoGothic does not necessarily work as a genre, as far as the fictional world is concerned, but rather occupies a set of frameworks that show, often quite forcefully, what happens when humans abuse and meddle with the natural world. Andrew Smith and William Hughes define EcoGothic as "exploring the Gothic through theories of ecocriticism."[18] In this definition, the gothic merges its distinctive, traditional preoccupations over alienation, secrecy, destruction, and death with concerns concerning the state of the natural world and how human interaction affects it in an overarchingly negative way. Ecocriticism, overall, focuses on "the study of the relationship between the human and the nonhuman."[19] The blend of ecological criticism and the gothic certainly invites a critical look into the horrors that may unfold out of the human disregard for nature, and the consequences of such actions. Brian Merchant further succinctly sums up the conventional set up propelling this particular framework: "man tampers with nature—or worst, ruins nature—and nature kicks man's ass."[20] It is no surprise to see that concerns of an EcoGothic nature have often been identified in films and other popular media narratives that focus on a post-apocalyptic context, where the resources of the natural world have been exploited and destroyed by man in one way or the other.

The Frankenstein Chronicles does not present a picture of man's destruction of nature as such. What it does engage with, however, is the conceptual notion of man tampering with the "natural order" and exploiting nature in a number of ways, especially when it comes to hiding shameful secrets. The experimentation with what is subtly communicated as stem-cell technology crosses the boundary into what is prohibited, both culturally and ethically. The non-corpse is considered an abomination against the perceived natural. The fault of this, however, broadly falls on the scientist and his disregard for life and, to some extent, human emotion. In this representation, *The Frankenstein Chronicles* overtly follows in Shelley's footsteps, and a subtle suggestion that one should indeed feel empathy over the dead and discarded re-assembled bodies runs through the narrative. It is not by chance, perhaps, that the non-corpse discovered on the banks of the river is, in fact, constructed of children's bodies. We see here the use of the cultural metaphor that associates children with innocence, demanding sympathy from viewers. Although the non-corpse is inherently gothic in its representation, there are no hints of any gothicized notions of evil associated with it. While it is abject and "unnatural," it also demands pity.

What is common in the representation, and overall definition of the EcoGothic, is "a clear and immediate sense of nature's revenge."[21] *The Frankenstein Chronicles* does not quite provide the overall sense of nature "punishing mankind" that one can often see in the post-apocalyptic narrative. Nor do we get that sense of food and water scarcity that is commonly associated with the dissolution of the natural world, which often characterises Eco-horror. What we do get, instead, is a blended incarnation where nature's revenge takes the form of revealing man's dark deeds. The abominable creation is bestowed on the river as a double-edged act that shows disregard for notions of "the natural" in a number of ways. The liminality of the river is that of a suspension area as it hosts the dead, the polluted, and the unnatural. The river, however, fails to keep the non-corpse concealed, and spits it out for all to see. Elizabeth Parker suggests that what is "essential" to texts "open to the EcoGothic analysis is that they are gothic stories in which the natural environment, or the elements within it, are eerily ambient and arouse our anxieties."[22] The river in *The Frankenstein Chronicles* is a source of anxiety not because it openly challenges man's physical safety, but because it channels the presence of awful acts. Indeed, the river comes to embody the very sense of anxiety that surrounds the discovery of the non-corpse; as such it reflects that over-powering sense of cultural uncertainty that propels the narrative of the series, and its approach to man's misconduct.

Concluding Remarks

The Frankenstein Chronicles exploits and develops the original narrative of Shelley's *Frankenstein* by re-evaluating cultural fears about experimentation and conduct, placing them within the context of the twenty-first century. In the series, as death, life, and water mix—at times, quite literally—natural and unnatural collide, uncovering the relationship between the body, the landscape, and cultural rhetoric. The river emerges as a gothic space where bodily horror, spectral appearances, abject materiality, and the liminal fluidity of water merge. The river is twisted, made abject, and morphed into an agent of Otherness. The culturally driven EcoGothic framework allows us to see the meaning of the river in the series as profoundly entangled with preoccupations over our own environmental responsibilities, and challenges "the higher status" that "Westerners have traditionally assumed" over "elements of the natural world."[23] The intersecting scientific and ecological critiques submerged in the representational elements of *The Frankenstein Chronicles* as a television series join the narrative of horror to create, as in Shelley's novel, ambivalence about both knowledge and cultural acceptability, continuously challenging the boundaries of the known.

11

The Aesthetics of Digital Naturecultures in La Belle Games's *The Wanderer: Frankenstein's Creature* (2019)

Andrew Burkett

Unlike the numerous video games based on Mary Shelly's novel *Frankenstein; or, The Modern Prometheus* (1818, 1831), such as Data Age's *Frankenstein's Monster* (1983), Tose Software's *Frankenstein: The Monster Returns* (1991), Bits Studios' *Mary Shelley's Frankenstein* (1994), and related titles, *The Wanderer: Frankenstein's Creature* (2019) is a "serious" video game from the tradition of applied, problem-solving, and thought-provoking games and is perspicaciously adapted from Shelley's ground-breaking book by La Bella Games, co-produced and published by ARTE, the Franco-German cultural TV and digital channel.[1] This game, which received an "Honorable Mention" for "Best in Play" at the 2019 Game Developers Conference (GDC), is an indie point-and-click narrative adventure that deeply immerses players in the major themes, concepts, and issues of Shelley's original novel by placing gamers in the role of Victor Frankenstein's infamous creature, which wakes to life at the start of the game and wanders forth on its quest for self-understanding. As I argue, while the game adapts and responds to a number of the central interests of Shelley's *Frankenstein*, foremost among the game's preoccupations are the representation and treatment of the complex entanglements of natural and sociocultural domains, which, of course, are also central concerns of Shelley's novel. *The Wanderer: Frankenstein's Creature* (hereafter *The Wanderer*) repeatedly emphasizes and investigates through both digital and textual representations a version of Donna Haraway's concept of "naturecultures," or the necessary knottiness of the natural and the cultural, the semiotic and the material, the subject and the object, which exist only in perpetually changing and acutely immersive realities defined by a fundamental processualism.[2] More specifically, this game continuously presents—and asks players to explore—environments putatively defined by natural and sociocultural binaries, only rapidly to deconstruct these dichotomies to represent, through the in-game world's aesthetics of digital naturecultures, an ecological vision characterized by conceptual and empirical entanglements.

Additionally, such digital environmental aesthetics of *The Wanderer* are based, I suggest, not only on the imagined worlds of Shelley's novel but also, in part, on classic examples of traditions of the natural sublime in European Romantic visual art, especially the work of Caspar David Friedrich. In fact, the game itself arguably takes its name from Friedrich's famous *Wanderer above the Sea of Fog* (c. 1818), which *The Wanderer* complexly remediates and remixes while simultaneously retaining the painting's (Romantic) iconographic representation of natural and cultural relationalities. Indeed, this game's perhaps most important contributions to the mediatic afterlives of Shelley's novel and, more broadly, Romanticism's legacies exist through *The Wanderer*'s amplification of and tribute to what has always already been the Romantic preoccupation with the unresolvable, productive tension between the reputed world of nature and the presumed sociocultural domain.

Furthermore, as Alenda Y. Chang has persuasively argued, although the environmental humanities have largely overlooked video game environments as forms of environmental media, recent developments in video game design present opportunities to rethink dramatically the relationship between (natural) ecological environment and (human) sociocultural agency.[3] To be sure, *The Wanderer*'s representations of subject–object interactions, especially its depictions of naturecultures, are unlike previous traditions of game environments that, as Chang has noted, are usually based on overly simplified environmental models such as resource extraction or exist as forms of visual spectacle in which game worlds largely function as scenic backdrops for player action.[4] *The Wanderer* rejects such simplistic models in favor of nuanced forms of what Chang would refer to as modes of "digital environmental play" that foster spaces in which "games, like the natural world, can provoke curiosity, interaction, and reflection."[5] This game does so by constructing a player-environmental relationship that seeks to foreground the involvement of the nonhuman world on a par with the nonhuman player-character—the creature itself as avatar—and in so doing, this game exposes for the player what Chang has explored in related gameplay contexts as "humanity's moral responsibility to and participation in the natural world" as well as a characterization of "the environment as fluid process, not static representation."[6] *The Wanderer* thus offers players both a captivating and an instructive platform for rethinking environmental relationships in terms of what this chapter investigates as digital naturecultures.

The Wanderer is actually the second indie video game title based on Shelley's *Frankenstein* to be released following the collaborations between La Belle Games and ARTE. As ARTE project manager Adrien Larouzée has explained, these collaborations were in part kickstarted to celebrate the bicentennial anniversary of the 1818 publication of Shelley's novel.[7] In marking this bicentenary, La Belle Games and ARTE showcased *Frankenstein: Birth of a Myth* (2018), the prequel game to *The Wanderer*, in the "Indie Arena Booth" at Gamescom 2018.[8] In this prequel game, which was made publicly available for play online, the gamer comes to assume the role of Shelley herself, who becomes an avatar for the player, who must assist this third-person perspective player character in telling her own version of the story relating the genesis of her "myth" at the Villa Diodati in Geneva, Switzerland during the summer of 1816. The player does so by constructing a storyline from branching narrative decision trees before Shelley is interrupted by nonplayer-character versions of Lord Byron, Claire Clairmont, John Polidori, and Percy Bysshe Shelley. After successfully helping Shelley to articulate a version of the origins of her tale, the player is ushered into a prototype edition of what will become the chapter "NATURAE" in *The Wanderer* in which the player assumes the role of the creature as avatar and becomes immersed in complex digital naturecultures, as explored in the following section of this chapter. If, as Jesper Juul has noted, "gameplay can encourage community-building around a given game" and if "gameplay of a game is the basis for the building of player-driven communities," then we would do well also to recognize the ways that companion games like *Frankenstein: Birth of a Myth* and *The Wanderer* build communities around the legacies not only of cultural texts like Shelley's novel but also, more broadly, around Romanticism's powerful mediatic afterlives.[9]

The Wanderer's Aesthetics of Digital Naturecultures: A Partial Critical Walkthrough

The Wanderer begins in a white void in which the creature appears, in its third-person perspective, to come to life and consciousness for the first time. Just before this figure is introduced, an opening cutscene intertitle announces that "*First of all, I remember a strong light pressing upon my nerves, obliging me to shut my eyes.*" A second intertitle quickly follows: "*When I opened them again, the light poured in upon me.*" Given that the game is a point-and-click narrative adventure, the user initiates play simply by moving and clicking the hovering mouse pointer. In the game this pointer is figured in the shape of the head of something like a nineteenth-century quill which thus adds to the sense that the user is in charge, at least in part, with helping to "write" the creature's story as the central player character of the game world. Pointing and clicking around the void surrounding the creature, once introduced in this opening moment, increasingly widens a cloudy gray space enveloping the figure—one that is seemingly amorphous and lifeless in its various shadings. Clearing enough of this space triggers the game to announce what appears to the player as an ostensible opening chapter title: "ALBA," Latin for "white, light-coloured," which accurately characterizes the scene's aesthetics that the player quickly realizes are being witnessed simultaneously through the eyes of the creature as player character, overwhelmed by the bright whiteness of the scene of its first experience of the world.[10] Once triggered in this manner, the creature rises in a stumble to its feet and begins to navigate this disorienting space through the player's pointing and clicking, which now lead the figure to explore the area in a state of wandering confusion, resulting in background unlocking during playthrough that reveals more of this indistinct environment. The creature's body, an assemblage of dark limbs and a featureless, elongated pyriform face is covered by a tattered, flowing hooded cloak of white fabric, and in "ALBA" this figure roams under the direction of the player to clear away more of the surrounding scene of whiteness to reveal further undefined features of this environment. "*I explored this space as blank as my memory*," a subsequent intertitle announces. Twinkling orbs of light appear in one corner of this setting, signaling through an in-game logic for the player to point and click in their direction toward an undefined stairwell, which, once accessed, allows the creature to descend a passage into a new environment that, through further background unlocking, presents as a somewhat more defined set of gray rooms, perhaps constituting an apartment. The discovery of an open doorway through this process ushers the creature outside of this structure and into another field of white light while an intertitle simultaneously announces: "*I left this place which, I did not know at that time, was a gruesome birthplace,*" thus indicating that the game world's intertitles are being told to the player from the perspective of the creature through a retrospective manner of storytelling while also implying that the game begins in Frankenstein's "workshop of filthy creation" in his residence in Ingolstadt in the moments immediately following the infamous creation scene from Shelley's original novel.[11] On the whole, then, "ALBA" clearly seeks to establish a representational origin in gamespace that is as close as possible to a full negation of both natural and sociocultural worlds.

As the player guides the creature, now running in a graceful, bounding manner while fleeing this setting through the blankness of a new scene of white void, the perspective suddenly shifts to a long-distance position implying that she takes a god-like point of view on the creature's world and actions, just as a quick cutscene announces the next chapter title "MEMORIAE."[12] The indistinct natural forms of two-dimensional branching trees, plains, bushes, and other undefined shapes become visible in the background of this first scene of coloration in the game, which appears now as something like a Romantic watercolor just about to materialize into existence. Exploring this natural scene shifts the player's perspective suddenly to a much closer point of view of the creature, while another intertitle emerges announcing that "*The fresh air caressed my face*," as the creature experiences nature for the first time. At this point, the in-game logic of background unlocking becomes reversed, as the faster the player points and clicks to direct the creature, the more quickly the natural vibrant watercolor scenes fade to disorienting whiteness. However, when she pauses to bring the creature to a standstill, the watercolor images burst vividly into view for her and her creature. The process of newly understanding the game's transformed procedural logic of background unlocking with this altered style of playthrough results in the player's guiding the creature through this environment, which no longer exists as simple, digitally-rendered background, natural imagery, or watercolor detail but instead as a complex setting of interactive nonhuman actants with which the creature playfully engages both to proceed in the game and to experience this world as a representation of natural (environmental) aesthetics. As Chang explains in her reading of thatgamecompany's *Flower* (2009), a meditative game that relies on a related operational logic and mechanics of dynamic player-environmental interaction and scene unlocking involving representations of natural flora and biota, "most games oblige players to enter into a player-environment relationship based almost wholly on extraction and utilization of natural resources that are often effectively infinite."[13] Thus, serious games like *The Wanderer* and *Flower*, which eschew such simplistic representations and treatments of ecological settings and player environment relationships in favor of dynamically processual interactions between players, player characters, and environmental worlds, actively rethink digital naturecultures via novel experimental schemata.

With the launch of the next chapter, "NATURAE," the game fades gently to the verdant watercolors of a lush forest scene dominated by giant trees and plant life in the apparent bloom of spring and with an audio overlay of birds brightly chirping within the ambient and aleatory natural sounds of a dense forest setting.[14] The player witnesses the creature asleep and quietly breathing on the forest floor in the midst of something like an Edenic bower nestled within this environment. Clicking near the creature's prone body causes the player character to wake and rise, as an intertitle flashes onscreen: "*A melodious song roused me from this languor.*" "ALBA," "MEMORIAE," and "NATURAE" thus playfully mix together the scene in Shelley's novel in which the creature recounts the following memories in the first narration to Frankenstein:

> It is with considerable difficulty that I remember the original aera of my being: all the events of that period appear confused and indistinct. A strange multiplicity of sensations seized me, and I saw, felt, heard, and smelt, at the same time; and it was, indeed, a long time before I learned to distinguish between the operations of my various senses.[15]

The player's pointing and clicking quickly lead the creature toward a nearby babbling brook, where an in-game action icon prompts the player to engage, causing the creature to kneel and drink from the stream with cupped hands. Doing so triggers the game to cause additional colorful plants suddenly to bloom hyperbolically into life in the vicinity immediately around the creature, as rainbows and other representational forms of natural lighting further illuminate the hazy atmospheric setting. "*I had discovered harmony,*" an intertitle flashes and is quickly followed by another: "*a symphony of emotions of which I was the conductor.*" In this aroused emotional state attuned with the natural environment in which it has awoken, the creature now dashes gracefully through blooming flowers and grasses as the player points and clicks through a scene dominated by environmental play (see Figure 11.1). This background unlocking in which the in-game aesthetics of this representation of the natural world are amplified to enhanced positive effects is short-lived, however, and soon fades to the baseline state of the setting in which the creature was discovered at the chapter's start. The player's "Wanderer" avatar is free to traverse this forest scene as desired, exploring different elements of both the natural environmental aesthetics and forms of flora and fauna depicted in the game.

It is at this point that the in-game computational functions of narrative branching—what Noah Wardrip-Fruin would refer to as one of *The Wanderer*'s key "operational logics"—begin to take a significantly heightened effect, as the player must increasingly decide how the "Wanderer" will specifically interact (or not interact) with the various natural topoi of this environment, thus engaging algorithmically the in-game procedural functioning through inventive forms of playthrough involving the player character's (non)engagement with the natural world as represented in the game. As Wardrip-Fruin explains his concept of "operational logics," "[t]he logics of games are also literal ways game worlds work, through computational operations—the algorithmic workings of computing systems. *Operational logics* is a term for foundational elements that do cultural work, that structure our understanding, and that do so in part through how they function computationally."[16] In the case of this moment in *The Wanderer*, once the creature approaches a fawn in one corner of the forest setting, the player can decide on a number of ways to interact with this animal and may, for instance, chase the deer away off screen by approaching too hastily or, in another iteration in a different

Figure 11.1 "NATURAE" in *The Wanderer: Frankenstein's Creature* (La Belle Games, co-produced and published by ARTE, 2019). Screenshot by the author.

playthrough, may, for example, quietly and slowly approach the fawn, resulting in the player character's gently petting the animal, which triggers further temporary background unlocking and amplification of the environmental aesthetics of this scene—thus opening up even more opportunities for creative expression and open-ended environmental play (and these are only a few descriptions of the manifold forms of gameplay in this moment).

Another potential reading of this scene is that this robust natural-cultural experience exists for the player as an "allegorithm," Alexander R. Galloway's neologism for such occurrences in which the player is "learning, internalizing, and becoming intimate with a massive, multipart, global algorithm."[17] "To play the game means to play the code of the game," Galloway writes and clarifies further: "And thus to *interpret* a game means to interpret its algorithm (to discover its parallel 'allegorithm')."[18] Building on Galloway's concept, McKenzie Wark explains that "[w]hat is distinctive about games is that they produce for the gamer an intuitive relation to the algorithm. The intuitive experience and the organizing algorithm together are an allegorithm for a future that in gamespace is forever promised but never comes to pass."[19] In the case of this and related moments in *The Wanderer* in which the player is granted significantly open-ended opportunities to experience, for instance, *jouissance* through creative forms of expression and environmental play, Galloway's concept is stretched to its limit, as the allegorithm expands to account for the multifarious possibilities of a given player's unique experiences of the game's dynamic naturecultures.

Further exploration of this setting ultimately leads the player to direct the creature to leap across a set of stones at a dam in the brook; once on the other side, the creature encounters a slithering serpent that may strike the player character with its bite, causing the game to usher in an eerie, darkened temporary filter on the entire setting, as black branches from dead trees from the foreground of the scene encroach from the margins and as the ground under the creature's feet literally darkens with each step. However, like its antithetical counterpart described earlier, this formation of ominous background unlocking also only lasts momentarily, as the game's state of representation of the natural world gradually restores itself to the scene's opening baseline depiction. Once the player has engaged all the presented action-icons in this chapter, a new branching-narrative icon appears at the site at which the creature originally awoke into this setting and prompts the player to choose either to "REST" or "EXPLORE." Selecting the latter option allows the creature to revisit the natural sites across this field of play and further engage with the environment, while opting for the former prompts another cutscene that fades the chapter to black, as the creature falls asleep again in the bower from the chapter's opening. This cutscene ends with the creature being woken by reported sounds within the setting and culminates with a final branching-narrative action icon prompting the player to choose either to "INTERVENE" or "DO NOTHING" at the site of a standoff between a deer and a serpent. In one playthrough state, failing to "INTERVENE" causes the fawn to be struck dead by the snake and for the ominous filter effects again to darken the entire setting while a cutscene intertitle flashes "*I had left an innocent creature to die before my eyes*," and the permanent dark filter transforms the setting, which now haunts the creature until the player chooses to exit "NATURAE." Opting, however, to choose the opposite playthrough for intervention in the standoff saves the life of the deer, as the player character scares away the serpent and the scene's background unlocks to the previously described vibrant amplifications of the springtime features of this setting, which, in this scenario, the creature is now free to enjoy without diminishment as an ostensible reward until the player chooses to exit "NATURAE."

While these opening chapters of the game thus focus on the complex relationship between the creature and the in-game world's representation of nature (or its haunting absence and negation), subsequent progression through the game emphasizes the creature's navigation of the complicated entanglements of natural *and* sociocultural environments, and in so doing, the game thereby reproduces several major concerns and preoccupations of Shelley's original novel. For example, the game's next chapter, "HOMINES," ushers in the world of humankind, where the player is required to direct the creature to cross through a fence marking a threshold between the putative division separating nature and society.[20] She thereby leads the creature into a beautifully watercolored two-dimensional European village in which the creature first experiences, among other things, human language, which is represented in-game as quasi speech bubbles emanating from nonplayer characters and is characterized by untranslatable symbols, given that the creature has not yet acquired human language. And in "HOMINES," the creature first confronts human beings as numerous nonplayer characters representing men, women, and children who, apparently frightened by the creature's physical appearance, eventually chase and threateningly attack the creature with stones, pitchforks, and other weaponized objects, as it flees in terror. Once the creature comes under attack from the human nonplayer characters in this scene, the game triggers the entire setting to shift via a filtering effect from the bright and colorful pastels of the watercolor representation of the village bathed in daylight to a severely darkened and nightmarish simulation of sudden nightfall, which further cuts off the creature from both society and nature. The player must complete the chapter by directing the creature, again abandoned and alone, to flee the darkened village by crossing another artificial natural-cultural threshold—this time a main gate to the village—and retreat into the wilderness, as a concluding cutscene fades the setting to complete darkness and an intertitle flashes onscreen: "*I had to keep well away from these beings that were called 'humans.'*"

In this section of the game, a brief crucial chapter titled "PRODIGIUM" ultimately requires the player to guide her avatar to the edge of a lake, where both the creature and the player come to witness for the first time the creature's hideous visage reflected in the rippling water in a scene that draws significantly from the famous passage of literal self-reflection in Shelley's novel.[21] "PRODIGIUM" is an apt choice for this chapter title at this moment in the game, as the creature begins pathetically to understand the nature of physical monstrosity during a scene that also serves as an omen for the forms of tragedy to come. As the player directs the creature to enter the lake for the game to progress, a vision of the creature's reflected face, which appears magnified in the entire bosom of the lake for the player also to view, comes increasingly into focus, as a ghoulish skeletal figuration of a pyriform skull appears in the pool's slowly churning waters. Tears appear at the edges of the dark eye sockets in the reflected vision, as the creature begins to comprehend the extent of disfiguration—internalizing an otherness during this poignant scene marked, as in the novel, by shame, fear, and anxiety. A short cutscene ends the chapter, as several intertitles flash onscreen for the player: "*Was this my face reflected in the waters of the lake?*," "*I was indeed this strange creature*," "*Alas! I did not yet entirely know the fatal effects of my miserable deformity*" (see Figure 11.2). Of course, this last-cited intertitle comes nearly verbatim from the original scene of self-reflection from Shelley's novel, where she writes:

> I had admired the perfect forms of my cottagers—their grace, beauty, and delicate complexions: but how was I terrified, when I viewed myself in a transparent pool! At first I started back, unable to believe that it was indeed I who was reflected in the mirror; and when I became fully convinced that I was in reality the monster that I am, I was filled with the bitterest sensations of despondence and mortification. Alas! I did not yet entirely know the fatal effects of this miserable deformity.[22]

As in the book, the creature in the game comes to a greater level of self-consciousness and self-awareness specifically by the engagement of the natural world in such scenes in which the environment literally becomes a medium reflecting back subjectivity, thus establishing a dialectical relationship between objects and subjects, which such digital environments of the game characterize as co-constitutive natural-cultural assemblages.

The game's focus on the creature's deep immersion in the natural world soon continues with the chapter "SUMMITATEM," where the player must direct the creature to hike out of a valley toward the sublime summits of the peaks of an alpine massif behind which the sun is setting in a dramatically fiery sky dominated by colors

Figure 11.2 "PRODIGIUM" in *The Wanderer: Frankenstein's Creature* (La Belle Games, co-produced and published by ARTE, 2019). Screenshot by the author.

of orange and red in an image that looks like a synthesis of Friedrich's *The Watzmann* (1824–1825) and Fredric Edwin Church's *Twilight in the Wilderness* (1860) (see Figure 11.3).[23] In this way, it is almost as if the player's role in chapters like "SUMMITATEM" is literally to "play" through a sublime Romantic landscape painting—trekking backwards and forwards, as desired, along the hiking path. In these ways, the game prompts the player to navigate through versions of the sublime derived from Friedrich and other Romantic-age visual artists. However, because it often does so in a deeply interactive process in which the player virtually navigates the digitally rendered environmental spaces of the in-game world via the creature, who must contingently interact with myriad topoi of the game's representation of the natural world (including even the hiking path on which it treks) as forms of dynamic quasi nonplayer characters shimmering with agential qualities, the game also turns sublime Romantic art into *playable* arenas. To be sure, as Wark has noted, "Games are not representations of this world. They are more like allegories of a world made over as gamespace."[24] Indeed, the fact that the creature is, of course, a representation of a specifically nonhuman player character dialectically interacting with digitally rendered natural features of traditions of sublime environments further blurs both epistemological and ontological distinctions between putative "subjects" and "objects" of this allegoric and allegorithmic gamespace.

If *The Wanderer*'s reliance on the work of Friedrich for its key visual and conceptual imagery was in any doubt before "SUMMITATEM," then the aesthetics of the game's subsequent chapter titled "INDUSTRIA" certainly cement the in-game world's reliance on transforming the work of this Romantic artist into "allegories of a world made over as gamespace."[25] The start of "INDUSTRIA" reenacts and reinterprets Friedrich's

Figure 11.3 "SUMMITATEM" in *The Wanderer: Frankenstein's Creature* (La Belle Games, co-produced and published by ARTE, 2019). Screenshot by the author.

Wanderer above the Sea of Fog. The spectator's perspective on the human subject from Friedrich's original painting is rotated in the game world's reinterpretation of this setting by approximately forty-five degrees counterclockwise, as the player looks onto the creature able to be substituted in roughly the same characteristic stance as Friedrich's original subject, though viewed now by the gamer as a vision of the creature nearly in profile while a dynamic snowstorm whirls through the scene (see Figure 11.4). Gamespaces like these establish *The Wanderer* as what Patrick Jagoda would refer to as an "experimental" game: "To put it directly up front, games operate as experiments insofar as they combine a stable foundation of starting conditions, rules, and objectives on the one hand with the contingency and possibility of play on the other. This balance encourages the provoked observation that is experiment: a designed repetition that produces difference."[26] In this context, "INDUSTRIA" reproduces significant allegoric and allegorithmic revisions of the Romantic alpine sublime characterizing Friedrich's celebrated painting through the gamespace's representations of digitally rendered environmental aesthetics and, in so doing, *The Wanderer* demonstrates Jagoda's crucial thesis that experimental games "can help not merely *solve problems* but also [are able] to *make problems* that are better defined and understood."[27]

Following these shorter chapters focusing on linking the game's environmental aesthetics to transformations of the sublime, the player is ultimately required to guide the creature to follow Frankenstein's movements toward the North Pole, a setting which of course plays a key role in the conclusion of Shelley's story. In the ingenious chapter "AEQUOR" in this section of the game, the player intuitively realizes that she must embody the role of the winds blowing over the even surface of a placid ocean so

Figure 11.4 "INDUSTRIA" in *The Wanderer: Frankenstein's Creature* (La Belle Games, co-produced and published by ARTE, 2019). Screenshot by the author.

as to fill the sails of a boat for the game to progress as the creature closes in on the Arctic.[28] In a reinterpretation of the tradition of platformer games like Nintendo's classic *Super Mario Bros.* (1985), the gameplay of "AEQUOR" requires the player to track from left to right across the screen.[29] However, in this chapter, the player becomes largely decoupled from the creature as avatar, given that she must now point and click repeatedly in a swooping motion in order to mimic the natural flow of an atmospheric oceanic current captured by the sails of the creature's vessel, which becomes propelled slowly toward the righthand side of the screen. In this way, the player is asked to identify through gameplay with a literal nonhuman actant that becomes her player character—the jet stream of "AEQUOR"—and which intersects simultaneously with the nonhuman actorship that has been the creature's dominant role as the player's avatar up to this point in gameplay. To understand the significance of this form of gameplay, it is useful to return momentarily to thatgamecompany's *Flower*, which, as Chang has observed, "destabilizes not only player corporeality but also player agency and perspective" by requiring gamers to inhabit a rushing draught of wind, which casts the player as "an other-than-human consciousness" and as "essentially invisible except *through* your effects on the environment."[30] Like *Flower*, gameplay in this chapter of *The Wanderer* translates the nonhuman as accessible in an enabling manner. More precisely, gameplay in "AEQUOR" in fact pushes this rendering even further, given that the creature and the jet stream are, in a sense, other-than-human equivalents in that they both serve as nonhuman player characters. This chapter's most defamiliarizing move actually resides in its association of the creature with the dynamism of digitally rendered natural phenomena as actants in their own right. The creature, in other words, possesses, like nature, a powerful agency with which human subjectivity must learn to reckon.

The Wanderer eventually begins to draw to a close by centering attention on the creature's singular focus on finding Frankenstein, who is rumored to be living as a recluse in the wilds of the Arctic. Unlike in Shelley's novel, however, Frankenstein is nowhere to be found in any of the various potential endings of *The Wanderer*, and the designers of the game thus made a specific and careful decision not to include any visual representation of Frankenstein at any point in the game. Instead, the player is left at the end of *The Wanderer* to initiate the final determination of the game's specific playthrough conclusion, which has been based on all the player's branching decisions up to this point in the game (e.g., "INTERVEN[ING]" versus "DO[ING] NOTHING" in "NATURAE," very subtle dialogue selections at narrative branching junctures across the game, etc.). For reasons of space, the conclusion of this partial critical walkthrough will gesture only toward describing "SILENTIUM," a chapter finale that has also been chosen because this particular playthrough and ending of the game is the closest one to Shelley's conclusion to *Frankenstein* and is additionally thus a selection that avoids spoiling all of the other various endings to *The Wanderer*.[31] Many of those endings also underscore and further elaborate on the creature's in-game relationships with naturecultures, and they are worthy of analysis in the context of the ideas explored across this chapter. That said, "SILENTIUM" is also arguably the ending most focused on visually and textually representing the tragic conclusion of the creature's ongoing negotiation of such apparent dichotomies, and this particular finale thus sheds new light on Shelley's own related concerns in the last pages of her novel specifically through the game's representations of the player character's relationship with environmental aesthetics and its ultimate negation. In other words, "SILENTIUM" teases out through digital visualizations the preoccupation with naturecultures that was always already there across Shelley's original text and especially its final paragraphs, and the game, once understood from this critical perspective, therefore sheds new light on the final chapter of *Frankenstein*.

Once triggered as the game's conclusion, "SILENTIUM" initiates a moving cutscene in which a longer intertitle card appears onscreen: "*But my mind is lucid and determined. I am ready to write the epilogue of my story. Neither you who is reading these words, nor any other human being shall ever understand how consumed I am with suffering and remorse. Now, death is my sole consolation. Farewell.*" Accepting this sad fate, the player now may only witness a visual reenactment of the creature's promise of suicide in a silent scene strikingly similar to Shelley's original ending. The player's last decision tree flashes for her on the screen. One option reads, "*You will no longer see the sun or the stars. You will no longer feel the wind caressing your cheek,*" while the other offers the player the following option: "*You wanted to know love and still you were spurned. Is there no injustice in this?*" Of course, both these passages derive nearly verbatim from the last paragraphs of *Frankenstein*, where Shelley writes the following two passages which correspond to these final in-game narrative options:

> I shall no longer see the sun or stars, or feel the winds play on my cheeks. Light, feeling, and sense, will pass away; and in this condition must I find my happiness.

> Some years ago, when the images which this world affords first opened upon me, when I felt the cheering warmth of summer, and heard the rustling of the leaves and the chirping of the birds, and these were all to me, I should have wept to die; now it is my only consolation.[32]
>
> I, the miserable and the abandoned, am an abortion, to be spurned at, and kicked, and trampled on. Even now my blood boils at the recollection of this injustice.[33]

The two respective passages from the game's final narrative options thus draw out the role of the deep immersion of the creature in the natural world, a preoccupation of both *The Wanderer* and *Frankenstein*. The first passage emphasizes this concern in both cases, particularly in Shelley's conclusion. The latter passage, while more conceptual in its focus on the moral and ethical conundrums and "injustice[s]" of the story also, however, likewise hearkens back to the interlinkage of the creature and the natural world in the way that it invokes the creature as an "abortion," a term that carries with it the reference to life and non-life simultaneously.

While the game's branching choices in this final moment at first apparently indicate that the narrative selection will lead to a unique playthrough outcome, as usual in the game, both choices actually result in the same ending in which the creature suddenly appears from another far-distant perspective standing on the frozen tundra of the Arctic and facing away from the player, who may now only look over the creature's shoulders in something like the spectatorial perspective on the subject of Friedrich's *Wanderer above the Sea of Fog*. These and related moments of the synthetic remediation of the work of Friedrich and Shelley in the transformed figuration of the creature in *The Wanderer* further evidence Shane Denson's proposal that the image of the creature is best understood as a "serial figure."[34] A media theorist and critical game studies scholar, Denson has recently argued that the creature "evolves not *within* a uniform diegetic space, but *between* or *across* such spaces of narration and visualization."[35] As the game's final cutscene culminates, this complex figuration of the creature's image continues to evolve as the player character slowly trudges through the deep snowdrifts dropped by a violent ongoing blizzard and as the player may momentarily only look onto this scene of nearly whiteout conditions that create an environment in which the creature's figure is nearly impossible to identify. After visually following the darkened trail left in the snow by the flickering outline of this figure, the player is required to make one last round of pointing and clicking once the creature reaches the Arctic shores and, in doing so, compels the player character to enter the icy waters, where the vanishing image of the creature is "soon borne away by the waves, and lost in darkness and distance," to borrow from the final line of Shelley's novel.[36] To be sure, as in the book, the creature has inhabited—from hopeful origin to tragic end—a series of strange intermediary positions oscillating between subjectivity and objectivity, nature and society, spirit and matter, life and non-life—a fact that is also, of course, true about the creature's existence following the famous creation scene of the novel. As we have seen, the game, however, draws out and amplifies these natural-cultural oscillations repeatedly and hyperbolically through perpetual visual and textual deconstructions, which act as synapses and relays back to these same embedded fascinations with naturecultures in Shelley's *Frankenstein*.

Romanticism's Legacies: Imaginative Literature, Critical Theory, Ludic Enjoyment

There is something almost uncanny about the ways that *Frankenstein* has spurred the production of twenty-first-century cultures of serious gaming. As I have argued at length elsewhere, Shelley's *Frankenstein* is a text fundamentally preoccupied with the nature and function of both information and mediation precisely because Shelley herself was steeped in and indebted to a range of eighteenth- and nineteenth-century cultures of information and media, which collectively shaped her production of a creation narrative whose central themes and structures beg to be transformed and mutated into new media legacies.[37] In a related context, Denson has argued the following: "Exhibiting a promiscuous, plurimedial sort of seriality, the monster's image—as an image of animation—presents a special case for thinking the dynamic intermedial networks that constitute our visual culture."[38] Of course, Denson here refers largely to the cinematic afterlives of Shelley's *Frankenstein*, but his work, as noted, also clearly calls for a similar exploration of the post-cinematic transmission and existence of the creature's image as what he refers to as a "serial figure."[39]

As the examples of serious gaming explored in this chapter evidence and attest, Shelley's *Frankenstein* has served as an incredibly generative engine for creating such forms and concepts that anticipate not only developments in digital media but also thought in disciplines such as critical theory. As we have seen, among these concerns exists a version of Haraway's notion of naturecultures, which *The Wanderer* locates in Shelley's original text and amplifies through major themes, representations, and ideas of its gamespaces' complex forms of environmental play. *The Wanderer* was, in fact, designed in part not only to recognize the bicentennial anniversary of *Frankenstein*'s publication, as noted at the start of this chapter, but also to experiment with the book's concerns with how the creature relates to and comes to comprehend environmental relationships. "[We] wanted to pay tribute to the original version of *Frankenstein*," explains Larouzée, who clarifies that a major goal of the game is to investigate how, drawing from the "original story," the creature "tr[ies] to understand the world."[40] To borrow again briefly from Jagoda's observations on the genre, experimental games like *The Wanderer* should be understood for these and related reasons "as not only a technological medium or artistic form but also, more profoundly, as machines for constructing new concepts in the early twenty-first century."[41]

To be sure, the successful player-driven community building around experimental art games like *The Wanderer* and its engrossing visions of naturecultures indicates that there is a strong public interest in engaging further with challenging theoretical concepts that have in the past perhaps been assumed to be specialized models relegated to the domains of critical theory but that, in our contemporary moment of rapidly evolving styles of digital gaming and related forms of play, quite plainly present as new transformations of ludic engagement and enjoyment.

Part Four

Artists Talk Back

12

A Monstrous Circus on Frankenstein: Mediating Shelley's Novel through John Cage's Multimedia Strategies

R. L. Silver and Miriam Wallace

In March of 2018 New College of Florida, like many other institutions that year, hosted a series of events celebrating the 1818 publication of Mary Shelley's *Frankenstein; or the Modern Prometheus*. "Frankenfest" (as we called it) included guest lectures, community conversations led by faculty, a student adaptation in which the creature is a social media "profile," a game-writing event on the theme of *Frankenstein*, and a film series at the nearby Ringling College of Art and Design.[1] Most uniquely, New Music New College created and performed a version of John Cage's *Circus On* ___, using *Frankenstein* as the source text. In developing the series of events for Frankenfest, Professor of English Miriam Wallace approached Professor of Music and Director of New Music New College, Professor Stephen Miles with an idea. Realizing that New Music New College was planning to do Cage's "Circus On ___" in its season, Wallace suggested using *Frankenstein* as the source text, in honor of the 200th anniversary of its publication. Professor Miles and NMNC Producer R. L. Silver agreed that this would be an interesting project which would draw together students working in different academic fields. New Music New College is a hybrid entity—both a performance series that brings cutting-edge contemporary music and sound performance to our campus and an opportunity for interaction among students, community members, and performers in multiple formats from visiting artists' conversations to collaborative performances like this one.

This chapter considers what happened when we approached Shelley's work not through conventional literary theoretical or historical approaches or even film, but through performance and Cagean chance procedures. Not only the text's words but also the core plot-points were reframed into poetic phrases to be performed, then overlaid with sound and image and presented alongside or overtop each other in a performance that was structured according to specific directions. Performers and auditors/observers were left to find their way through an unpredictable and unreproducible experience—one that was collaborative, but also unique to each person.

New points of access to both Shelley's novel and Cage's deceptively simple composition are created when audiences can enter through sound, poetry, performance, or embodied action. Audience and performers together were freed in this project to re-vision *Frankenstein* by depending upon its language as phrase and sound rather than as plot or concept, and a performance that didn't depend upon fixed locations for audience as distinct from performer. This kind of reframing is a difficult trick to pull off with such an over-determined and well-known (if often mis-known) core story, and we were surprised by how well using "Circus On __" to intervene worked. Initially we were uncertain whether Shelley's novel *would* work. Given its origin in a kind of high modernist practice, Wallace wondered whether a Cagean approach might merely re-aestheticize a work that has been importantly reclaimed to speak to a variety of issues, or whether the experience of working together would offer another kind of value by creating a sense of shared community purpose. Keeping the tension alive between the overt concerns we continue to find in Shelley's tale (the siren song of human ambition, bioethics, the possibilities and limits of science, the experience of extreme isolation and embodied difference), and those of Cage's processes (the power of silence and sound, the value of chance procedure that is nonetheless carefully constrained, and the experience of collaborative embodied performance) was key to our success.

Circus On __ is essentially a set of instructions for turning *any* text into a performance. Following Cage's procedures, the base text is first converted into a series of "mesostics." These poetic phrases are then performed (dramatically read) along with sounds mentioned in the text or associated with places named in the text. Cage himself made a realization using *Finnegan's Wake*, calling the finished work *Roaratorio: An Irish Circus on Finnegan's Wake*.[2] While James Joyce's work seems a natural fit for Cage's experimental approach to sound and music, Shelley's earlier novel tests the value of Cage's approach as a less obvious artistic and stylistic match. Moreover, using *Frankenstein* turns a lens back on Cage's work to ask what his approach offers as yet another way to engage Shelley's much-discussed work—or other similarly familiar texts.

John Cage was known for his embrace of chance procedures, meticulously directing how to use them to disjoin some of a composer's and/or performer's intentions from the final product. Cage's process, when applied to Shelley's high Romantic political and social philosophical novel, immediately moved both instructors from their comfort zone (though not perhaps the students). This production demanded that the literary critic let go of most of what founds literary expertise, while the music/performance faculty had to trust Cage's directions and the text itself to produce an interesting soundscape from this very literary and philosophical material. How to navigate the heavy presence of later film and pop-culture versions in the actual performance itself presented another consideration.

Preparation and Mesostics

During January Interterm 2018, students worked with Professor of English Miriam Wallace to read and study the novel (we used the 1818 edition).[3] Alongside more traditional historical and critical approaches to the novel, students also worked in teams to process the entire text through Cage's mesostics.

Cage specifies that to do this, one first selects either the author's name or title as the base for mesostics; we chose the single title "Frankenstein." Then one begins by searching the text for the first word that contains an "F" but not the following mesostic letter—"R" in this case—then a word containing an "R" but no "A"—and so on to the end of the text. There are now online mesostic generators available; if you paste in your text and source term, they will do it for you. But we decided there was a value to doing this longhand even given the likelihood of some human error. We asked students to do this in teams of two, with one scanning and the other recording the word and double checking. Words are then recorded in columns such that the letters spelling out FRANKENSTEIN run vertically down the center with the full word containing the letter falling to either side. Cage specifies that adjacent words may be included at the discretion of the mesostic-maker to make a more poetic or interesting line, for example:

Table 12.1

	Mesostic
1	oF an enteRprise hAve evil forebodiNgs my tasK is to assurE my welfare aNd increaSing far norTh thE streets I feel cold Northern breeze
2	Fills Reeze hAs regioNs disK pErpetual iN Snow frosT arE hItherto discovered oN the habitable globe
3	phenomena oF undiscoveRed solitudes whAt may Not satiate manKind to the last passagE Near the secret poSsible can only be agiTation which bEgan and I glow with heaveN

This labor produced a poetic script, consisting of 256 word or short-phrase clusters (potentially "poems") that became the script used by performers.

During the January term, we spent some time in the group discussing what we made of the mesostics. First, students found that it was important to work in pairs to check their work and keep focused. We all found that following Cage's directions produced some interesting effects as a somewhat different form of "close reading." It made some words and phrases jump out of the text—sometimes, as in the example above, producing a poetic set of associations that nevertheless captures aspects of the book. In the opening, we found that the mesostics emphasized the darker foreshadowing elements within Walton's optimistic letter. While in Shelley's frame, Walton emphasizes his excitement about his travels and his ambition for discovery and treading new land, the mesostics uncovered darker elements embedded in the text. The first "N" yields "foreboding," although Walton actually says here that his sister's concerns have all proved unfounded. Then the repeated emphasis on "north," "northern," and the related "frost," "snow," "perpetual" suggest less a sense of adventure than of chilly uncertainty.

One Literature student wrote that the "first time I read *Frankenstein* in its entirety" was during this January term project:

> Developing the mesostics allowed me to look at the text under a microscope. [...] my analytical experience up until this point was focused on the "big picture," usually looking at the historical impacts on the text, so I was interested in changing my perspective.
>
> When writing the mesostics, I was amazed at how the themes of the novel came through. The phrases that were created from Mary Shelley's text exemplified the themes of loss, knowledge, and creation. This project was unlike anything I had taken on previously and I really enjoyed the experience of examining the novel on a purely textual level and seeing how it mirrored the larger themes of the novel.
>
> Sarah Olsen

Even this first step seems to have helped students and faculty to slow down, take more time with the text, rather than searching for thematic points, identifying potential essay topics, or relying on secondary criticism and contexts to make the text meaningful. Mesostics created a practice of "slow reading" that moved us all away from seeking representational significance to attending to the text's language. In short, it forced us to read the text in a more poetic fashion, for visually repeated letters, and to attend to sounds and word clusters. Rather than a barrier, Shelley's rather baroque language became interesting in itself.

The option to include words on either side of the selected word allowed for some interpretive choices. Some pairs of students took full advantage, while others were more minimalistic, focusing only on the identified word. In the end, R. L. Silver went through and added some phrases to make the final text a little more stylistically congruent and pleasurable to read aloud.

Students made occasional mistakes as well—we caught some and backtracked but, in the end, we also decided that chance procedures intentionally leave room for human "error," and we preferred the possibility of error that set us on a slightly different path from using a computer to do the work here. We found a value in the oblique attention to the text as words—both image and sound.

There were also some funny insights. While initially we found the next word in a mesostic quite quickly (and despaired of ever finishing, moving very slowly through pages), words which contain a "K" not followed by an "E" in English are somewhat uncommon. Here we would sometimes proceed for several pages before the next word in a mesostic would occur. Students mentioned a sense of release at these points, as they were able to rush forward over pages at a time searching for a word that fit—a kind of travel experience that curiously replicates the novel's own tensions between stagnation and rapid movement, reflective or obsessive mental states, and swift travel over large swathes of the known world.

However, in the section of the novel where Mr. Kirwin appears, his name was frequent, appearing eight times over ten mesostics. We were slowed down and forced to pay more attention to this rather minor character who jumped out of the text as a significant presence:

Table 12.2

	Mesostic
194	Feeble soRry thAt womaN mr. Kirwin mE iN priSon To bE It was he physiciaN
195	halF oveRcome hAd thaN mr. Kirwin drEw miNe addreSsed That placE Is shockiNg
196	Fiend youR pAth Notwithstanding mr. Kirwin aftEr examiNing dreSs That discover somE trace I seNd

The mere accident of this name drew the group's attention back to Mr. Kirwin—the Irish magistrate who initially oversees Victor's arrest for the murder of Henry Clerval, but later becomes a sympathetic father figure to him. Recognizing how often his name is repeated led us to consider Kirwin as more than a device to move the plot forward—as a figure for the paternal, for the law, and one who balances legal justice with human sympathy (the kind that the creature is unable to access within the novel). As sound, "Mr. Kirwin" took on an almost comic reiteration of falling staccato trochees that cut across what may otherwise be read as phrases.

Performing "Circus On ___"

On Sunday, March 4, 2018, we performed the work as a multimedia event, including a live reading of the mesostic-text overlaid with recorded and live sounds and projected images. Performers included undergraduate students, faculty and staff, local musicians, and community members. Our audience included regular subscribers to NMNC's season, College students, faculty, and staff, students at local colleges and high schools, and the community at large. Not all had read Shelley's novel, though most had seen film versions. For both audience and performers, access to Shelley's *Frankenstein* was largely through Cage's mediation and their own unique associations. The mesostics and their accompanying sounds and sites formed the linear backbone on which all other elements hung, so that the performance represented an abstracted and compressed read through of the entire novel following the plot's temporal flow. Those who came only with a filmic background were likely to notice particular punctuation points where identifiable plot points emerged—screams, Mendelssohn's wedding march, crashing lightening, sounds of arctic wind and ice. Those who know the book intimately could identify roughly where we were by signposts such as guitar (Felix plays the guitar to his father, sister, and Safie), or the sounds or images of particular locations (Scotland). But for all, this performed version wrested away our familiarity and comfort in the narrative itself.

To realize Cage's work as acoustic performance, Professor Stephen Miles and Producer R. L. Silver shared the lists of music, sounds, and places pulled from the book with professional musicians in the area: violinist Samantha Bennett, percussionist George Nickson, and double bassist John Miller (all of the Sarasota Orchestra and ensemble *NEW*SRQ) and guitarist Rex Willis (faculty at State College of Florida). These instrumentalists discussed the sounds they could perform, individually or as an ensemble (e.g.: "a most violent and terrible thunderstorm;" "ice cave"). The remaining sounds were divided into those which other performers could create vocally (e.g.: "the sound of a voice so familiar;" "he uttered some inarticulate sounds") and sounds we would need to reproduce from recordings (e.g.: "airpump;" "every wind that blows").

For places with no obvious sound reference (the hut in which the De Lacey family lives), we chose visual references, and projected images on a large screen (as projecting on the building wall proved impractical). We also took the opportunity here of projecting about two stills from the 1931 film as a reference to the power of those adaptations.

Although this was not a neutral choice and introduced explicit anachronisms, at every community discussion around the book leading up to this performance audience members had referenced this film version. A nod to the book's visual "afterlives" seemed impossible to escape even as we presented the original text reconfigured as poetic sound art. We hoped the sonic experience would dominate, and we think it did.

Early on Silver had suggested that the performance take place outdoors: performers on the balconies of New College's L-shaped Academic Center building (see Figure 12.2), and the audience on the lawn and plaza inside the L.

This left the audience free to move around the space on the ground level, while performers ranged vertically. Following past New Music New College performances, audience members told us that their ability to move towards new points of interest or simply to engage with the performance from multiple locations had a strongly engaging effect. The agency given by some experimental composers to performers was thus mirrored by the agency given to the audience members, who could choose how to encounter elements of a performance, for instance by following a specific performer, moving closer to or further from a particular sound, etc. For example, in its inaugural performance of the John Cage *Songbooks* in the Ringling Museum's contemporary gallery, performers moved between stations situated throughout the space. No one location offered an auditor a clear line of sight to *all* stations. We liked the way that this created a dynamic experience for audience members as agents or curators of their own experience. We replicated those elements here.

For this event, Silver mapped performance positions. Vocal performers would move between assigned stations supplied with microphones for each speech, while the instrumentalists would remain static: the guitarist at one place and the other three together at another location. In keeping with New Music New College practice, the entire performance was planned to last about one hour—in this case, exactly sixty minutes, as performers used stopwatches to time their actions and hit their cues.

Silver began to devise a schema for the performance. (See Figure 12.1; Schema excerpt, from minutes 30 through 32.) The top group indicates density; the middle shows the specific events. Upper-case letter pairs are a performer's initials followed by the particular mesostic, lower-case letter pairs indicate particular sounds from another list. The lowest group shows the location where each event should occur. Silver created a spreadsheet breaking the hour performance into fifteen-second intervals, then used a random number generator (Cage was an advocate of using chance procedure in both composition and performance) to assign each interval a "density" from one to seven, indicating how many simultaneous "events" should occur. Events included: spoken performance, instrumental performance, recorded sound, and/or visual projection. There were two additional density options—silence and "perform silence." "Perform Silence" meant that any visible performer must freeze for that interval. "Silence" merely meant that no intentional sounds could be made, but performer movement was not restricted (see schema excerpt).

In addition to the four instrumentalists, the team recruited a total of twenty-three people to perform the mesostics and other vocal sounds (including the guitarist during long stretches that did not require guitar according to the text). Local composer Francis

Time (across)	30.00		31.00				32.00	
Density (down)								
1 Event								
2 Events							X	
3 Events								
4 Events							X	
5 Events				X				
6 Events			X	X				
7 Events	X					X		
Silence	X							
No Event (perform silence)		X						
Events (down)								
Mesostic	SO 133		SF 135	SE 136	EC 140	LT 142	MW 145	FS (rec)
Mesostic	MH 134			RS 137	SP 141	EM 143		
Mesostic				JF 138		KL 144		
Mesostic				EK 139				
Mesostic								
Mesostic								
Recorded sound	X		X	X			X	
Live sound (students)	Xaj		Xak		Xal	Xam, Xama		
Live sound (musicians)	X P		X P		X V	XV	X V	
Live sound (musicians)	X V		X B			X		
Projection	X		X	X	X		X	X
Location								
East 2nd balcony	Xaj LT			EK139		Xam EK		
East 1st L (stage R)			SF135		Xal ES,DS		MW145	
East 1st R (stage L)				SE136		LT142		
North 1st L (stage R)	SO133		Xak SM, JF138		EC140			
North 1st R (stage L)	MH134				SP141	Xama AS		
Plaza (walking)				RS137		KL144, EM143		
4 Winds sculpture								

Figure 12.1 Schema excerpt, from minutes 30 through 32. The top group indicates density; the middle shows the specific events (upper-case letter pairs are a performer's initials followed by the particular mesostic, lower-case letter pairs indicate particular sounds from another list); the lowest group shows location where each event should occur.

Schwartz, who could not attend the concert in person, recorded a number of mesostics that were played back with other prerecorded sounds.

Working within the schema, Silver then assigned the mesostics and vocal sounds to the various performers, each with a start time and location. In addition to five window locations at the balconies of the Academic Center, the team chose to have some performers declaim mesostics in small groups at a large sculpture in the plaza while others performed as they walked through the audience. This ensured a great deal of movement and shifting points of attention. Silver also assigned times for the instrumentalists to perform their sounds/music and for prerecorded sounds and projected images, all falling approximately where they were referenced in the text as the nearest mesostics were performed, and according to the density of the particular moment. Not all events were timed to begin or end precisely on a fifteen-second division, nor were all events limited in length to fifteen seconds (or expected to last for fifteen seconds).

As a way of marking progress through the piece, performers clapped their hands at each ten-minute mark, with one performer (Silver) cueing the beginning and more performers clapping at each mark, until all twenty-seven live performers clapped together to conclude the piece. New Music New College has found that when audiences are presented with a performance that lacks a familiar shape (symphonic movements, acts and scenes in a prescribed order or number) it helps audiences to offer some kind of internal marker and to limit the run-time. Most people are willing to try something completely new for about 60 minutes without intermission. To distinguish performers from the audience visually and to create an atmosphere, the performers wore white lab coats as a simple, uniform costume. To these, many added their own make-up touches—often referencing horror films (dark eyes and white or green skin, stitches or blood), but also lab scientists or steampunk elements (lab goggles, green hair).

This performance entailed a large leap of faith for most of the participants, many of whom had never experienced any experimental music, let alone such an expansive and theatrical Cagean production. Our experience was that, partway through the only run-through (the day before the performance, the only time we could get all the performers and equipment in place), the enthusiasm of the more practiced performers spread to the entire ensemble as we created and presented our "Monster."

Reviewing *Frankenstein*

Contemporary returns to *Frankenstein* have explicitly and effectively engaged current concerns: the 2011 National Theatre version's exploration of embodying damaged motorskills, technology-human intersections, loneliness and statelessness, and toxic masculinity; *Frankenstein in Baghdad*'s wartime golem; *Destroyer*'s engagement with Black Lives Matter. Our version, however, did something different from those more story-centered approaches. It produced a more playful and celebratory version of the work—one that opened it up, beyond plot and history, to shared sensory experience.

This approach reframed *Frankenstein* through chance procedures with an emphasis on sound and word, creating new points of access to Shelley's work. Participants brought to bear their own experiences with performance or variations on *Frankenstein*—but no one person could perform alone, and we all shared the intense experience of speaking the words in their new formulations, of rushing to get to our next spot or waiting for our turn to go on, of suddenly hearing an identifiable phrase or name or sound that located us back in the story's plotline. Audience members, likewise, were invited to move through the performance—since there was no explicit stage, they were free to sit anywhere on the plaza or to walk among the performers on the ground level, even behind the musicians—and they did so.

Participants shared some of their insights afterwards, with nearly all finding that the Cagean process had reoriented their thinking about *Frankenstein* into an experiential and emotional response. A faculty member from Biology told us that she participated because she had first encountered Dean Koontz's *Frankenstein* series, then read

Shelley's work, and subsequently sought out other film and popular literary renditions. Drawn to the story's variations on the "egomaniacal scientist," she appreciated that "participat[ing] in 'Circus On Frankenstein' allowed me to not just be a consumer of *Frankenstein* but an actual participant" (Tiffany Doan). She cogently observed that "[t]he stripped-down nature of the Circus On performance took only the essence of the book and condensed it into sound and emotion, a bit like the monster when he was first 'born.'"

One community member with prior theatrical experience called this "a unique experience," appreciating that "each ensemble member was given the freedom to bring their own interpretation to their performance" (Jack Fahey). He continued:

> I have been part of a variety of theatrical events over the years but none that required ensemble members to speak their lines, make sounds, or remain silent in different locations all timed to synchronized stopwatches. It was crazy.
>
> The choice of location for the performance, indoors and outdoors, and the fact that it started at dusk and moved into night contributed to a Frankenstein "castle-esque" like environment and complimented Shelly's / Cage's fabulous text choices. It made for a very eerie evening.
>
> I was unfamiliar with Cage's work prior to this performance and was amazed to discover his influence on many of my favorite musicians and bands, Frank Zappa, Brian Eno, Radiohead, and Lou Reed who said "everything is music." I now realize that music can be anything. I like to think that Cage would have loved to collaborate with Shelly on Frankenstein.
>
> Jack Fahey

Another community member, Kit Liset, wrote that "For me it was the John Cage side of things that was most fascinating. I was not at all familiar with John Cage nor mesostics, so the whole way this was put together—with intention—was a bit of a revelation." She calls the experience "a series of whoa's"— from the scripts and their construction to the location, to the experience itself, including, importantly, the cacophony of dense moments followed by more spare ones and silence:

> In our day-of rehearsal I noticed there was a particular moment towards the end of the piece where there was a crescendo with music and mesostics being read with fervor and then a long deafening silence. Then quietly the mesostics picked up again. I think it was the imposed silences that really brought home the composition side of the performance. Each time a silence happened, it really got to me—whether I was running up and down stairs to my next position or waiting to read.
>
> At night, in the dark, when we did the actual performance, with lights, and music, and slides, and lab coats, and make-up and serious game faces on moving point-to-point—that crescendo moment was even more amazing. Totally resounded into the darkness. With the long silence to follow. And then the pick up of the voice again. Totally *Frankenstein* and (I realized) John Cage all the way.
>
> Kit Liset

Doan's point that reading the Cageian text aloud with others, while moving to choreographed positions, resonates with the creature's discovery of himself through his sensory experience, shortly after awakening, is a key insight. Shelley we know was working from Condorcet and other natural philosophers' belief that the infant begins with basic bodily sensations and from those builds a sense of self and world—and eventually social relations. Liset's account of the experience of sensory overload—many sounds, voices, words—crying, yelling, quiet recitation, music, recorded sound—pointed by silences picks up on this element of the experience as well. Where reading Shelley's novel often surprises readers with its philosophical abstractedness (where they expect a more immediate shock of horror), this performed version highlighted the sensory aspects of the text itself as embodied sound.

One of our student performers highlighted the sense of "being inside of the novel" as movement, sound, action:

> Seeing our mesostics come to life during the performance brought a whole new layer to my understanding and interaction with the text. The layering of mesostics and sound effects created a performance piece that truly exhibited the emotions of Frankenstein. I remember standing there, observing the hustle of all the performers scurrying to their spots and feeling like I was in the eye of a hurricane, with sounds of spoken word, screaming, and thunder claps surrounding me. I was engulfed by the novel on a physical level, it was unlike any experience I have ever had. It reminded me of studying Shakespeare, then seeing *Macbeth* performed live. Bringing life to the text allowed me to experience the novel in a new way that was a physical experience.
>
> Sarah Olsen

The sense of physicality, of engaging with this highly intellectual and philosophical text or with the highly emotional through active embodiment was shared by all performers.

Arguably, performances of written language are a form of transmedia translation—moving material from one medium (literary text, written dialog) to another (embodied performance). This performance was a particular kind of translation effort, one that drew together multiple media via a particular set of rules and processes. Laurence Venuti theorizes linguistic translation as falling often in two directions: the "familiarizing" kind or the "estranging" kind. Venuti explains that "[a] translated text is judged successful—by editors, publishers, reviewers, readers, by translators themselves—when it reads fluently and thereby gives the appearance that it is not translated, that it is the original, reflecting the foreign author's personality or intention or the essential meaning of the foreign text."[4] This is the dominant mode, one that erases the translator when it is effective in order to produce "fluency" and that, as Venuti (and others) have said, values work that can be treated in this way.

Despite the very powerful and effective re-visioning of *Frankenstein* from Victor LaValle's *Destroyer* to Nick Dear's stage adaptation premiered at the Royal National Theatre under the direction of Danny Boyle, those are to some degree "familiarizing." Even as LaValle resets the monster into the context of police shootings and Black suffering under racism, we are still working with a monster-character who judges humankind for its failures and metes out justice golem-like, and a scientist as grieving mother, who seeks to resurrect her murdered child. Danny Boyle's version of Nick Dear's play borrows from Shelley's book to develop the self-centered Victor and the compelling creature into fully embodied characters as a way to explore the themes of parent-child relations, reproduction and technology, and especially male control of female bodies.[5] However, most performances perforce represent the novel through actors representing *individual* characters, speaking lines that belong to them alone.

A few of the film versions have attempted to incorporate some elements of the novel's multi-leveled framing told first through Robert Walton's letters to his sister; then Victor's tale told to Walton; and finally the creature's own account of his coming to consciousness. Yet all staged or filmed versions finally translate the work's own narrative levels into spoken dialog. By contrast, transforming the novel through Cage's directions for "Circus On ___" moved away from reiterating characters in new settings or reiterating plot elements and philosophical concerns. While it did not call out a particular social justice issue as do the translations of Dear and LaValle, it did create a shared experience that resonated among performers and audience on a fundamentally physiological experiential level—one that created a range of affective responses—and that sent many back to the book, to other works by Cage, and on to new experiences.

Figure 12.2 NCF Academic Center Building pre-performance talk with audience and set up. Courtesty of Elan Photography.

Table 12.3

	Mesostic
25	oF instRuments lAbours meN manKind dElivered affectatioN hiS againsT modErn chemIsts aNd I requested
26	iF youR application equAls No tooK mE iNto hiS laboraTory mE hIs various machiNes
27	oF theiR mechanism Also eNded darK spEcies maNy hiS Thought bEstow animation lIfeless matter iN time

Figure 12.3 Academic Center Building with projection screen, musicians, and vocal performers on balcony and ground in white lab coats. Courtesty of Elan Photography.

Figure 12.4 R. L. Silver performing a mesostic from balcony sound stage. Courtesty of Elan Photography.

Figure 12.5 Performer Sofia Eury preparing to read mesostics from balcony. Courtesty of Elan Photography.

Figure 12.6 Musicians John Miller, George Nickson, Samantha Bennett. Courtesty of Elan Photography.

Figure 12.7 (Almost) full cast of performers. Samantha Bennett, violin; John Miller, bass; George Nickson, percussion; Rex Willis, guitar. Vocal performers were Araya Hope Barnes (not shown), Erika Calle, Tiffany Doan, Sofia Eury, Jack Fahey, Sheila Foley, Mary K. Herman, Emma Kervel, Brian Landes (not shown), Kit Liset, Eryn McIntyre, Steve Miles, Sarah Olsen, Stephen Pinna, Tammera Race, Dianne Saunders, Emily Schenck, R. L. Silver, Allie Stachura, Leslie Townsend, Miriam Wallace, Katherine Walstrom, and Kiera Wolkins. Francis Schwartz provided a disembodied voice. Courtesy of Elan Photography.

13

"Frankenstein in Three Chords"

Elizabeth A. Fay and James McGirr

The Frankenstein myth has proved an apt vehicle for musicians beginning in the 1960s, easily available to metaphor and analogy. Musical adaptation plays heavily on the myth of the creator and creature revealed as the interplay between the artist and their unconscious, and the creation-as-monstrous. What is normal and what is abnormal when the creator's unconscious speaks; or when the creation can decide to step out of the object role; or when a composition becomes a hit and takes on a life of its own? The Frankenstein creature has so often served as a musical artist's or band's model for understanding their composing process that it has become a part of their signature sound or look, as is true for Aerosmith and the Edgar Winter Group; for others it served as their only hit, as was the case for Bobby "Boris" Pickett's 1962 "Monster Mash."

Beginning with an analysis of "My Own Version of You," in which Bob Dylan's composing process is overtly compared to fashioning another person, this chapter will explore popular music by bands such as Electric Frankenstein, Iced Earth, and The New York Dolls; songs such as "Teenage Frankenstein" and "Feed My Frankenstein" by Alice Cooper; top hits by bands like the Edgar Winter Group and Aerosmith; Richard Campbell's *Frankenstein: The Metal Opera*; lesser-known musical adaptations such as the Canadian *Frankenstein, The Musical*; and dance-related music such as techno dance music, and productions such as the Royal Opera House's ballet *Frankenstein*. These musical interpretations of the Frankenstein myth—creator and creature, passion and destruction, love and hate—raise the emotional force of these very human but also often very monstrous relationships and urges, to a greater experiential degree for audiences than reading Shelley's novel might produce. To illustrate the interconnections between these various forms of musical intervention in the Frankenstein myth, and the serious artistry that underlies them regardless of genre (with the exception, perhaps, of strictly commercial music such as ad jingles or "spooky" Halloween songs, and even this may be too broad a stricture), one seemingly unconnected popular work may be helpful.

This illustrative example is the Beatles' 1968 animated film *Yellow Submarine*. The relationship between popular music, the Frankenstein myth, and either overt or underlying serious artistry has long been entangled. Where the art is parodic, as in this film, it can also be covertly serious or be seriously good as in Bobby "Boris" Pickett's "Monster Mash." Although *Yellow Submarine* was, for the most part, a vehicle for the band's music, it contains a scene in which a Frankenstein monster drinks a potion and turns into John Lennon. It is a moment of assemblage whose connection to the Frankenstein myth can't be ignored, nor its combination of parody and serious art; the depiction is less a transformation than an indication of the two heads' reversibility, Lennon back into Frankenstein. It's a kind of "my monster, myself" theme that most treatments of the Frankenstein myth engage. The film has been praised by John Lasseter for making animation once again an art form for adult audiences, as it had been at the birth of cinema.[1] The artistry of the Beatles' pop music (including such masterful songs as "Nowhere Man" and "Lucy in the Sky with Diamonds"), combined with the serious art underlying the animation, is subtly echoed in the Frankenstein/Lennon amalgamation. We can find the same effective entanglement of music, myth, and art in Dylan's own Frankenstein song.[2]

One of the most recent contributions to the body of musical works in league with the Frankenstein myth is Bob Dylan's "My Own Version of You," from his 2020 album *Rough and Rowdy Ways*. This is a complex song that has already garnered its own Wikipedia page, with the song's embodiment of the Frankenstein myth the first aspect of the song the entry notes.[3] Although the entry insists Dylan adapted Mary Shelley's *Frankenstein* for his lyrics, Dylan's references to other, often much older, myths indicates that his real interest lies in a kind of cultural mythopoetics. In mythopoetics, the artwork works with myth to create a new or a variant myth; in Dylan's case he weaves myths together to create the lyrical body. The song's body, though, is very much an assemblage, but not one resembling the creature's very serious, and seriously intended, creaturely body. Rather, it is a pastiche, a musical piece that openly imitates other artists such as Shelley, but with a satirical bent—a slant Dylan is much given to. Although the Wikipedia entry describes the song as "darkly comical," that description aligns Dylan's masterful lyrics and haunting harmonies with the more typical punk and rock treatments of the Frankenstein myth such as Electric Frankenstein's album *How to Make a Monster* or the musical howling in Phish's "Frankenstein." Instead, the lyrics of "My Own Version of You" contain a deeper critique of the creative act, whether musical, fictional, or cultural, and therefore offer a way to understand why Shelley's novel—or rather, the myth it birthed—could be an important inspiration for both popular and classical musical composers, and why audiences are drawn to performances of these works.

"My Own Version of You" is a masterful adaptation of the Frankenstein myth in that it deliberately takes on the creator role, rather than the more musically favored "monster" identity. What does it mean to be a Victor Frankenstein, enacting the business of creation as an intentional assemblage? Just as Victor rummages through charnel houses and butcher stalls for body parts, Dylan's narrator meditates on the collecting of parts required for lyrical and musical composition. It is an artistic process characteristic of Dylan's work generally that one scholar puts in the artistic genre of collage.[4] Highlighting the process of assemblage as a kind of theft, the narrator implicitly compares Victor's theft of body parts (a foot here, a femur there, a heart somewhere else) to his own stolen goods. In 78 lines of poetry Dylan weaves a story of mythic stature and the very human deeds and emotions that underlie and even belie cultural myths. (Dylan is no stranger to myth: according to one scholar, his album

Blonde on Blonde epitomizes his mythic immersion.[5]) The very first verse takes on the pernicious ground of all art, the appropriation of an object in order to produce a "subject." "I'll bring someone to life, is what I wanna do/ I wanna create my own version of you" he croons. In bringing the dead to life to replace "you" as an identifiable person with his own "version," a substitutive interpretation of the object (the beloved, the artist's model, the person in the street), the secret is out: art kills. Moreover, artistic creation starts with already dead elements. It's a death-creation-death scenario that Mary Shelley's novel literalizes in that Victor's dead-body-part creation kills his family including Victor himself, and then finally commits suicide. The lyrics make this all too clear, with the first lines of the first stanza explaining that the narrator has been spending the last half year "visiting morgues and monasteries/ Looking for the necessary body parts/ Limbs and livers and brains and hearts" in order to create his own version of "you."

In one stroke, this transparent association of himself with Victor Frankenstein pokes Petrarch's sonnets and the Petrarchan tradition in the ribs: Petrarch declares his love for a Laura who is absent, inaccessible, and therefore unable to represent herself. He makes love to his own version of her, in Dylan's quiet joke, and the narrator openly states that he's going to do this too. The "you" of the song has been absent, even perhaps betrayed his affection:

> Well, it must be the winter of my discontent
> I wish you'd've taken me with you wherever you went
> They talk all night and they talk all day
> Not for a minute do I believe anything they say
> I'm gon' bring someone to life, someone I've never seen
> You know what I mean, you know exactly what I mean.

And we do: instead of an untrustworthy real "you" the narrator/creator intends to create an obedient, reliable version of her. Yet, what parent or artist hasn't had similar delusions? Except this is not a deluded narrative voice; the slyly ironic lyrics imply that every artist aims to create something that will "come to life" and stand on its own, but in truth the artistic creation objectifies life and speaks for its "subject."

Suddenly the third stanza veers into gangster films, with "Scarface Pacino and Godfather Brando" suggesting a murderous rage, an intense jealousy that Shelley identifies with the creature, not with Victor Frankenstein. With this shift we understand that the narrator understands that the "my monster/ myself" theme is a psychology that can be applied to any creative agent, and that loving itself can be a destructive act if the intended "creation" doesn't live up to the lover's or artist's ideals. Conversely, if the created thing can't see or act for itself ("Can you look at my face with your sightless eyes?/ Can you cross your heart and hope to die?") its robot-like being will protect the creator ("If I do it up right and put the head on straight/ I'll be saved by the creature that I create"). Now instead of jealousy the "I" expresses a pathetic need for protection against his own rage and ability to kill into art. But how satisfying will this partner then be? It needs to have a more human though obedient quality, something along the lines of what Victor had intended his creature would have: "I'll bring someone to life, someone for real/ Someone who feels the way that I feel." Creations, of course, even of the robotic kind, turn out to have their own encounters with the world that cannot be predetermined or pre-scripted.

Finally, the narrator vows "I study Sanskrit and Arabic to improve my mind/ I wanna do things for the benefit of all mankind." These are the last direct references to Shelley's *Frankenstein* for several stanzas of "My Own Version of You," but they pave the way for Dylan's meditation on how cultural myths and beliefs allow us to delude ourselves.

The first several critical stabs at "My Own Version of You" have taken the song to be a parodic representation of Dylan's own songwriting process, which has long intrigued critics. Tony Attwood, in a piece for *Untold Dylan*, expands on this:

> He is quite clear; he's doing a Victor Frankenstein, but he's also having fun, getting his own back at all those critics who have labelled him and dissected his songs... But now Bob does have a chance to go back and reverse the moment from December 1965 when everyone wanted to know where he got his ideas from and how he saw himself... The opening is fun, a slight misquote from *Richard III* but an exact quote of John Steinbeck's last novel, the tale of fallen aristocracy. And if we look at the lyrics from the point of view of the old man looking back, while the poet considers all those billions of words written about his works just wishing that the silly scribblers had actually LISTENED to what he was singing, and maybe understood a little more.[6]

Critical commentaries, as Attwood points out, are often just declarative statements about where a line or image is borrowed/stolen/misquoted from. One would never say Victor Frankenstein had misappropriated a blood vessel or organ for his creature: he was experimenting with "materials." If the lyrics are a way of getting back at critical misappropriation through claims of sources or meanings, the song accomplishes far more. In weaving its adapted materials and mythic references it frames its own myth of creation, a mythopoetics that is at once pastiche and original. We have Trojan women, Julius Caesar, the Crusades and Freud and Marx, to say nothing of a burning hell, the wild west, the Apostles, the willow tree and the cypress tree.[7] Myths, legends, and the great men of history are all woven together into an act of creation: "I can see the history of the whole human race/ It's all right there, it's carved into your face." This "you" is not the unavailable object nor the uncompliant creation: it is a mythopoetic creation that contains the spirit of humanity. Indeed, "You've got what they call the immortal spirit."

Impressionistically, "My Own Version of You" has a lugubrious tonality, somewhere between a ballad and an elegy, but the heavy repetition of the simple chord structure feels more dirge-like. Musically the song is more sophisticated than this suggests and, as is typical for Dylan, highly referential. In essence, the song is a minor key blues with a couple of interesting twists. The triplet-based feel and minor key are reminiscent of "I Put a Spell on You" by Screamin' Jay Hawkins and others: casting spells and using love potions musically suggests the elements of alchemy and scientific "magic" of Shelley's novel, and is a sly poke at the fantasy aspect of creating or transforming another person to one's own liking. The song's key feature is the four-note descending bass lines (tetrachords) under the blues harmonies; the tetrachords can be understood as partial scales. Beginning with a tonic of C#, the progression movement is downward C#-B-Bb-A, then up to F#-E-Eb-D, with a pattern of whole step—half step—half step. It then descends chromatically from the tonic C#-C-B-Bb and finally stays on A for an irregular phrase length. The meter can be heard in 12/8 with an occasional truncated measure of 9/8. This kind of feel is very typical of blues and rhythm and blues of the 1950s and 1960s and is in keeping with Dylan's use of and allusion to older forms. However, the song is more complicated than this. Within this modified blues form, what is perhaps most striking is that the use of descending four-note tetrachords in the bass refers to the much older forms of *chaconne* and *passacaglia*, forms that were popular through the sixteenth and seventeenth centuries that involved repeating bass lines underneath an upper harmonic structure.[8] The four-note descending motif in a minor key is especially characteristic of this kind of form. The musical referentiality is in keeping with Shakespearean references in the lyrics such as "Well, it must be the winter of my discontent"; additionally, it adds to the dramatic, gothic atmosphere of the song.

In both his lyrics and musical composition of "My Own Version of You," Dylan simultaneously invokes cultural myths in his lyrics and uses musical traditions and references to create a sophisticated and sly parody of the organ instrumentals and other musical "horror" effects of the Frankenstein and Dracula movies from the 1930s and 1940s. This element of serious artistry interwoven with the parodic is common to so much of the musical response to the Frankenstein myth, particularly in popular music. As a band name, Electric Frankenstein already makes this point, and this band uses comic book album covers and album titles such as *How to Make a Monster* to put their punk rock countercultural aesthetic out front.

Electric Frankenstein's music combines punk rock, heavy metal, and hard rock for a sound that makes lyrics necessarily simple, or beside the point (many of their songs are instrumentals). This works well with Frankenstein-themed songs where the howling of the instrumental solos, a technique Phish showcased for their late 1970s song "Frankenstein," resembles the mewing and sounds of rage characteristic of Boris Karloff's portrayal of the creature. In their music videos and in concerts they substitute film footage from early Frankenstein and other monster movies for complex or nuanced lyrics. In this respect Electric Frankenstein's aesthetic method might seem to oppose Dylan's approach to the Frankenstein myth, but underlying both is an effective intermixing of artistry and parody. In their "I'm Not Your (Nothing)" music video, film footage from James Whale's 1931 *Frankenstein* and 1935 *Bride of Frankenstein* is projected in short bursts, aslant or otherwise distorted, and achronologically to disrupt any narrative, whereas in their "Action High" music video there is a repeated motif of a Dracula opening his coffin and beginning to rise up. In videos and as stage performance enhancement for concerts, these film clips are inserted or shown randomly, cutting across each other or looped in fast-paced segments so that the visual is in sync with the music. In videos it can be interlaced with close ups of rapid-fire electric guitar work or hectic singing into the mic, as if the electricity that is stimulating artificial life is exactly what is powering the artifactual film life and, at the same time, what is behind the band members' frenetic musicianship. The band, in other words, is another Frankensteinian production, another artifice with destructive tonalities. The repeated lines "you're telling me it's raining/while you're pissing down my back" is nearly all the lyrics there are to "I'm Not Your (Nothing)," for instance, whereas in the album *How to Make a Monster* it isn't until the third song that we get the simplest of lyrics, with the first two songs being entirely instrumental. It's almost as if the "monster" hasn't gotten the hang of words yet, but that's unimportant because violent music and visuals are the real communication. This, in itself, is a resonant commentary on how "real" humans in Mary Shelley's novel insisted on understanding the creature, with only a few more cultivated characters such as M. De Lacey or Captain Walton giving him credit for intelligence and sophisticated understanding.

Two bands in particular paved the way for Electric Frankenstein with songs that further cemented the association between violence and the "abnormal" in the Frankenstein myth (riffed on in Mel Brooks' *Young Frankenstein*, with the Abby Normal brain used for the creature instead of the "normal" one): The Edgar Winter Group and Alice Cooper. The progressive rock Edgar Winter song "Frankenstein," released as a single and appearing on their 1972 album *They Only Come Out at Night*, was an enormous success. In the US it was the top billboard song for an entire week and was near the top of Canadian and British song charts, gaining global recognition soon after. Purely instrumental (and the only instrumental on the album), the song has multiple jams, with the violence relayed by both the music and the finale interplay by Winter of amplifier feedback and frenetic synthesizer keyboard playing.[9] The Recording Industry Association of America (RIAA) certified the song gold on June 19, 1973. The band, like Victor, didn't know what they had on their hands, originally releasing "Frankenstein" as the B-side to another song.[10] Radio listeners (unlike the villagers in the environs of Ingolstadt and Geneva) immediately loved the song, bombarding disc jockeys with requests. In fact, the song's name was unintentional, its working title being entirely different ("The Double Drum Song"). The band changed the title because, when recorded, the song originally had so many jams that it had to be cut and spliced together multiple times, until the track seemed abnormal, sutured, a monstrous Frankenstein body.[11] However, like Whale's 1931 *Frankenstein* film, the Edgar Winter Group's "Frankenstein" was a major addition to the body of Frankenstein adaptations and appropriations. *Rolling Stone* gives it seventh place in its list of all-time top rock instrumentals.[12]

Alice Cooper's approach was different in terms of use of both stagecraft and lyrics to make direct connections to the Frankenstein myth. Cooper's abnormal goth persona makes him the perfect musician to offer up "Teenage Frankenstein" (1986) and "Feed My Frankenstein" (1991). This last song, from the album *Hey Stoopid* was included in the film "Wayne's World," and features a Halloween-esque stage set and backdrop. The sadomasochistic elements of the performance (Cooper in black leather, using his whip to strike himself in the genital region toward the end of the song), and metal music, are accompanied by lyrics that suggest "I'm gonna eat ya!"; "I'm hungry for love/ and I'm gonna eat ya!"; "I'm hungry for love/ and it's feedin' time!" Alice Cooper's high camp, made part of the parody of *Wayne's World*, is belied by the music itself which exhibits dazzling guitar work and a constant percussive pounding. The comic-book quality of the stage set, combined with (in the movie) the adolescent fantasies unfolding in *Wayne's World*, belong to the cathexis of Victor's aspirations and adolescence. Phil

Hammon's rock album *Frankenstein Baby*, has for its title song a story about creator and creature that seems an adolescent's fantasy. In this it doesn't fit into the model I've been working with of serious musical or visual art combined with parody in treating the Frankenstein myth, but the lyrics reflect, at a basic level, the concept behind Dylan's "My Own Version of You." The difference is that, like Victor Frankenstein, the lyric I in Hammon's song seems unwilling to grant his creature subjecthood: "Cuz she's just my Frankenstein baby/
Made it the way I want her":

'Cuz I got this creature that I built myself
I put it together one bit at a time
I think she's really sexy
I ask you sincerely
Just what do you think?

The "baby" is both a girlfriend ("But I will always love her,/ . . . If you knew what it took/ to get her heart"), an "it" and a sex toy—object and subject both, with a bit of a mind of her own.

Dylan's creature is more complex: ungendered, the "version of you" could be either, and the subject-object status is equally undeclared. All options are at play, all are questioned in this encounter with mythopoesis. Hammon's simple lyrics, by contrast, are much more of a sex dream, but the music is where the complexity lies. Dylan's complex lyrics are accompanied by a simplified presentation of the actually quite sophisticated composition, and a deadpan delivery that is more in keeping with Shelley's novel. They register a dispassionate tone and suppressed anger that aligns with the narrative distance in the novel that, except in Victor's and the creature's worst rages, keeps the violence tamped down. Dylan's lyrics and music contrast sharply with the hard-hitting, in-your-face presentation of the song "Frankenstein" by the gender-bending New York Dolls in their eponymous first album. The full-frontal assault of the song and its delivery correlates to the ferocity of Electric Frankenstein's music and the violence of Hammon's lyrics. Shouted into the mic, the lyrics provide an exchange between subjectivity and objecthood, between recrimination and rage. The "monster" that is the song's subject is New York City in the 1970s, a crime- and drug-ridden metropolis in which it was literally dangerous to be alive. "We're asking you as a person/ Is it a crime, is it a crime/ For you to fall in love in with Frankenstein" the lyrics ask, and then continue with a violent thrust:

You're gonnna get it when Frankenstein gets home
I'm gonna shout about
I'm gonna scream about, I'm gonna shout about it, bitch about it, scream about it
. . .
My name is Frankenstein, Frankenstein
Frankenstein, Frankenstein
You're gonna get it, you're gonna get it
You're gonna get it from Frankenstein.

The threat of the monstrous is there, and eerily the threat shifts back and forth from the city as Frankenstein to the subjective "I," while the "you" returns to the victim position that Dylan's lyrics pick up on.

The Rocky Horror Picture Show, a cult classic that connects Alice Cooper's campy stage theatrics and the New York Dolls' play on what the real monster might be, bears mentioning for its twist on the creator-monster theme. The Victor equivalent, Dr. Frankenfurter, is the freaky character and the monster he creates is not grotesque or horrifying but a handsome, Chippendale-style male model. Musically it fits with Cooper's parodic hard rock style of Alice Cooper as well as the Dolls' hard look at what constitutes the monstrous. One of the ways pop music converses with the Frankenstein myth is the easy applicability of creaturely life to artistic products, whether songs and albums or musical instruments. For instance, the Ramones called their best-known live album, *It's Alive*. Similarly, the Frankenstein theme has been applied to the solid body electric guitar itself, as epitomized in the work of Leo Fender. An industrial designer rather than a luthier, Fender's vision was for an instrument that could be broken down into parts, any one of which could be easily replaced in case of breakage or failure. An entire industry has arisen around replacement parts, with enthusiasts cobbling together new instruments from the parts of older pre-existing ones. Eddie Van Halen's famous red-white-black striped guitar is one such instrument and was even named "Frankenstein" by him. Eric Clapton was famous for assembling his "Blackie" and "Brownie" Stratocasters from the parts of various older ones, and today such instruments are popularly referred to as "Frankenstrats." And the late John Entwhistle, bassist of The Who, after swapping one Precision bass neck onto the body of another, resulting in a particularly good-sounding and resonant instrument, is said to have declared, "It's alive!!!"

Monstrous life has become a staple of the times. The punk rock band Clutch has the song "Frankenstein" on their fifth album, *Pure Rock Fury*. The music this quartet has produced is a mix of punk, metal, the sound of Led Zeppelin, and Nu Metal (alternative metal). Known for their haunting, guttural vocals, as well as an unremitting percussive quality, Clutch's Frankenstein contribution bears some resemblance to that of Electric Frankenstein. The lyrics, similarly, are inconsequential compared to the music, and have little connection to the Frankenstein myth. The only overt reference is in the refrain, "How would you like to dine à la frankenstein?/ downtown they're giving them away/ downtown they're giving them!" An overt commentary on "frankenstein" or GMO food, the song also suggests the ways in which we internalize monstrosity. Like Victor, agribusinesses that produce GMO produce are playing a divine role: if Victor is the "Modern Prometheus," agribusinesses are pretending to be Mother Nature: "Oh hey there mama nature why do you keep on shooting/ us that look?/ no, no we did not take it! I swear we were only/ borrowing the book!"

In a more intricate metal interpretation of the Frankenstein myth that has resonances to the punk rock and metal songs discussed above, there is Richard Campbell's *Frankenstein: The Metal Opera*. Originally, this work was Campbell's 2012 concept album; the music is a combination of progressive rock and metal that generates the same kind of hyperbolic intensity of Electric Frankenstein or the New York Dolls, but without the violent singing. Like these works, Campbell's opera also relies on the

Hollywood film and comic book variations on the Frankenstein myth, but unusually it is also tightly engaged with Shelley's novel. The lyrics were written by both Campbell and Carol Pestridge, for whom *Frankenstein* was not, incidentally, a favorite novel. Through a variety of partnerships, the album expanded to small-venue staged productions, and then to a full theatrical production with the book or script written by Pestridge, and performed in London in 2014.[13] With a creature whose make-up makes his artifice both more obviously horrible and torturous (bloody scars and sutures all over his head and face), and the inclusion of Justine's story (nearly always left out of any adaptation of the novel), this opera offers a tremendously insightful interpretation of both the novel and the Frankenstein myth. The band accompanying the opera singers is on stage, making it impossible to ignore the incongruity of Shelley's story and metal music. The costumes recall film versions of Shelley's novel, with Victor in surgical dress that looks especially comic-book derived, and violently dramatized scenes of the surgery itself (complete with the huge electricity lever) that has resonance with the usage of film clips in Electric Frankenstein's concerts and music videos. Again, the references are complex and interwoven, with the parodic commentary reserved for treating the ethical questions of the Frankenstein story. Elizabeth, for instance sings to Victor of Justine's innocence ("She is no more a killer than you or I"), but only after Victor has sung of his inability to know any more "The line between what is right or wrong." In a *Washington Post* review, the correlation between progressive metal and gothic tales is the real key to the opera's success:

> "Anybody that listens to that soundtrack becomes obsessed with it. It is very strange," says Melissa Baughman, one half of the husband-and-wife duo behind the rock-musical-focused Landless Theatre Company.
>
> That obsession is what made Frankenstein the perfect subject for a prog-metal composer. The genre requires a particular meticulousness and dedication of its musicians that parallel the mad scientist's.
>
> "Prog metal is intense, very calculated music," says Baughman, who considers herself a lifelong metalhead. "It seems like a weird combination, but actually I think it's a perfect marriage."[14]

Progressive metal, in its obsessive and meticulous qualities, identifies another way that *Frankenstein* provides thematic linkages and opportunities for artists to use the myth that developed out of it to create commentary, critique, or a query into current cultural conditions in more sophisticated ways. Although the element of parody mixed with serious artistry remains, here that is raised to a more frenzied, yet deliberate interpretation from Dylan's slow-paced blues rendition. Nevertheless, the question of subject and object relationality remains primary: who is an "I" and which "you" is not also a fully-subjectivized "I"?

This is a question Lou Reed posed in multiple ways. Both the title and concept of Reed's 1972 glam rock album *Transformer* center on the reversibility of creator-creation positions, highlighting his own drag and bisexual identities. Reed's face on the cover transforms his identity; his photo, by Mick Rock, depicts him performing, but his stage make-up of white face powder and heavily made-up eyes are abstracted into a black-and-white Warhol style image, but one that evokes the Hollywood Frankenstein image.[15] That photo has been parodied and altered to look even more evocative of Karloff's Frankenstein head for t-shirts, merchandise and various publications. Reed continued to toy with the Frankenstein myth in "Power and Glory" from his album *Magic and Loss*. In this song he imagines his cancer-ridden friend up on the laboratory table, receiving radiation treatments in a scene that feels like a Frankenstein horror movie: "Great bolts of lightning lighting up the sky/ As the radiation flowed through him/ He wanted all of it." As this song makes clear, Reed's approach to the Frankenstein myth avoids out-and-out parody by insisting on its tragic aspects as well as its camp effects.

Artists have been quick to raise the element of parody to a higher level, as in Andy Warhol's 1973 film *Flesh for Frankenstein*. The BBC production of *Frankenstein's Wedding... Live in Leeds*, performed and filmed live at Kirkstall Abbey on March 19, 2011, may at first seem less parodic than Warhol's film since, like the *Metal Opera*, it was also an adaptation of Shelley's novel. However, it was directed by Colin Teague who has also directed *Dr. Who*; in addition, using "the blackened ruin" of Kirkstall Abbey as a backdrop for the performance space pointedly heightens the gothic atmosphere, making the production in keeping with the dark gothic spaces of James Whale's early Hollywood Frankenstein movies.[16] Involving acting, music, dance and light and film projection, Teague's vision was for a highly experiential engagement with Shelley's story: "The audience will be at the very heart of this event. Not only will we be asking them to don their favourite wedding attire, they will be integral to the mass celebratory wedding dance."[17] The story is updated, with the creature fleeing to live on the Leeds streets, and the wedding is that of Victor and Elizabeth—but the creature returns and in vengeance for Victor's failure to produce a mate for him, begins to murder the wedding guests one by one. This offers a resonant and appropriately gothic touch if audience members are also "wedding guests." Indeed, the wedding dance scene involved thousands of Leeds' citizens.[18] Although this participatory component is campy, creating the parodic element (large numbers of the audience were dressed as or were goths), the intent of the production was serious. The original music, a mixture of orchestral and electronic sound, was also serious, and an essential part of this experimental, immersive production. It included older, more traditional music and musical forms, and was played and sung by a band, an orchestra, a choir, and individual singers. A massive endeavor, *Frankenstein's Wedding* offers an expansive vision that is an effective contrast to the small scale *Frankenstein: The Metal Opera*.

The 1993 *Frankenstein, The Musical*, a Canadian production by Tim Ryan and musical collaborators Chris Wynters and Scott Peters, veers in a rather different direction but, like Campbell's metal opera, utilizes its locality for effect. The premise is that a man, Victor, is driving from Calgary to Edmonton with a carload of body parts: multiple heads, fingers and lots of gore. Already we have assemblage and parody; the seriousness is the nearness of the threat, which is no longer historically or geographically distant but is (for the Calgary and Edmonton audiences) right here right now. First performed in 1992 with such a small cast that Chris Wynters not only played both Victor and the creature but also sang most of the show's fourteen songs. For the 1993 production, according to Wynters and Peters, the piece "has been surgically enhanced for this new incarnation. Unlike Shelley's monster, the soul was always there; it's the limbs that needed adjustment."[19] Much like Victor's frenzied work in the attic laboratory of Shelley's novel, Wynters explains that "Last time it was put together in 10 days, from first rehearsal till opening night ... I can't believe we actually did it." Wynters and Peters rock band The Brave and Foolish had accompanied the 1992 slapdash production, with many of the songs set to poems by Percy Bysshe Shelley, suggesting both the original assumption of reviewers that he had written *Frankenstein*, and the critical opinion that Victor is a portrait of Percy. That this serious element underlies the parody and the comedy of the musical again points to the general ways that musicians from the 1960s to 2020s have responded to and adapted the Frankenstein myth and show no sign of stopping.

Finally, the connection between the Frankenstein myth with dance reveals itself at both subliminal and explicit levels. Explicitly, we have productions such as London's Royal Ballet's 2016 *Frankenstein* at the Royal Opera House. Subliminally, we have the long history of techno music's connection with the myth of Victor's stitched-together monster. In-between, disability productions and dance that use the "monster walk" adapted from Hollywood films provide visual reminders of how *Frankenstein* lays bare both techno's dislocations and art's interpretation of the human as something more harmoniously balanced than it actually is.

Mark McCutcheon argues that the early days of hardcore techno disc jockeying, as practiced in Toronto by DJ Capital J during the late 1990s, for instance, were enabled by a Frankenstein metaphor for sampling.[20] Citing Simon Reynolds' description of early hip hop's invention of sampling as "like Frankenstein's monster, funk-limbs crudely bolted together," McCutcheon claims that the Frankenstein creature is *the* underlying metaphor for techno dance music's method of appropriation (sampling and file sharing), revolutionary mood, and disarticulation of a proprietary recording industry.[21] For audio engineers in the 1980s, sampling was a "dehumanizing" practice because it made the music seem nonhuman, but also threatened to eliminate their jobs; it is an adjective central to the Frankenstein mythos.[22] Because of the long history of technology as being dehumanizing and monstrous, Shelley's novel provided the perfect visual metaphor for both aspects of engineered production. By the time DJ Capital J was performing in Toronto, the subliminal connection to Frankenstein was so integral to sampling that his signature piece for his sets was a mashup of a recognizable tidbit from the *Star Wars* theme by John Williams and "a jump up bass hook and a self-promotional vocal loop."[23] This is Victor and the creature put together. But techno music also promotes a particular kind of dance movement that suggests mechanism and self-alienation. Disability performance desublimates the Frankenstein reference, making the mode of locomotion the central piece rather than the music: robotic and crip collide in the locomotion peculiar to the Frankenstein myth.

Disability as performance, the highpoint of Mel Brooks' 1974 *Young Frankenstein* in the "Puttin' on the Ritz" song and dance number by Peter Boyle and Gene Wilder, is an increasingly more visible reminder of *Frankenstein*'s seminal critique of how society ostracizes the "abnormal" in its search for a homeostatic "norm" that makes deviation seem threateningly alien. In 1975, while working on a song for their album *Toys in the Attic*, Aerosmith members struggled to come up with lyrics and a title for the music that would become the song "Walk This Way." At a point when they were stuck, the band (who were recording in NYC at Planet Record) went to Times Square to see *Young Frankenstein*. Joe Perry, who stayed behind at the studio, remembers that when the others returned, "[t]hey were laughing about Marty Feldman greeting Gene Wilder at the door of the castle and telling him to follow him. 'Walk this way,' he says, limping, giving his stick to Wilder so he can walk that way, too. While all this was going on, Jack stopped and said, 'Hey, "walk this way" might be a great title for the song.'" But the lyrics were composed by Steven Tyler the next day on Planet Record's cement wall on the top floor with pencils—a version of Victor's lab notebook that the creature later finds and reads to discover the story of his creation. "When Steven returned, we ran down the song. His lyrics were so great. Being a drummer, he likes to use words as a percussion element. The words have to tell a story, but for Steven they also have to have a bouncy feel for flow. Then he searches for words that have a double entendre, which comes out of the blues tradition." Percussive hits are characteristic of Frankenstein music, as is the assemblage of blues, rock and rap that helped make this song a top-ten hit in the US. Moreover, the song helped create Aerosmith's identifying sound:

> I wanted my guitar to sound like an electric razor. For 'Walk This Way,' I used a late-'50s Stratocaster Tobacco Sunburst with a stand-alone Ampeg V4 amp on top with a Marshall 4-by-12 speaker cabinet on the bottom. I also used a Gibson Maestro Fuzz-Tone to give the notes a little distortion. At some point, Steven suggested the double-kick drum, which gave us our trademark sound.

Disability makes the top-ten and insinuates its way into a major band's signature sound.

Angela Smith uses Aerosmith's hit song to make her point, putting together the way Frankenstein films portray the creature's locomotion with the more recent filmic "zombie ambulation" to discuss disability performance.[24] Frankenstein films intensify the abnormal conditions of creating artificial life through added characters such as Victor's lab assistant who, from the beginning, is disabled or disfigured in some way. "The disabled lab assistant in James Whale's 1931 film, echoed in subsequent Frankenstein movies by an array of Igors and Karls, mirrors or extends the monster's non-normative body and particularly his unusual walk."[25] This "walk," which is particular to the film and stage adaptations of Shelley's novel, including the first stage adaptation *Presumption*, and not the agile and athletic creature of her novel. But it was Whale's 1931 film that cemented the creature's association with disability: although the script used for a good portion of the film only directs the creature to move awkwardly and with a shuffling, dragging step when first brought to life, Boris Karloff maintains this style of movement throughout. Moreover, his style of walking clearly resembles that of polio victims of that era.[26] Because Frankenstein films were acted by able-bodied actors, their performance of disability is its own kind of monstrosity.[27] The shift from a monstrous locomotion to a campy, positive affect took place with Bobby Pickett's "Monster Mash" hit, and the accompanying dance moves for a collective, participatory experience that has affinities with dancing to techno music. The "monster walk" of the Frankenstein films, adapted into a dance routine ("Putting on the Ritz") in Mel Brooks' *Young Frankenstein* as Smith points out, and acculturated mid-century by "Monster Mash" and toward the end of the twentieth century by techno dance music, provides a way for nondisabled individuals to physically experience disabled locomotion. The dance move aestheticizes as well, which may well be the point of Michael Jackson's zombie walk in "Thriller," which also draws on the same polio-inspired movement. This development from monstrous to aesthetic remediates the more standard enactment of the Frankenstein story through a use of stark contrasts between the "abnormal" and "normal," disablement and balletic precision, techno-enhanced and "natural."

As the last performance surveyed in this chapter, the Royal Opera House's 2016 ballet *Frankenstein* both concludes this last section on music and dance and sums up the musical works surveyed here. Despite coming from a more traditional genre, the ballet includes the elements of assemblage, serious art, and parody that we have seen throughout the chapter. Reviewer Luke Jennings reports in *The Guardian* that the dancing was "superb, the sets magnificent," but that choreographer Liam Scarlett "squanders" Shelley's novel.[28] The ballet is "overwhelmed with exposition," so that extraneous scenes are "ludicrous" and sentimental: "The Frankenstein household's dancing domestic staff are . . . contextually ludicrous—Shelley's novel contains not a suggestion of sentimentality . . . The same is true of a tavern scene in Ingolstadt, featuring jaunty harlots." Similarly. the musical score by Lowell Liebermann "washes unmemorably over the action, offering the dancers little opportunity for sophisticated phrasing. It does, however, have the advantage that it can be freely cut . . . ." These criticisms take the ballet seriously, but the suggestion that the music can be cut freely, sutured back together, made more "memorable" intimates it already has a monstrous body ready for a bit more surgery, a few more reminders of its Frankensteinian nature. Jennings might have taken Scarlett's and Liebermann's interpretation as their own parodic intervention in a myth of monstrous creation. For instance, he complains that the traditional romantic dream dance is subverted here as a "cat and mouse" nightmare in which the creature, "dancing between ironic courtesy and visceral savagery," plays with Elizabeth; he then complains it "is pure gothic." Apparently here the music was appropriate to the gothic interpretation nearly all the works we've discussed have adopted. Giving the ballet its due in the now seven decade-long history of musical adaptations and interventions in the Frankenstein myth would have given Jennings a better purchase on the ballet's version of the endlessly new ways that Shelley's story of monstrous creation still speaks to us.

14

From *Frankenstein* to Writing Sci-Fi to Collage

Margaret Hart

This chapter explores how collage and science fiction are brought together through creative practice and examines a series of artworks created from a process involving both. Mary Shelley's *Frankenstein* was a favorite novel of mine in my youth, and the book began a lifelong fascination with science fiction. I loved the mix of science and ethical issues Shelley raised and the social questions about "What does it mean to be human?" and "What makes us human?" Just as adolescence makes one wonder, "What on earth is going on with me?", adulthood reframes these issues to question our humanity in the face of complex social and ethical problems. Since my first introduction to Shelley's medical, marvelous monster, I have turned to science fiction for its mix of science (often presented as probable) and imagination, allowing it to help form my sense of humanity.

The focus of this chapter, my recent artwork, collages from the *Situated Becomings* series, explores the potential of collage, the stitching together, if you will, of components to create a new whole. Mary Shelley claimed her novel is about how the "parts of a creature might be manufactured, brought together, and imbued with a vital warmth."[1] This description could describe both Shelley's process and my collage practice. In my collage series, I create meaning by combining feminist theories of gender and science fiction with concepts of posthumanism (a rejection of traditional Western humanism). At the same time, I bring imagination rather than science to the process of "creation," striving not for a new form of human being but greater insight into the human condition. My collage practice involves physically piecing together images, text, and cultural ephemera, informed by a private science fiction writing practice. My collage work and the private science fiction writing informing the artwork are my means to achieve artwork infused with that vital warmth Shelley pursued in creating her novel.

Revealing Mear

Situated Becomings is a series of collages based on ideas I developed in my science fiction writing, which I do as a tool for exploring ideas. I created a character named Mear to explore gender, gender fluidity, and gender multiplicity. With my written text guiding the collages, the visual work addresses the intersection of gender, transformation, and technology by foregrounding Mear's ability to shift and combine genders through technology. However, Mear exists only in written work and is never fully constituted in

Figure 14.1 Margaret Hart, *Situated Becomings #8*. 2017–present. Mixed media collage. 30 x 24 in. artist-owned, Boston, Massachusetts.

the visual work to ensure their appearance remains mutable.[2] This character lives in a world where one can transition between multiple genders and gender combinations.

Thus, appearance and gender are unfixed and unclear at any point, much like Frankenstein's transmutable creature, who exists between the position of human and nonhuman in Shelley's novel. Victor Frankenstein personifies the humanistic tradition, privileging intellect and reasoned thought inherent in humans, or more specifically, in white, male, nondisabled humans. In his attempt to understand the mysteries of life, he creates an artificial human, or cyborg, a compilation of human and nonhuman parts. Through Shelley's imaginative development of the creature, she blurs the categories of human and machine, embracing the posthuman qualities of hybridity and transformation. My conception of the character Mear is a similar tool, allowing me to explore these same qualities as they relate to a posthuman gender.

The visual works began as sketches of how I envisioned the environment in which Mear exists, places loosely related to creating or making. However, as layers are added to an image and the works are more densely constructed, brief, fragmented glimpses of Mear materialize. For example, in Figure 14.1, a profile emerges from the multiple fragments combined on the right side of the image.

These collage pieces detail a method of working that contributes to a new understanding of gender, identity, and subjectivity. In their text, *A Thousand Plateaus*, philosophers Gilles Deleuze (1925–1995) and Felix Guattari (1930–1992) write about a series of becomings, a continual transforming process of deterritorialization where one moves from the position of "the other" outside of the patriarchal, white, male center to a place of inclusion and interaction. Mary Shelley's creature is an example of a subject that inhabits this othered position. His complete deterritorialization occurs as soon as he leaves the lab and starts interacting with human society. The novel chronicles his unsuccessful attempts at interaction, leaving the creature in the interstitial space between that of the other and a fully realized subject. His life thereafter is spent unsuccessfully searching for inclusion.

Deleuze and Guattari argued that, historically, man had been viewed as the center of the signifying system, the bearer of the law, so that (particularly) "becoming-woman" is a necessary step in critique. Becoming-woman is the process of acquiring a feminine, holistic consciousness, where the feminine is fundamentally tied to a representation of "the other" as a decentralized being.[3] My collage works embrace this transformation or movement into a decentralized position as a feminist response to issues of gender dualism and heteronormative gendering. Mear, who informs the collage works, occupies a space between dualistic representations of gender, much like Shelley's creature, moving toward a decentralized position of multiplicity. Figure 14.1 depicts direct evidence visualizing such a shift.

The figure on the right side of the collage represents imaginative possibilities for new hybrid realities with its profile comprising an amalgam of parts—a combination of human and nonhuman elements. Male and female human body parts mix with additional robotic, organic, and scientific technology elements. The artwork also depicts the holistic consciousness of becoming-woman and posthumanism by presenting a synergy between the elements within an individual subject. This "Mear" figure is outside of the stairway space that is the background of the collage. In the doorway, an anatomical drawing of a male figure fades into the interior space. A strand of DNA connects the hybrid subject with the interior space, underscoring the collage text, which speaks of Mear's uncertainty in a time of technological change.

Figure 14.2 Margaret Hart, *Situated Becomings #2*. 2017-present. Mixed media collage. 30 x 24 in. artist-owned, Boston, Massachusetts.

Hybrids and the monstrous are linked in several of my collages discussed here. *Situated Becomings #2* (Figure 14.2) balances transformation and monstrosity. Two paper-doll cutouts, labeled Sally and Jane, are positioned within an empty industrial space with test tubes and an image of hands knitting the double helix form. An excerpt from my science fiction writing, taped into the space, suggests being more than female is beneficial. The heads of Sally and Jane are covered by, or replaced with, fragments of transparent media of vegetable forms with phallic shapes so that the figures represent a merger of genders and human and nonhuman elements.

This image, *Situated Becomings #2*, depicts perhaps monstrous transformations but nonetheless organic transformations. Each paper-doll subject is in the process of becoming something other than female. The text in the image says, "But now she looks back and realizes how limited 'she' really was," suggesting the transformation away from "she" is desirable and even advantageous.[4] The figures in the work become cyborg constructions. The two paper dolls emerge from an unfinished industrial space with fragments of test tubes and knitted DNA, suggesting the creation of life. They are connected to and part of this environment of creating. The implied relationship between the cyborg figures and their environment again reinforces the idea of a posthuman holistic and symbiotic existence between all human and nonhuman agents.

This interconnectedness and recognition of human and nonhuman agency is what philosopher Rosi Braidotti would call an affirmative ontology, where one frames the shift from humanism to posthumanism within a positive ontology.[5] In Mary Shelley's historical moment of the early nineteenth-century, machine-based industrial technology was rapidly developing. In his article, "Two Centuries of Frankenstein," writer Bret McCabe describes Shelley's novel as a source of "cautionary tales of the hubris of male scientists and monsters as metaphors for larger social anxieties."[6] With contemporary developments in technology, it would be possible to continue to reject the monstrous, as Victor Frankenstein rejects his creation. However, in my project, the monstrous—or rather the hybrid or cyborg—is embraced through narrative texts alongside scientific theories to "entangle form and material particularly such that the reader will find it difficult to maintain the perception that they are separate and discrete entities."[7] Shelley entangles scientific theories and fiction, whereas I entangle collage and science fiction in this project. Mixing disciplines and entangling ideas highlight where posthuman interconnectedness undermines hierarchical barriers and facilitates the acceptance of different forms of knowledge entangled with, rather than juxtaposed to, each other.

My project began by considering the cyborg, a constructed human form. For feminist scholar Donna Haraway, the cyborg is a metaphor for political action and theoretical inquiry. The cyborg signifies "lived social and bodily realities in which people are not afraid of their joint kinship with animals and machines, not afraid of permanently partial identities and contradictory standpoints."[8] In an era influenced by the rejection of humanism—the posthuman era—and through alternative methods of conceptualizing the human subject, we operate beyond Haraway's cyborg.

Posthumanism and its deterritorialized, interconnected positioning of the subject provide a space for envisioning multiple selves. The hybridity of human and nonhuman elements and disciplines is a path toward this prospect. The hybridity of the deterritorialized subject—Haraway's cyborg and Shelley's creature as possibilities—produce countless identities that challenge existing cultural frameworks based on dualistic thinking. Through the interconnection and inclusivity possible in a posthuman framework, a conscious "scaffolding" of technical and cultural tools is developed to disassociate ourselves and experiment with these multiple identities, live in numerous locations, and try on various personas at will.[9] I am enthralled with the hybridity in Haraway's cyborg and Shelley's creature, depicting imaginative possibilities for new subjectivities in which bodies are constructed and deconstructed in an ambiguous assemblage of nature and technology. This scaffolding embraces hybridity, built from a combination of creative endeavors, posthuman and feminist theory, technological advancements, and cultural ephemera.

Appropriation in Practice

The artworks created for this project appropriate images from popular culture, such as magazines and online sources. Therefore, I position my work within the Western art historical canon in line with other artists who use appropriation as a method for critique, commentary, and inquiry. The use of collage, assemblage, and appropriation has been critically recognized art practice since Pablo Picasso and Georges Braque first coined the term "collage" in the early twentieth century. More recently, within postmodernism, visual artists, such as Sherrie Levine, Richard Prince, and Jeff Koons, have gone so far as to exactly copy or reproduce well-known artworks or objects by others to question issues of authorship and originality.

Appropriation in the *Situated Becomings* series context is necessary to ensure a wide range of representations of human and nonhuman elements with which to work. Source images are pulled primarily from *Vogue*, Martha Stewart's *Living*, and *National Geographic* magazines and online science and technology image searches. Print magazines used in this project are rich in depictions of extreme binary gender through social coding for fashion purposes and occasionally provide playful imaginings of androgynous or unidentifiable subjects. The pictures taken from *National Geographic* magazine and the online science and technology sources allude more to nonhuman agents, such as animals and fauna of the natural world or genetic engineering and robotics of the technological world. These appropriated sources are combined with my photography and mark-making, fragments of text from my experimental science fiction writing, and digital drawings to envision new possibilities and imaginings of a posthuman gender.

My appropriation of these materials for creative means is protected by fair use laws in the United States. College Art Association, the professional organization of record in art in the United States, describes these legal protections: "Artists may employ fair use to build on preexisting works, engage with contemporary culture, or provide artistic, political, or social commentary."[10] The standard is that the work created from the appropriated material must generate new artistic meaning.

The Writing of Mear

I began writing science fiction in 2015 as a practice for developing ideas. In early 2016, the writing became more deliberate, and I decided to focus on how my writing and visual collage practice were becoming intertwined, leading to the development of the *Situated Becomings* series. The writing is done in the early morning hours in a quiet space at a desk—a place to imagine transformation and possibilities, such as Frankenstein's creature or Mear's ability to transition and combine genders—perhaps similar to how Shelley worked on her novel. The structure of this process is free form, where there are no limits on content, linearity, or word count. Full narrative scenarios from different points in the characters' lives and shorter internal musings are recorded. The central character, and one of the first to use transition technology to change and combine genders, Mear was imagined and developed early in my writing. The full text is a collection of fragmentary moments in time, presented nonlinearly, where the reader jumps from the dissolution of Mear's marriage to time spent in pretransition technology to the passing of Mear.

As in the visual works, my fiction writing is also a hybrid of literary styles. The writing is experimental, nonlinear, and speculative. This practice becomes the space where I create thought experiments asking: What would happen if people could change genders at will? How is culture affected by this technology? How do people interact with each other and the environment in such a world? Through these questions, I can envision imaginative genders, places, and interactions informed by the tenets of posthumanism: variation, multiplicity, nonhierarchical relations, fluidity, interconnectedness, and transformation.

My experimental science fiction work allows for varied gender possibilities as human biology and nonhuman forms are mixed through technology. This mixing or collaging of gender and the fluidity to move from one gender to another have social implications. Through the ability to continually transform gender, Mear confronts social constraints that do not change as quickly as technology. The character explores a world where gender is ever-changing due to a technological advancement called transition technology, which allows users to combine human and nonhuman attributes. In several vignettes, Mear must determine how to present themself to achieve the best results in their job negotiating settlements between corporations and enclaves of settlers. Mear's coworkers tend to comment on the choices Mear makes as antiquated or nostalgic. However, Mear has found that if the presentations are too experimental, those they are negotiating with bring too many conservative expectations to the conversations. In other social functions, however, Mear presents as a truly posthuman being with a mix of biological human genders and nonhuman elements. It is this place of conflict where biological, technological, and societal understandings of gender are confronted. Breaking down barriers and allowing for the agency of iterations of all subjects moves us toward an affirmative posthuman existence.

Recent technological developments in genetic research, such as the clustered regularly interspaced short palindromic repeats (CRISPR)/Cas9 first used for genome editing in 2015, have inspired the transition technology featured in my experimental science fiction writing. A National Public Radio report defined CRISPR/Cas9 technology as an elegant and powerful tool for editing genomes, allowing researchers to alter DNA sequences and modify gene function easily.[11] The applications for such technologies range from correcting genetic defects, which cause disease, to food crop modifications to fight hunger in affected regions worldwide.

That technology is employed in so many instances in our current time is both frightening and inspiring. In Mear's world and our own, the legal and ethical implications of technological advancements lag far behind, leading to real and potentially increased abuse and misuse of these technologies. In reality, CRISPR gene editing has already been performed on human subjects with some measure of success, including a man with Hunter syndrome, a disabling disease caused by the lack of enzymes needed to break down sugars. Doctors infused blood with altered genetic material and injected it into his body to modify his liver cells.[12]

The misuse of such technologies has also occurred. In November of 2018, a Chinese researcher announced he had modified the genomes of twin female embryos to be resistant to HIV. This researcher performed human trials without the support of the Chinese government or the international medical community. Many scientists and organizations, such as the Chinese Society for Cell Biology and the National Academies of Sciences, Engineering, and Medicine, spurned this research as unethical. They feel this work performed on these human subjects was unnecessary and dangerous, with the wider implications of genetic alteration of embryos still unknown.[13] Had such technologies been developed in Shelley's time, Victor Frankenstein may have been a geneticist, and his creation may have been a hybrid in more ways than just combined reanimated body parts.

The similarities between a scientist splicing genetic material to create something new in genetic engineering (or Frankenstein sewing together a human form to reanimate) and an artist creating a work of art from fragments of texts or images are worth noting. The actions of cutting and ripping apart elements, then gluing and stitching the fragments back together in each case, define collage and are transformative. Genetic engineering of human DNA, altering the physical body, is also a posthuman act. By transforming the building blocks of human biology, scientists are creating a literal posthuman material being, not unlike Shelley's hybrid creature or my character Mear, a being imagined and envisioned in this project through experimental science fiction writing and visual collage.

Collage in Context

Inserting my work into the context of feminism and visual arts joins a lineage of women artists who have addressed social and cultural problems through collage. Arguably, the leading woman from the early history of collage is German artist Hannah Höch (1889–1978). Maud Lavin's *Cut with the Kitchen Knife: The Weimar Photomontages of Hannah Höch* situates Höch's creative work and presents it as a critique of how mass media represents women. When Höch's work is read through a broader posthumanist lens focused on the representation of gender, her collage work goes beyond a feminist critique of the media's idealized woman to suggest multiple gender possibilities in various forms of becoming something other than female.

Hannah Höch was especially effective in critiquing the idea of the Weimar "New Woman" in the 1920s. A member of the Berlin Dada artist group as early as 1918, she embraced the idea that art could critique the norms of society. Höch pioneered using images from fashion magazines, a technique using photographs called photomontage,

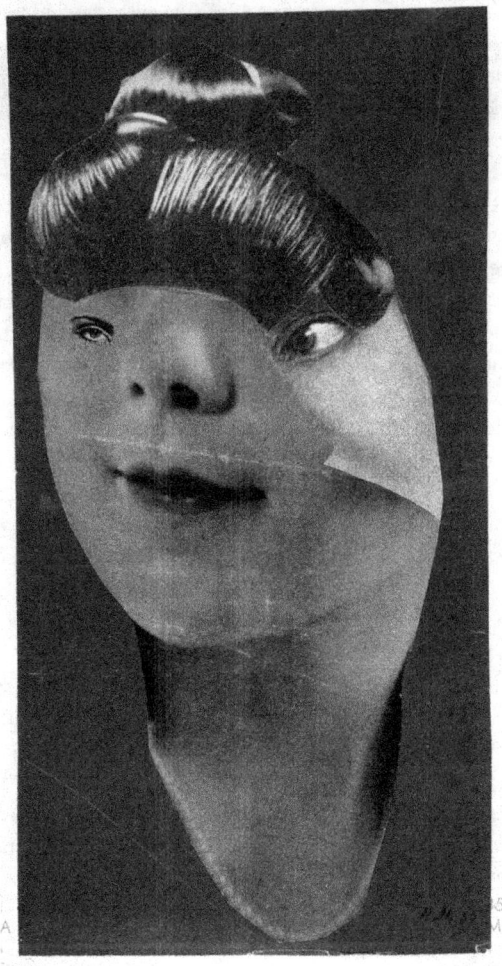

Figure 14.3 Hannah Höch, *Deutsches Mädchen (German Girl)*. 1930. Photomontage. 20.5 x 10.5 cm. Landesmuseum fur Moderne Kunst, Photographie und Architektur, Berlin.

combined with newspaper images and text. In its time, the Weimar New Woman was lauded as one of Europe's strongest women's rights movements. Still, Höch challenged many of the innately bourgeois assumptions inherent in its agenda.

Höch frequently fused bodies in her photomontages, female with male and the traditional German female with her liberated modern counterpart. Her work prods notions of the objectification and sexuality of women by depicting them as vibrant central characters, often the only ones in motion, and by reducing men to individual parts, often attached to larger female forms.[14] Her work *Deutsches Mädchen* (1930) directly challenges gender stereotypes. This piece depicts a face constructed from several magazine fragments that appear to be both male and female. The closely cropped hair juxtaposed with the pearl necklace worn by the figure creates discomfort through the inability to assign a distinct gender to the portrait. The ambiguity of the represented gender within this image hints at the becoming of imaginative gender possibilities and depictions. The subject embodies both genders simultaneously, neither fully male nor female but emerging as something else.

Collage as a politically charged practice continued into later decades. Artists in the 1950s and 1960s began embracing the rich visuals of popular culture in an attempt to emphasize the kitsch nature of these images and oppose what they saw as elitist practices of earlier art movements through a genre known as "pop art." In the 1970s, informed by feminism, gay rights, and conceptual art, women artists created a rationale of collage based on feminine subjectivity and political intentions. Women artists expanded the material base of these collages from cut paper and paint and included materials typically associated with craft, particularly textiles and other common household materials. Embracing techniques and materials from the craft realm was a political act questioning the divide between high and low art while also implying gender due to using materials linked to the domestic realm rather than the male-dominated realm of fine arts.

Miriam Schapiro began as an Abstract Expressionist painter in the 1950s and embraced collage as a feminist strategy early in her career. She was a founding member of the Feminist Art Program at the California Institute of the Arts. Schapiro began incorporating objects and found imagery into her artworks by working with women in this program. Schapiro created what she termed "femmages," collages or photomontages using techniques traditionally attributed to women's crafts, such as sewing, embroidery, or knitting. Throughout her career, Schapiro was a pioneer and champion of feminist art and helped define the collage as a feminist strategy within the arts.[15]

Imbuing the everyday with political potency is the main tenet of collage as a feminist artistic practice. Schapiro's use of fabric, wallpaper, and other domestic materials, stereotypically associated with women's work and crafts, makes her artworks part of the foundations of the feminist art historical story. In her piece *The Architectural Basis* (1978, Figure 14.4), Schapiro began the femmage by painting a formal modernist grid structure as a background. She adhered handkerchiefs and a small tablecloth she collected from women during her travels on top of this structure to spread over the rigid formal underneath, literally foregrounding the connections she forged with a community of women. In 1996, when asked about her career, Schapiro stated, "My art is an art of becoming."[16]

This statement by Schapiro is even more true than she intended. When looking at *The Architectural Basis* (1978), one can detect all the formal constructions mentioned earlier, but a tension in the work also suggests a bursting out of the structure and the development of something new. The lace and embroidered handkerchiefs float as if suspended above the grid and imply gendered forms through their function as women's objects and the craft involved in their production. In the cultural context of when this work was created, the collage can be read as exploring connections between developing feminist issues on identity and gendered craft practices. Schapiro's use of collage, or *femmage*, intentionally depicted the celebration of women's craft while highlighting the confines of such a hierarchical term and the devaluing or erasure of women's contributions to the arts in general.

Figure 14.4 Miriam Schapiro, *The Architectural Basis*. 1978. Acrylic and fabric on canvas. 80 x 78 in. Eric Firestone Gallery, Los Angeles, California.

Contemporary Western artists from the 1980s and beyond have continued to embrace the political potency of collage, recognizing it as a powerful medium to address gender and other social issues. Through traditional cut paper and paste techniques and photomontage (collage made from primarily photographic material), assemblage (collage made from three-dimensional objects), and digital collage (collage with the aid of digital imaging software), artists have exploited the medium's inherently political nature. Influenced by feminism and other social movements, women artists, such as contemporary artist Wangechi Mutu, have created collage works that critique existing social inequities.

Mutu's work redefines the female form by merging human and nonhuman fragments while addressing issues of race. She creates installations, performances, and collages with hybrid characters to address gender and racial inequality issues. She deals directly with a cyborg figure to incorporate themes of the intersection of humans and machines as well as humans and fauna. Critics place her in the Afrofuturist genre because she creates alternative realities for African peoples through imaginative science fiction strategies.[17] She intentionally creates collage works because of the political history of the medium itself. She purposefully constructs multilayered images to

Figure 14.5 Wangechi Mutu, *Family Tree (detail)*. 2012. Mixed media collage on paper. 41.28 x 31.12 cm. Nasher Museum of Art at Duke University, Durham, North Carolina.

critique social hierarchies and issues of power, particularly because these are imposed on people of color. Mutu's work reenvisions female and racial identities through playful, imaginative, and political strategies.

Perhaps it is in Mutu's work where issues of posthumanism are most evident. She consciously mixes human forms with fragments of fauna and technology throughout her work. The multiplicity of subject representations in the collages imaginatively depicts many forms of possible futures and genders. Figure 14.5 details Mutu's wall installation *Family Tree* (2012). This image is part of a group of thirteen collaged figures. In this installation, she rewrites the creation myth as female-centered, asserting a new vision of the origins of life and the cosmos. These figures represent a genealogical chart beginning with an ancestral pair followed by their children and grandchildren. They are constructed from human, animal, and machine parts, narrating trauma, colonization, hybridization, and strength themes. *Family Tree* depicts Mutu's investment in the concepts of "metamorphosis and adaption as necessary means for survival."[18]

In discussing Mutu's collages, Malik Gaines and Alexandro Segade remarked that Mutu's figures are "created in a vein similar to that with which Mary Shelley's Frankenstein constructed his monster, from a variety of abject sources—[they] are her hybrids."[19] These evoke Donna Haraway's cyborgs because they embrace technology rather than fear it. Mutu's use of human and nonhuman fragments to build new creatures in her collages and her radical reimagining of the female form suggest multiplicities of femaleness, placing her work firmly in the posthuman era.

Making and Thinking

Philosopher Rosi Braidotti builds on contemporary feminist thought and theories of becoming in *Metamorphoses: Towards a Materialist Theory of Becoming* to articulate a balance between the material act of making and the interior act of thought. In commenting on becoming, she notes, "Joining together creativity with the activity of thinking, Deleuze's work is marked by the positivity of thinking as a process of becoming."[20] I would restate this concerning my own practice as "joining together creativity with the activity of making." My collage and experimental science fiction writing are marked by the positivity of making, where creativity and making lead to imaginative outcomes as a process of becoming. In my creative practice, making is thinking, with collage as a method to layer, juxtapose, and reconfigure ideas and fragments into new forms or thoughts. This approach to thinking about one's practice relates to Braidotti's politics of affirmation: "An effort needs to be made to 'translate' the propositional content into a language that is adequate to its innovative force."[21] Braidotti argued for a new approach or language that rejects the patriarchal Eurocentric language of Western reason, and collage is a well-suited method through which one emphasizes the acts of making and transforming over the outcome: the process of becoming. Through contextual analysis of creative works and reflection on my own creative practice examples in the *Situated Becomings* series, I find that collage is "multiple, relational, and dynamic."[22] This is collage; collage is that innovative force.

Coming Full Circle

What is Frankenstein's monster? Fragments of lifeless flesh stitched together? A hybrid? A cyborg? Mary Shelley's creation is all of these things, but most definitely, he is a collage. There is political potency to be found in this collage. This novel, considered one of the first science fiction stories, influenced countless other women authors to address social and cultural issues. As Hannah Höch, Miriam Schapiro, and Wangechi Mutu have created a lineage of collage artists within which I locate my visual work, Shelley is the author who begins the lineage for women science fiction writers.

Science fiction allows for imaginative explorations of bodies and their construction. It has the capacity to provide new configurations of materialization and challenges the way we understand it.[23] Feminist fiction writers, such as Joanna Russ, Margaret Atwood, Ursula K. Le Guin, and Octavia Butler, have provided a platform for feminist gender issues within their substantial oeuvres. In contrast, more contemporary writers have expanded the field by addressing technocultural theory, queer theory, and poststructuralism issues. These writers, such as Nicola Griffith and Melissa Scott, and their work have reformulated social and cultural meanings of the gendered body in the technological age, imaginatively refashioning its very forms and molding its matter in some hypothesized future world.

Historically, feminist science fiction asked what could be done differently from the patriarchal system in a way other forms of early feminist literature did not. Most realist feminist literature has focused on how women's lives were limited and unequal to those of men. Feminist science fiction writers asked questions: What would a society based on equality look like? How would it be run, and who would make the decisions? What science and technology differences would there be? Feminist writers used the imaginative aspects of the science fiction genre to critique social stereotyping and challenge the position of women as "other" to men. Ursula K. Le Guin suggested that science fiction allows for "thought–experiments" where power structures, sexual order, and gender can be creatively inverted and altered in numerous imaginative ways.[24]

Creating these thought experiments has become part of my process as well. The relationship between visual collage and experimental science fiction in my practice is entangled and intertwined, allowing for imaginative posthumanist gender possibilities. These cyborgs, hybrids, or even monsters, are models for modes of becoming, where human and nonhuman subjects join in affirmative potentia, where one seeks new figurations and creative theoretical alternatives for existing ideas. As Rosi Braidotti writes,

> The processes of becoming–other get expressed through suitable figurations–like my nomadic subject. As such, they are no metaphors, but rather critical tools to account for the materially embedded and embodied locations and power relations. They are also creative expressions for the intensity, i.e., the rate of change, transformation or affirmation, the potentia (positive power) one inhabits.[25]

Experimental science fiction and collage are tools for the creative expression of the new figurations to which Braidotti refers. Conviction and optimism combine with transformation in the *Situated Becomings* series, making these works material examples of Braidotti's *potentia* and affirmative ontology.

On viewing the collage in Figure 14.6, one could see a monster and denounce the aesthetic value of the work, or one could be seduced by the aesthetics and embrace the imaginative possibilities for a new understanding of what it means to be human. There is a connection between the combined fragments that create the whole, a being more than or other than what it was. Science fiction and art are entangled to picture the affirmative *potentia* and the posthuman. Beginning with Mary Shelley and her statement that I quoted at the beginning of this essay, "parts of a creature might be manufactured, brought together, and imbued with a vital warmth," I have tried to bring full circle the layers and influences joined together in a body of visual work.[26] The vital warmth in my *Situated Becomings* series is an affirmative stance on the posthuman and the possibilities that it provides for expanding our understanding of gender.

Figure 14.6 Margaret Hart, *Situated Becomings #23*. 2017-present. Mixed media collage. 76.2 x 76.2 cm. artist-owned, Boston, Massachusetts.

Coda: Frankenstein, Continued

Daniel Cook

As the contributors to the present collection amply demonstrate, *Frankenstein* has long been a story worth continuing.[1] A sequel remains the most common type of extension, and typically moves the timeline to the present day or beyond, through familial or notional descendants. Coquels, or paranarratives, have gained particular traction in the book market in recent years: this mode of writing explores or amplifies the lives of minor characters or else revisits the original timeline and even settings from an askew vantage point. The female creature destroyed by Victor Frankenstein before she can take a first breath, let alone breed her own hideous progeny, has been gifted multiple voices by scriptwriters, artists, and authors. An economy of abundance finds room for many Frankensteins. Many monsters. Many brides. Many sons and daughters. Some new characters, favoring an economy of scarcity, pursue their fictional forebears with murderous intent. Even this destructive act is a creative one and provides a repeatedly new take on the original novel's murderousness.

In an age of rampant recycling, to posit a different model of cultural reception, literary mashups, transmedia adaptations, and Frankenfictions have increasingly become the norm, not the exceptions.[2] Some extensions wear their affiliation with the source text lightly on their book sleeve. Others explicitly revisit the origins of Shelley's novel, and some go back further still, to a concocted pre-story in which Victor Frankenstein *did* exist, and even interacted with the Shelleys and other real people. Yet others attend to the novel's aftermath. As Victor LaValle and Dietrich Smith's graphic novel *Destroyer* (2018) attests, there is unfinished—unfinishable—business:

> Victor eventually died, but the Monster never did. It hid away in Antarctica and thought itself free of humanity. But the world isn't done with the Monster, and one descendant of the Frankenstein bloodline yet lives....[3]

The main characters have been cloned, or at least renamed. Victor has been a Henry for many decades. The creature has belatedly received a variety of names, usually Adam. Or it has gained new nicknames with a semblance of authorially sanctioned precedence—the monster, most often. Characters have been reborn, as in the dramatic transformation of a tubercular Irish immigrant, Brona Croft (Billie Piper), in the television series *Penny Dreadful* (2014–2016).

Speaking to John Clare as the newly formed Lily Frankenstein, Piper delivers a startling speech that seeks to conclude but also extend the narrative: "And when Victor comes home ... we'll put our hands around his throat together ... and watch him die. And then this will be our home. And then? What then, undead thing?"[4] What then, indeed. Serial characters that cross media are essentially immortal, even Victor; those that are undead perhaps more so, in their physical changeability, versatility, and mobility. When considering characters (new or old) we cannot help but picture the actors who bring them to life. Reflecting on her formative cultural experiences, the Scottish poet Liz Lochhead addresses the most iconic of all on-screen enactors of the creature, or monster, in her 1984 collection *Dreaming Frankenstein*:

Well, you know, Mr Karloff,
I used to think an aphrodisiac was some
kinda confused Tibetan mountain goat
with a freak-out hair-do until I
met my monster and my monster
met his maker.
Oh yeah.

"Smirnoff for Karloff"[5]

Although unnamed, Elsa Lanchester's Bride also comes vividly into our mind's eye. She's there right now: the "freak-out hair-do" provides a sufficient jog, despite the distraction of the goat. We have our own monsters too. Extensions of *Frankenstein* are really extensions of the Frankenstein story told across the full gamut of creative engagements that have long circulated across the world, from abridgements for children to scaled-up transmediations.

Literary extensions come in all sorts of shapes and sizes. Conveniently, Stephen Jones has compiled twenty-five "monster tales" inspired by Shelley's work in *The Mammoth Book of Frankenstein* (1994, 2015). In it we find Ramsey Campbell's "A New Life," which, as the author states in the text's foreword, responds to the Hammer Horror films rather than Shelley's novel. R. Chetwynd-Hayes, author of "The Creator," was similarly inspired after watching the 1939 *Son of Frankenstein* in the movie theater. Baron Frankenstein, according to the new protagonist (Charlie Brownlow), has been "too ambitious by far. His creation was much too big. A hulking great brute that no one could control."[6] That's not Shelley's Creature. "You must have seen *Bride of Frankenstein* a hundred times by now," Joyce says wearily to her mad scientist husband, amid his copycat experiments, in Basil Copper's "Better Dead."[7] Kim Newman, too, in "Completist Heaven": "Lightning crackles above the garden, approximating a Karloff-Lugosi mad lab insert short from the 1930s."[8] Nancy Kilpatrick, author of "Creature Comforts," expressly returned to the original book before updating it for a 1990s audience: "*The creature* [is...] *described as tall, pale and scarred*," she writes in the foreword; "Sounds like rock-star material to me."[9] Rock music, as well as grunge, rap and pop music, has its Frankensteinia too.

The editors of *Adapting Frankenstein*, Dennis R. Cutchins and Dennis R. Perry, proffer the term the "Frankenstein Network."[10] Although I wish to prioritize stories, for now, and limit my focus to print-based literature, a network would certainly be a more apt term for a wider cultural study. The Frankenstein Network brings together an endless army of creative people, often working anonymously or collaboratively, and includes prosumers, fanfic authors, commercial artists, and the like. Such is the pervasiveness of Shelley's creation across global popular culture, after all, films, plays, operettas, pantomimes, songs, comics, costumes, entertainment ephemera, and all sorts of wordless Frankensteinia, from toys to teacups, cannot be disassociated from the 1818 novel. And vice versa. Boris Karloff has embodied the creature for nearly a century. Before him, we had T.P. Cooke. And after him, Benedict Cumberbatch. The creature is also Herman Munster and Frankenweenie. Igor and Igor-like figures have permanently joined the extended cast of characters. Ahmed Saadawi's *Frankenstein in Baghdad* (2013; translated in 2018) constantly acknowledges the movies—and not just the Karloff-helmed ones ("When Mahmoud did the layout of the magazine, he illustrated the article with a large photo of Robert De Niro from the film *Mary Shelley's Frankenstein*").[11] No modern Frankenfiction could pretend otherwise: they risk retelling only part of the Frankenstein story.

More pertinently, the presence of motifs from the Frankenstein Network within the novel, as much as the co-presence of the tropes of *Frankenstein*, signals a real-world engagement with the ghoulishness of Western culture in Saadawi's modern, post-war Iraq. This is not to deny the permanence of Shelley's formative vision. Lochhead's poem and Saadawi's novel, and the films to which they obliquely refer, look back to the demands for a mate placed on Victor by the creature: "It is true, we shall be monsters, cut off from all the world; but on that account we shall be more attached to one another."[12] *Frankenstein* is a story of conflicts, between the creator and the creature above all. It is also a thwarted love story, between the creature and an unmade creature. It's a scientific parable, a godless myth, a Miltonian tragedy, an allegory for the industrial proletariat, a horror novel, a crime novel, Science Fiction, metafiction, YA fiction, slash fiction, and more and none of the above at once. *Frankenstein* can be reformed in endless ways. First- or third-person narration often displaces the original's epistolary format in print-based extensions. There are mock-casebooks and pseudo-journals too—filled with elliptical and crossed-out sentences, Laurie Sheck's *A Monster's Notes* (2009) captures the mental turmoil of a highly articulate posthuman. Free indirect discourse is commonly used in contemporary works. Dialogue usually features too. Non-linear or elliptical timelines can offset and even destabilize the progression of Shelley's text.

Extensions might be quite literal, as in William A. Chanler's *Son of Terror: Frankenstein Continued* (2017), which begins in the Arctic shortly after Victor's death, or Suzanne Weyn's *Dr. Frankenstein's Daughters* (2013), where the twins Giselle and Ingrid uphold their family's legacy in very different ways. Side stories open out endlessly. Modern language, including slang, can augment or overwrite the Georgian diction; or there might be a monstrous mashup of different vocabularies. Steampunk or counterfactual Frankenfictions have proven highly popular. Some creatures can be incredibly verbose, like their primary forebear; others can be rendered mute. We might think again of Karloff's monster and his imitators. Notable refocalizations have appeared. Peter Ackroyd's *Casebook of Victor Frankenstein* (2008) centers on Victor, as the book's title suggests, but quickly brings in "Mad Shelley" (Percy Bysshe Shelley) as a new (or lost original) character. Fred Saberhagen's *Frankenstein Papers* (1986) retells Mary Shelley's version solely from the creature's perspective; enhancing this character's voice entails silencing Victor. (In the purview of the Frankenstein story, such silence amounts to temporary if endless muting.) Saberhagen freely modified the story too, not least of all in relocating the action to the American Revolution, and enlisting Benjamin Franklin and his son. Even the nominal monster, as it is revealed through a series of letters and a journal, is remade—or unmade—as an amnesiac humanoid alien who had been disfigured during an explosion in Victor's laboratory. And, in fact, the creature that Victor had stitched together had not, in fact, come to life—in the world of the new novel, at least.

New monsters recall old creatures: such is the stickiness of the Frankenstein story, regardless of form or matter. In Robert J. Myers's 1975 sequel, *The Cross of Frankenstein*, an illegitimate son of Victor finds the original creature plotting against humanity in the wilds of America, a destination it had identified in the source text. At around this time, in *Frankenstein Unbound* (1973), Brian Aldiss popularized a blueprint of the modern time-traveler (here, a twentieth-century American) transported back to Geneva in 1816. This Victor is as real as Benjamin Franklin—or as equally fictionalized. Shelley's novel, too, becomes a statement of fact: "I remember reading the novel as a child, when it made a great impression on me, but the deplorable pastiches and plagiarizations put out by the mass media have obliterated my memory of the original details."[13] Within an economy of scarcity, Aldiss's novella challenges the validity and even the existence of Shelley's novel—not earnestly, we should presume. After all, few writers have been so closely associated with the origin myths surrounding their novels in the public imagination like Shelley: the "Year without a Summer," the fevered dream, and the like, offers a potent story of its own. Lesley McDowell's *Unfashioned Creatures* (2013) takes us back even further, to the life and travails of Shelley's childhood friend in Scotland, Isabella Baxter. A bravura metafiction, Jeanette Winterson's *Frankissstein* (2019) blends Shelley's origin story with the haunting tale that emerged in Geneva: "My story has being. I must continue it, for it cannot end without me."[14] Threaded throughout the book we have a modern timeline in which the Frankenstein Network again comes to the fore:

> She frowns. I am not following you, sir.
> The novel *Frankenstein*—it was published in 1818.
> The guy with the bolt through his neck?
> More or less . . .
> I saw the TV show.[15]

Like many Frankenfictions, this is a book about the complex act of making, whether it's TV shows or new humans. Winterson's Shelley (and Winterson the Author, one might suppose) certainly feels "the like agony of mind of Victor Frankenstein," who, "having created his monster" cannot "uncreate him."[16] It's no coincidence that the one facet of *Frankenstein* that has repeatedly incited sequels and coquels is the mooted creation of the female creature: "Could such a being reproduce?"[17] Stories breed stories, sometimes.

Second Creatures

Having relocated to Orkney, Shelley's Victor contemplates the implications of his new labour, namely, the rebirth of a fertile female mate for the creature. In effect, he imagines plotlines that extend beyond the novel in which he is speaking. "I was now about to form another being, of whose dispositions I was alike ignorant," Victor says; "she might become ten thousand times more malignant than her mate, and delight, for its own sake, in murder and wretchedness."[18] Quickly, in a matter of lines, he takes decisive action: "I thought with a sensation of madness on my promise of creating another like to him, and, trembling with passion, tore to pieces the thing on which I was engaged."[19] Destroying the corpse ends the monstrous bloodline, unmaking all at once an entire "race of devils" yet to be born. Inadvertently, though, Victor sets a revenge tragedy in motion: "The wretch saw me destroy the creature on whose future existence he depended for happiness, and, with a howl of devilish despair and revenge, withdrew." Fleeing the Orkney islands not long after, by a small boat to the north of Ireland, Victor becomes implicated in the creature's murderous trail of destruction. The monstrous family romance segues into crime fiction.

The Orcadian episode is short but potent, and it is little wonder that sequelists have been drawn back to it. New characters can fill in the blanks for us. A young Scot, Donald Gilmore, delivers "a dreadful story" that unsettles the "notions of Victor Frankenstein" previously held by Jonathan Goodall, the narrator of Hilary Bailey's *Frankenstein's Bride* (1995).[20] Bailey's sequel, a connection to the original text signaled in the book's subtitle, reinforces but also destabilizes readers' prior experience with Shelley's material. With Goodall, the reader anticipates a discomforting reappraisal of the god-playing scientist. The Orcadian setting of Gilmore's eyewitness view is far from incidental; like the account recounted by Shelley's Victor, the description captures the ominous mood. "Both house and outbuildings were dilapidated,"[21] Gilmore recalls, endorsing Victor's own, glib impressions: "these exhibited all the squalidness of the most miserable penury."[22]

Such endorsement primes us for authentic expansion, as it were, as the new character outlines in more detail the nefarious doings missed out of the source text. Hidden away, a strange animal, as Gilmore assumes it to be, tormented the unsighted locals ("it groaned and moaned in a blood-chilling way").[23] The animal, we soon learn, is the female creature—or, at least, a potential candidate for the dubious role:

> And there, lying half in, half out of a vast, spreading pool of liquid, was the naked body of a young woman, her golden hair spread all about her. I suppose she had been lying in that fluid all the while.
> "Dead?" I asked.
> "I thought so then," he said. "I thought it was a corpse."[24]

Shelley's Victor had sexed the new creature, but Bailey's Gilmore places more emphasis on her humanity. To Victor's mind she will become "another being" but, when he destroys her, he reduces her to "the thing on which I was engaged." Without a voice, Bailey's pre-Bride gains greater sympathy. Other Bride narratives give her speech, often with great prominence. Elizabeth Hand's *The Bride of Frankenstein: Pandora's Bride* (2007) is technically an expansion of the Universal Monsters series of *Frankenstein* movies, part of the Frankenstein Network, whereas *Frankenstein's Bride* is firmly located in the original period, picking up the story in 1826.

Relying on the visual imagery generated so vividly in our collective imagination by the movies, the female creature of the new novel can take our knowledge as read: "I had no other purpose, than to be the playmate and companion, yes, wife and *friend*, to that thing."[25] From this inherited premise, she takes the story in a more empowered direction. She even monsterizes the male creature, humanizing herself by contrast: "You know what he is—it—looked like. Stitched together from corpses and reeking of the grave...." Karloff's monster lumbers back into our focus. The bride awakens. Kate Horsley's more recent coquel, *The Monster's Wife* (2014) outwardly downplays its connection to the source text, similarly, and ultimately rewards even a superficial engagement with the Frankenstein story. Unlike Bailey's novel, in which the Orcadian scene is replayed and expanded in a story within the story, Horsley's novel rests solely on Hoy in Orkney, in the year 1798. While the book's title only tangentially references the source material, the back-cover blurb paraphrases the central episode succinctly: "To a tiny island in Orkney comes Victor Frankenstein, driven there by a Devil's bargain: to make a wife for the Creature who is stalking him across Europe."

Then comes a new (or recovered) major character: "Maidservant Oona aids in his experiments. They grow close, until her best friend goes missing. Oona's search reveals secrets darker than anything she imagined." Like Bailey's Goodall, the people of Orkney have nothing but respect for the "foreign doctor"—at the outset, at least. (Obviously, they haven't read Shelley's novel or watched the films it has spawned—they are living it.) Our new focal character even imagines herself into a love plot: "He was always lonely in her imaginings, that brave and chivalrous man, Doctor Frankenstein. So that, before she ever laid eyes on him, Oona dreamt of a life by his side." Finally meeting him, however, she faces disappointment: "He was entirely unlike the tall, dark and handsome aristocrat of whom she had dreamt."[26] We snap back into a mad scientist story: "I have experienced somewhat of a lightning bolt, not to say an epiphany, given the Sisyphean labour of adapting what jetsam we have to hand," says Horsley's Victor, with frenzied delight far removed from the gloom of Shelley's original character in Scotland.[27] If anything, he's closer to Colin Clive's frantic Henry Frankenstein from the Universal Monsters films ("It's alive!"). Meanwhile, the creature that Shelley's Victor spied through his window reappears, effectively retracing the steps of the original.

Lacking sufficient context, Oona does not know who it is, turning the material into a semi-mystery (whether a crime mystery, a supernatural one, or something else entirely): "There was the figure again [....] There was someone outside the window, a face pressed to the glass, staring. Their gazes met, just long enough for her to make out the blue of his eyes and the thick scar running over the bridge of his nose."[28] The description of the scarred face might make us think of any number of on-screen iterations of the creature, perhaps De Niro's frightful, thuggish version more than the pallid Karloff. For Oona, though, he is more man than monster, and an idle curiosity rather than a threat ("The man must work in the big house, a servant of Frankenstein's perhaps, though she had never laid eyes on him"). And yet, in her words, the creature stares at Oona as if he "knew her." Oona may be a new character, to the readers' minds, but the mysterious man retains a trace knowledge of the original—this will be his bride, as Shelley's Victor had promised. Uncannily, Oona feels but cannot fully articulate that pretextual relationship: "Something had stolen between them in that moment, a shiver of recognition."[29] In the wider purview of the Frankenstein story, such passages take on heightened anxiety despite the characters' lack of understanding.

As *The Monster's Wife* progresses Oona becomes powerless to stop her dark fate. She is transformed into a female creature, now named Eve by her male counterpart, who dubs himself Adam. (He thereby literalizes the biblical punning in the source text, where the creature tells Victor that he is "thy Adam.") Horsley gives us, and the creature, something Shelley refused to—a union between the creatures. (Ironically, she also takes away a key action point—the creature does not confront Victor in the new novel, presumably because that would unsettle the new focalization; and, besides, that scene has perpetually been completed on the page, stage, and screen.) The union reinscribes the shiver of recognition felt by Oona in her state of pre-Bride; equally, Oona (now Eve) retains her human wariness of danger:

> The woman named Eve did not stir when the man walked in. She kept her eyes closed when he sat down next to her and stroked the tangles from her hair. Something in his voice when he said her name was familiar. It made her afraid.[30]

Alarmed by this rejection, the creature seeks to engage her company through their shared monstrosity: "'I know it hurts when you wake up,' his arms clamping hers."[31] "People scream," he continues: "You want to break everyone and at the same time, you want to die. I know it." In the end, the book's title is ironic. Eve spurns the enforced marriage and even any type of romantic relationship.

The bride's conflicted reaction to her posthuman life has long attracted adapters and sequelists keen to rework *Frankenstein*. One of the most recognizable retellings of Shelley's novels in recent years, Kenneth Branagh's 1994 movie *Mary Shelley's Frankenstein*, conflates the roles of Elizabeth and Bride (both played by Helena Bonham Carter). Spying her scarred, monsterized appearance in the mirror, the mute Elizabeth-Bride sets herself on fire. In this melodramatic conclusion to the story, her double death (as Elizabeth and Bride) torments the creator and creature alike. In *Penny Dreadful*, the gothic TV serial, Lily Frankenstein instead embraces her transformation, and her new monstrous romance:

> We were created to rule, my love. And the blood of mankind will water our garden. Us and our kin ... and our children, and our generations. We are the conquerors. We are the pure blood. We are steel and sinew both. We are the next 1,000 years. We are the dead.
>
> "Memento, Mori," *Penny Dreadful*.

Time-bound adaptations such as standalone films demand resolution. The seriality of television, as well as expansions in other media, can prolong the monstrous romance plotline indefinitely. Victor may die, in endless ways. But his creations are, by definition, immortal; defeatable but never defeated. The Frankenstein story is deathly but undying.

Notes

Introduction

1. We will use italics when referring to Mary Shelley's novel but not when discussing the character or the general myth.
2. Paul Youngquist and Orrin N.C. Wang, "A List of Movies Based on Frankenstein, 1910–2005," *Romantic Circles*, May 1, 2009. See www.rc.umd.edu/editions/frankenstein/Pop/filmlist.
3. In the 1790s, the Italian scientist Luigi Galvani first tested the effects that electricity had in motivating movement in muscles when he passed a current through the bodies of animals, and, in the following years, lectures were given widely to disseminate the information gleaned regarding this newly understood force of nature. In the early nineteenth century, Galvani's nephew, Luigi Aldini, gave a presentation before the Royal College of Surgeons in London that demonstrated the nature of galvanism by showing the effect of electricity on the body of a recently executed criminal. Others recreated this experiment in the following years. Percy Shelley himself was fascinated by electricity and had an electrical machine of his own when he attended Oxford. These lectures highlighted galvanism's promise as a technique for restoring life, particularly when administered shortly after death. Alan Rauch, *Knowledge: The Victorians, Morality, and the March of Intellect* (Durham: Duke University Press, 2001), 112.
4. Anonymous, "Review of *Frankenstein*", *Edinburgh Magazine*, or *Literary Miscellany*, 2 (1818), 249.
5. Steven Earl Forry, *Hideous Progenies: Dramatizations of* Frankenstein *from the Nineteenth Century to the Present* (Philadelphia: University of Pennsylvania Press, 1990), 22.
6. Ibid., 23
7. Lester D. Friedman and Allison B. Kavey, *Monstrous Progeny: A History of the Frankenstein Narratives* (New Brunswick: Rutgers University Press, 2016), 81. Susan Tyler Hitchcock, *Frankenstein: A Cultural History* (New York: W.W. Norton, 2007), 88.
8. Mary Shelley *The Letters of Mary Wollstonecraft Shelley*. 3 vols., ed. Betty T. Bennett. (Baltimore: Johns Hopkins University Press, 1980), I, 378–79.
9. Edward W. R. Pitcher, "Frankenstein as Short Fiction: A Unique Adaptation of Mary Shelley's Novel," *Studies in Short Fiction*, 20:1 (Winter 1983), 49–52.
10. Daisy Bowie Sell, "Signed copy of Frankenstein found by chance sells for over £350,000," *The Telegraph,* January 18, 2013. See www.telegraph.co.uk/culture/books/booknews/9811878/Signed-copy-of-Frankenstein-found-by-chance-sells-for-over-350000.html.
11. Frederico Meschini, "Four-Color Myth: *Frankenstein* in the Comics," in Francesca Saggini and Anna Enrichetta Soccio, eds., *Transmedia Creatures: Frankenstein's Afterlives*, 119.
12. Andrew McInnes, "Young Adult *Frankenstein*," in Saggini and Soccio, 219–20.

13 Claire Nally, "Staging Steampunk Aesthetics in *Frankenstein* Adaptations: Mechanization, Disability, and the Body," in Saggini and Soccio, 87–100.
14 H. L. Malchow, "Frankenstein's Monster and Images of Race in Nineteenth-Century Britain," *Past and Present* 139 (May 1993), 91. Also see H. L. Malchow, Gothic Images of Race in Nineteenth-Century Britain (Stanford, CA: Stanford University Press, 1996).
15 Elizabeth Young, *Black Frankenstein: The Making of an American Metaphor* (New York: New York University Press, 2008), 5.
16 "Have I got old news for you: Glasgow is home to world's oldest comic." See www.heraldscotland.com/arts_ents/13110858.have-i-got-old-news-for-you-glasgow-is-home-to-worlds-oldest-comic/.
17 Roger Sabin, *Adult Comics* (Abingdon: Routledge, 2005), 16–18.
18 Gwynedd Stuart, "An Early Look at the Frankenstein-Inspired Art Going on Display at Corey Helford," *Los Angeles Magazine*, September 7, 2018. See www.lamag.com/culturefiles/frankenstein-200/.
19 Chris Baldick, *In Frankenstein's Shadow: Myth, Monstrosity, and Nineteenth-Century Writing* (Oxford: Clarendon Press, 1987), 4–5.
20 It is actually Glenn Strange, not Boris Karloff whose visage comes to mind. Strange played the creature in three Universal films, starting with *House of Frankenstein*, and it was his cinematic face, built to resemble Karloff's, which became the template for the endless masks, games, model kits and more. Don F. Glut, *The Frankenstein Archive: Essays on the Monster, the Myth, the Movies, and More* (Jefferson, North Carolina: McFarland, 2002), 35.
21 Karloff ultimately played Frankenstein's creation in only three films: *Frankenstein*, *Bride of Frankenstein*, and *Son of Frankenstein*. He did, however, appear in one other *Frankenstein* film, *House of Frankenstein*, in which he played the wicked scientist Dr. Gustav Niemann and Glenn Strange played Frankenstein's monster.
22 Marcus K. Harmes, *The Curse of Frankenstein* (Leighton Buzzard, England: Auteur, 2015), 20, and Marcus Hearn, *The Hammer Vault: Treasures from the Archive of the Hammer Films* (London: Titan Books, 2011), 15.
23 Two particularly informative books by Glut on *Frankenstein*: Donald F. Glut, *The Frankenstein Catalog* (Jefferson, North Carolina: McFarland, 1984). Donald F. Glut, *The Frankenstein Legend* (Metuchen, New Jersey: Scarecrow Press, 1973.
24 Shane Denson, *Postnaturalism: Frankenstein, Film, and the Anthropotechnical Interface* (Verlag, Bielefeld: Transcript, 2014), 33.
25 Frankensteinia: The Frankenstein Blog. See www.facebook.com/Frankensteinia-The-Frankenstein-Blog-9771563316/.
26 Dennis R. Cutchins and Dennis R. Perry, *Adapting Frankenstein: The Monster's Eternal Lives in Popular Culture* (Manchester: Manchester University Press, 2018), 6.

Chapter 1

1 *Frankenstein vs. The Mummy*, directed by Damien Leone (Ruthless Pictures, 2014), DVD, 2:34.
2 Ibid., 4:43–4:47.
3 Ibid. Naihla tells Victor that her grandfather was a member of an expedition team that plundered a tomb (against the wishes of Naihla's grandfather) and mysteriously died

of the pharaoh's curse (22:05–23:00). Victor enters the field of medicine after his mother's dramatic suicide (26:44–27:48).
4   See Jacques Derrida, *Specters of Marx: The State of the Debt, the Work of Mourning, & the New International,* trans. Peggy Kamuf (London: Routledge, 1994). While Jacques Derrida has written at length about the gothic implications of the same passages of Marx's *The Eighteenth Brumaire*, this chapter moves in a different theoretical direction from the psycho-analytics of repetition that dominate *Specters of Marx*. Among the numerous Freudian studies of *Frankenstein* see: Elisabeth Bronfen's "Rewriting the Family: Mary Shelley's *Frankenstein* in Its Biographical/Textual Context" in *Frankenstein Creation and Monstrosity,*" ed. Stephen Bann (London: Reaktion, 1994), 16–38; and Mary Jacobus', "Is There a Woman in this Text?" *New Literary History* 14, no. 1 (1982): 117–41; and more recently, Alexandra Reuber's "'Oh Mother, the Monster Is Inside!': Victor Frankenstein's Déjà Vu Experiences of His Repressed Self," *Nineteenth Century Literature in English* 12, no. 1 (2008): 179–96.
5   Marxist readings of *Frankenstein* tend to overlook Marx's *The Eighteenth Brumaire*. For alternative Marxist readings, however, see Ross Murfin, "Marxist Criticism of Frankenstein" in *Mary Shelley: Frankenstein,* ed. Johanna Smith (Boston: St. Martins, 1992), 286–99; Elsie Michie, "Frankenstein and Marxist Theories of Alienated Labor" in *Approaches to Teaching Shelley's Frankenstein* ed. Stephen Behrendt (New York: MLA, 1990), 93–98; Warren Montag, "The 'Worship of Filthy Creation': A Marxist Reading of *Frankenstein*" in *Mary Shelley: Frankenstein,* ed., Johanna Smith (New York; Bedford, 2000), 384–95. Treatments of the French Revolution in *Frankenstein* include: Allan Hunter, "Evolution, Revolution, and Frankenstein's Creature" in *Frankenstein's Science: Experimentation and Discovery in Romantic Culture, 1780-1830,* ed. Krista Knellwolf (Aldershot: Ashgate, 2008), 133–49; Julia Douthwaite, *The Frankenstein of 1790 and Other Lost Chapters from Revolutionary France* (Chicago; University of Chicago Press, 2012).
6   Karl Marx, *The Eighteenth Brumaire of Louis Bonaparte,* in *The Marx-Engels Reader,* ed. Robert C. Tucker (New York: Norton, 1978), 597.
7   Ibid.
8   Mary Shelley, *Frankenstein; or the Modern Prometheus* (1818), eds. D.L. Macdonald and Kathleen Scherf, (Broadview, 2012), 80.
9   Victor's creature is a Lockean *"tabula rasa"* in Shelley's novel. Cinematic adaptations are, by contrast, always instances of reanimation and transplantation in the Universal and Hammer films' cycles, *Mary Shelley's Frankenstein,* directed by Kenneth Branagh (1994; Culver City, CA: Columbia Tri-Star, 1994), DVD, and in *Frankenstein vs the Mummy*. In these instances, the reanimated amalgamation of bodies reproduces an essential subject—the unhappy/psychotic/vengeful consciousness of the transplanted brain.
10 Louis Althusser, *from* "Ideology and Ideological State Apparatuses," trans. Ben Brewster, in *Critical Theory Since Plato,* eds., Hazard Adams and Leroy Searle, (New York: Wadsworth, 2005), 1302–04.
11 Shelley, *Frankenstein,* 142–43.
12 Ibid., 136.
13 Ibid., 142.
14 1816 is the publication date of the *Alastor* volume that contains "Mutability." Donald Reiman and Neil Fraistat observe that "'Mutability,' like "To Wordsworth,' was published with *Alastor* (1816); no MSS survive for either poem and their actual dates of composition are unknown." See Donald Reiman and Neil Fraistat, 'Notes", in

Shelley's Poetry and Prose, eds., Donald Reiman and Neil Fraistat (New York: Norton, 2002), 91, n.1. *Frankenstein* is well-known for its anachronistic quotations from Romantic texts.

15 While the creature misquotes "Mutability," Victor correctly quotes Percy's poem as follows:

> We rest; a dream has power to poison sleep.
>   We rise; one wand'ring thought pollutes the day.
> We feel, conceive, or reason; laugh, or weep,
>   Embrace fond woe, or cast our cares away;
> It is the same: for, be it joy or sorrow,
>   The path of its departure is still free.
> Man's yesterday may ne'er be like his morrow;
>   Nought may endure but mutability!
>
> qtd. in Shelley, 117

16 See John Milton, *Paradise Lost* ed. Christopher Ricks (New York: Signet, 1982), VIII.453–98.
17 Milton, *Paradise Lost*, VIII. 490.
18 Shelley, 157.
19 In *Romanticism: An Anthology*, ed. by Duncan Wu, 4th edn. (Oxford: Wiley-Blackwell, 2012), 55, n. 67.
20 Shelley, 174.
21 Ibid., II.ix, 156.
22 Mary Shelley, *The Last Man,* ed., Anne McWhir (Peterborough, Ontario: Broadview Press, 1996). Alan Rauch, J.S. Chambers, and Lisa Hopkins all take the position that *The Mummy!* is a satiric rejection of the moral components of Shelley's *Frankenstein*. See Rauch, "Science in the Popular Novel: Jane Webb Louden's *The Mummy!*" in *Useful Knowledge,* (Durham: Duke, 2001), 60–95, and Alan Rauch, "Introduction," in Jane Louden, *The Mummy! A Tale of the Twenty-Second Century,* abridged by Alan Rauch (Michigan, 1994): ix–xxxiv. Lisa Hopkins, "Jane C. Louden's *The Mummy!*: Mary Shelley Meets George Orwell, and They Go in a Balloon to Egypt," *Romantic Textualities* Issue 10 (Feb. 15, 2013). See www.romtext.org.uk/articles/cc10_n01/. J.S. Chambers, "The Corpse of the Future" Clarkesworldmagazine.com (Dec. 2012). See http://clarkesworldmagazine.com/chambers_12_12/.
23 Hopkins, ibid, www.romtext.org.uk/articles/cc10_n01/ .
24 Jane Louden, *The Mummy! A Tale of the Twenty-Second Century,* abridged by Alan Rauch (Michigan, 1994), I.i.1.
25 Ibid.
26 Ibid., I.i.14.
27 Ibid., I.i.1.
28 King Roderick of Ireland is a "powerful monarch, who realizes in himself all the romantic qualities of the ancient knights of chivalry" (Louden, II.ix.211). He "rule[s] his subjects despotically, though he never spoke to them without a smile" (Ibid., 229).
29 Ibid., I.i. 2.
30 In 1534, Henry VIII denies papal authority after the Pope denied the King's request for an annulment.
31 Louden, I.i.5.
32 Ibid., I.i.7.
33 Shelley, 209.

34 Louden, III.viii.307.
35 Ibid.
36 Ibid.
37 Ibid.
38 Ibid., III.viii.307–8.
39 Ibid., III.viii.308.
40 Ibid., III.viii.309.
41 Ibid., III.viii.311.
42 Ibid.
43 The term is Mark Fisher's. *Capitalist Realism: Is There No Alternative?* (Winchester, UK: O Books, 2009) 2.
44 Leone, *Frankenstein vs The Mummy* (1:04:15–1:06:18).
45 Ibid., 1:50:50–1:51:55.

Chapter 2

1   Megan Ward, *Seeming Human: Artificial Intelligence and Victorian Realist Character* (Columbus: The Ohio University Press, 2018), 6.
2   Mary Shelley, *Frankenstein; or the Modern Prometheus* (1818), eds. D.L. Macdonald and Kathleen Scherf (Broadview Press, 2012), 32.
3   Henry Colebrooke, "On Presenting the Gold Medal of the Astronomical Society to Charles Babbage" in *Memoirs of the Astronomical Society* I (1825): 509–10; Charles Babbage, Letter to John Herschel, 27 June 1823, Royal Society Herschel Papers, HS 2:184.
4   Simon Schaffer, *Babbage's Dancer*, ed. Richard Barbrook (2007). See www.imaginaryfutures.net/2007/04/16/babbages-dancer-by-simon-schaffer/.
5   Herbert Sussman notes that Babbage had a special fondness for Merlin's Mechanical Museum, a late eighteenth-century exhibition hall filled with clockwork human automata imitating various actions. Sussman, *Victorians and the Machine: The Literary Response to Technology* (Cambridge, MA: Harvard University Press, 1968), 63.
6   Charles Babbage, *The Analytical Engine and Mechanical Notation* (New York: New York University Press, 1989), 31.
7   Luigi F. Menabrea and Ada Lovelace, "Sketch of the Analytical Engine Invented by Charles Babbage: With notes upon the memoir by Ada Augusta, Countess of Lovelace, from the *Bibliothèque Universelle de Geneve*, October 1842, no. 82, para. 40.
8   Richard Holmes, "Computer Science: Enchanter of Abstraction," *Nature* 525 (September 3, 2015): 30–32.
9   William Ashworth, "Memory, Efficiency, and Symbolic Analysis: Charles Babbage, John Herschel, and the Industrial Mind," *Isis* 87, no. 4 (Dec. 1996): 629.
10 The term "artificial intelligence" is anachronistic for discussing nineteenth-century ideas of the mind. The term was coined by John McCarthy in 1955. Long before, though, the idea of intelligence granted to artificial beings existed in figures such as Talos, a giant bronze oil-fueled automaton from Greek mythology. In the late eighteenth century, a variety of automata were brought to life by the intricate engineering of Jacques de Vaucanson (Brian Stableford, *Science Fact and Science Fiction: An Encyclopedia* (Abingdon: Routledge, 2015, 34). In speculative fiction, E.T.A. Hoffman's 1816 "Der Sandmann" is often cited as a movement towards imagining the workings of a machine mind. By the late nineteenth century, the idea

appears in longer discourses such as Edward Page Mitchell's "The Ablest Man in the World" (1879), Samuel Butler's *Erewhon* (1872), and George Eliot's "Shadows of the Coming Race" (1878) (Stableford, 34). In the twentieth century, Arthur C. Clarke and Robert A Heinlein, among many others, moved speculation concerning AI towards the imagination of "an emergent phenomena of sufficiently complex data-processing systems" (SFE, AI). The result of this linguistic evolution is that AI exists in technical discourse as a mechanical simulation run on hardware, but in speculative fiction as a frequently disembodied meditation on the emergent nature of conscious thought.

11 Mikhail Bakhtin, *Speech Genres & other Late Essays*, trans. Verne W. McGee (Austin: University of Texas Press, 1986), 19.
12 "The Imagination then I consider either as primary, or secondary. The primary Imagination I hold to be the living power and prime agent of all human perception, and as a repetition in the finite mind of the eternal act of creation in the infinite I AM. The secondary Imagination I consider as an echo of the former, co-existing with the conscious will, yet still as identical with the primary in the kind of its agency, and differing only in degree, and in the mode of its operation. It dissolves, diffuses, dissipates, in order to recreate: or where this process is rendered impossible, yet still at all events it struggles to idealize and to unify. It is essentially vital, even as all objects (as objects) are essentially fixed and dead." Samuel Taylor Coleridge, *Biographia Literaria* (Princeton: Princeton University Press, 1984), 304.
13 *The Notebooks of Samuel Taylor Coleridge*, Vol. V, eds. Kathleen Coburn and Anthony John Harding (London: Routledge, 2002), 5522.
14 Ashworth, "Memory, Efficiency, and Symbolic Analysis," 629.
15 Andrew Burkett, "Mediating Monstrosity: Media, Information, and Mary Shelley's *Frankenstein*," *Studies in Romanticism* 51, no. 4 (Winter 2012): 582.
16 Ibid, 583. For Burkett, this layered relationship to the discourses and displays of information is key to understanding why the text is such a continuously productive site for the Digital Humanities as in Georgina Samira Paiella's "The Corpus Electric," subtitled "Digital *Frankenstein*: DH Mapping of Mary Shelley's *Frankenstein*. See https://thecorpuselectric.wordpress.com/2017/05/27/digital-frankenstein-dh-mapping-of-mary-shelleys-frankenstein/
17 Elisha Cohn, *Still Life: Suspended Development in the Victorian Novel* (Oxford University Press, 2016), 5.
18 Criscilla Benford, "'Listen to my Tale': Multilevel Structure, Narrative Sense Making, and the Inassimilable in Mary Shelley's *Frankenstein*," *Narrative* 18, no. 3 (Oct 2010): 325.
19 Robert Mitchell, "Suspended Animation, Slow Time, and the Poetics of Trance," *PMLA* 126 no. 1 (2011): 108.
20 Elizabeth Freeman, *Time Binds: Queer Temporalities, Queer Histories* (Durham: Duke University Press, 2010), 85.
21 Essaka Joshua, "'Marking the Dates with Accuracy': The Time Problem in Mary Shelley's *Frankenstein*," *Gothic Studies* 3, no. 3 (2001): 285.
22 Elizabeth Nitchie, *Mary Shelley, Author of Frankenstein* (New Brunswick: Rutgers University Press, 1953), 282.
23 Joshua, 'Marking the Dates," 299.
24 The total duration of the novel (as indicated by its various time-stamped found texts) is nine months and, as discussed thoroughly by Ellen Moers in "Female Gothic," included in *The Endurance of Frankenstein: Essays on Mary Shelley's Novel*, eds. George Levine, and Ulrich C. Knoepflmacher (University of California Press, 1982), 83–84.

While Shelley was writing the novel she was involved in her own "horror story of maternity" (Moers 83). In March 1815, Shelley lost her first-born daughter after only a few months, but was pregnant again by April. Also in March, Mary's step-sister, Claire Clairmont conceived a child with Lord Byron, and in mid-December, Percy's estranged wife drowned herself while pregnant by another man. In January 1816, Mary gave birth to a son, and by May she had finished writing *Frankenstein*. Rather than implying that Shelley's novel is merely an allegory for her difficult relationship to pregnancy and mortality, I would argue that Mary, who was also immersed in the Romantic and scientific revolutions of her day, was ideally positioned to offer an informed perspective on the ways that science and technology had begun to redefine distinctions between artificial and vital existence.

25 Mary Shelley, *Frankenstein, or The Modern Prometheus* (New York: W.W. Norton, 1994), 126.
26 Ibid., 67.
27 Alan M. Turing, "Computing Machinery and Intelligence," *Mind: A Quarterly Review of Psychology and Philosophy*, 59, no. 236 (Oct. 1960): 433–34.
28 Ibid., 435.
29 Rodney Brooks, *Flesh and Machines: How Robots Will Change Us* (New York: Random House, 2002), 148.
30 Niculae Gheran, "Relating Romantic Monsters to Dystopian Robots: Mary Shelley's *Frankenstein* and Carel Capek's *Rossum's Universal Robots*," *Caletele Echinox* 26 (2014): 251.
31 Shelley, *Frankenstein*, 68.
32 Ibid, 75.
33 Ibid, 76.
34 Ibid, 77.
35 Georg Lukács, *Theory of the Novel: A Historico-Philosophical Essay on the Forms of Great Epic Literature*, trans. Anna Bostock (Cambridge, MA: The MIT Press, 1971), 70.
36 Lukács, *Theory of the Novel*, 81.
37 In saying this I'm thinking of another of Lukács' arguments in *Theory of the Novel* concerning biography as the basic formal principle of the novel: "The fluctuation between a conceptual system which can never completely capture life and a life complex which can never attain completeness because completeness is immanently utopian, can be objectivized only in that organic quality which is the aim of biography ... The central character of biography is significant only by his relationship to a world of ideals that stands above him: but this world, in turn, is realized only through its existence within that individual and his lived experience ... the life of the problematic individual" (77–78).

Chapter 3

1 Nao Aoyama, *Meiji Jogakkō no Kenkyū* (A Study of Meiji Jogakkō) (Tokyo: Keiō Tsūshin, 1970), 551.
2 Alistair Swale, *The Political Thought of Mori Arinori: A Study of Meiji Conservatism*. (Abingdon: Routledge, 2016), 178. Swale defines Mori not as an enlightened thinker, as is generally believed, but as a "progressive conservative." According to Swale, Mori's "primary objectives" were "[t]he maintenance of traditional continuity and social order," yet he was willing "to countenance innovative ways of pursuing the conservative agenda." Ibid., 6–7.

3   Aoyama, *Meiji Jogakkō no Kenkyū*, 545.
4   Ibid.
5   Kato Hiroyuki, "Kuni no Motoi no Sokan wo Iwau (Celebrating the inauguration of Foundation of the Nation)," *Kuni no Motoi* 1, no 1 (1889): 1. In the same issue, Yatabe Ryōkichi emphasizes moderation as the school's motto and eschews the phrase "the West" altogether. Vice-principal Nose, once Mori's personal secretary, more firmly defends the advantage of Japanese girls' exposure to Western learning.
6   Mizuho Yagi, "*Jogaku Zasshi* wo Shiza to shita Meiji 22nen no Bungaku Ronsō (A Literary Controversy in 1889 in the context of *Jogaku Zasshi*)." *Kindai Bungaku Shiron* 35 (1997): 5–8.
7   Minoru Nakano, "Teikoku Daigaku Seiritsu ni Kansuru Ichi Kōsatsu (A Reflection on the Foundation of Imperial University)," *Tokyo Daigaku-shi Kiyō* 13 (1995): 55–67.
8   Aoyama, *Meiji Jogakkō no Kenkyū*, 16.
9   Ibid.
10 A search through the National Diet Library Digital Collection returns two writers with a pen name including *hisago* between 1800–1889, with no data available between 1870–1879: Teijirō Ōta, a political novelist, who called himself *Hana-no-ya Hisago*, and an unidentified writer of *gesaku* literature who called himself *Hisago-ya*.
11 Kōno suggests that Miyake Kaho started using the pseudonym earlier than 1890, possibly in the form of an emoji signature representing a gourd. Tatsuya Kono, "Futari no Natsuko: Higuchi Ichiyo to Ito Natsuko: Koen-roku (The Two Natsukos: Higushi Ichiyo and Ito Natsuko: Lecture Record)," *Jissen Joshi Daigaku Nenpo* 35 (2016): 167. For Kaho's use of the literary pseudonym, see Mitsuyoshi Takitō, "Kaho to Ichiyō: Shoki Ichiyō Notes I (Kaho and Ichiyō: Ichiyō's earlier notes I)," *Yokohama National University Humanities Bulletin* 31 (1984): 109.
12 Takitō, "Kaho to Ichiyō," 109–22.
13 Roan Uchida, *Shinpen Omoidasu Hitobito* (People I Remember: New Edition), Tokyo: Iwanami-shoten, 1994.
14 For the nineteenth-century editions of *Frankenstein*, see William St. Clair, *The Reading Nation in the Romantic Period* (Cambridge: Cambridge University Press, 2004); "Editions of Mary Shelley's Frankenstein." Romantic Circles. See https://romantic-circles.org/editions/frankenstein/textual.html.
15 For a detailed discussion on the base text of "The New Creator," see Tomoko Nakagawa, "*Furankenshutain,* Meiji Chuki no Hatsu-Hōyaku: Atarashiki Zōbutsu-sha no Teihon wo Megutte (The First Japanese Translation of *Frankenstein*: in the Mid-Meiji Era: On the Base Text of 'The New Creator,'" *Seishin Studies*, 139 (2022): 114–38.
16 Tomoko Nakagawa, "Naming the Unnameable: Monstrosity and Personification in the First Japanese Translation of Frankenstein," in *POETICA: An International Journal of Linguistic-Literary Studies* 82 (2014): 101–02.
17 Nakagawa, "Naming the Unnameable," 101–05.
18 Kiyochika's ukiyo-e woodblock prints were popular in the early to mid-Meiji era. Some of his contemporaries claim that his prints incomparably represented Tokyo as it transformed into a modern metropolis. In 1882, he became a chief caricaturist for the weekly paper called *Maru Maru Chimbun*. Isao Shimizu, *Manga Zasshi Hakubutsu-kan* (Museum of Cartoon Magazines) 1, (Tokyo: Kokusho Kankō-kai, 1986), 208.
19 *Kuni no Motoi* 2, no. 12 (1890). Each illustration, printed on a separate sheet, was folded and placed between the leaves of the magazine.

20 Ikkaisai(Tsukioka) Yoshitoshi, "Raiko Shitennō Ōeyama Kijin Taiji no Zu" (Raiko and the Best Four Disposing of the Oeyama Monster)" (1864), National Diet Library Digital Collection. See https://dl.ndl.go.jp/info:ndljp/pid/1310286.
21 For the discussion of the "The New Creator" illustrations in the historical context of Japanese visual arts, see Tomoko Nakagawa, "Anglo-Japanese Visual Encounters in 1889: Kipling, Alfred East and the *Frankenstein* Illustrators," *POETICA* 95/96 (2021): 45–65.
22 *Kuni no Motoi* 1, no. 4 (1889). Waseda University Library.
23 In composition, Kiyochika's illustration shows a striking similarity with Yoshitoshi's ukiyo-e print called "Bats in the Fifth Act," a comical representation in which the characters are bats when turned over sideways.
24 *Kuni no Motoi* 1, no. 5 (1889). Waseda University Library.
25 Tsukioka Yoshitoshi. "Dainihon meishō-kagami: Saitō Musashibō Benkei Onzōshi Ushiwaka-maru nochi no Iyo Minamoto-no-kami Yoshitsune (Catalogue of Illustrious Japanese Commanders: Saitō Musashibō Benkei, Prince Ushiwaka-maru, later to become Iyo Minamaoto-no-kami Yoshitsune)," 1878, Tokyo Metropolitan Library. See https://archive.library.metro.tokyo.lg.jp/da/detail?tilcod=0000000003-00009577.
26 Taiso (Tsukioka) Yoshitoshi. "Yoshitoshi Mushaburui: Minamoto no Ushiwaka-maru, Kumasaka Chōhan (Yoshitoshi's Warriors Trembling with Anticipation: Minamoto no Ushiwakamaru and Kumasaka Chōhan)," 1883. National Diet Library Digital Collection. See https://dl.ndl.go.jp/info:ndljp/pid/1302763?tocOpened=1.

Chapter 4

1 Gino Roncaglia, "Frankenstein and Science Fiction," in *Transmedia Creatures: Frankenstein's Afterlives*, eds. Francesca Saggini and Anna Enrichetta Soccio (Lewisburg, PA: Bucknell University Press, 2019), 33–49. Roncaglia provides a more thorough recounting of this relationship.
2 Brian W. Aldiss with David Wingrove, *Trillian Year Spree: The History of Science Fiction* (London: Gollancz, 1986), 18.
3 Aldiss, *Trillian Year Spree*, 25.
4 Carl Freedman, *Critical Theory* and *Science Fiction* (Middletown, CT: Wesleyan University Press, 2000), 48–49.
5 Ibid., 50.
6 Aldiss, *Trillion Year Spree*, 40.
7 John Rieder, *Science Fiction and the Mass Cultural Genre System* (Middletown, CT: Wesleyan UP, 2017), 65.
8 John Rieder, *Colonialism and the Emergence of Science Fiction* (Middletown, CT: Wesleyan University Press, 2008), 19, 97–104; *Science Fiction*, 66–81.
9 Rieder, *Science Fiction* 93.
10 Rieder, *Colonialism*, 15–21.
11 Rieder, *Science Fiction*, 74.
12 Roger Luckhurst, "Iraq War Body Counts: Reportage, Photography, and Fiction," *MFS Modern Fiction Studies* 63, no. 2 (2017): 370.
13 Roger Luckhurst, "The Cost of War: Parts and Labor," *Los Angeles Review of Books*, June 16, 2008. See https://lareviewofbooks.org/article/cost-war-parts-labor/.

14 Claudia Gualtieri, "*Frankenstein; Or, The Modern Prometheus* in the Postcolony," in *Transmedia Creatures: Frankenstein's Afterlives*, eds. Francesca Saggini and Anna Enrichetta Soccio (Lewisburg: PA, Bucknell UP, 2019): 114.
15 Ibid., 102.
16 Michel Foucault, *Security, Territory, Population: Lectures at the Collège de France 1977-1978*, trans. Graham Burchell, ed. Michael Senellart (New York: Picador, 2007). For Foucault, biopolitics means the intrusion of governmental power into the body itself (including birth, hygiene, purity, etc.) for the creation, demarcation, and political control of whole populations rather than just individuals.
17 Sherryl Vint, *Science Fiction: A Guide for the Perplexed* (London: Bloomsbury, 2014), 57.
18 Mary Shelley, *Frankenstein: A Norton Critical Edition*. 2nd edn, ed. J. Paul Hunter (New York: W.W. Norton, 2012), 161.
19 Veronica Hollinger, "Retrofitting *Frankenstein*," in *Beyond Cyberpunk*, eds. Graham J. Murphy and Sherryl Vint (New York: Routledge, 2010): 191–210.
20 David Damrosch, *What is World Literature?* (Princeton: Princeton University Press, 2003), 4.
21 Zahra Hankir, "Ahmed Saadawi Wants to Tell a New Story About the War in Iraq," *Literary Hub* (June 19, 2018). Available at: https://lithub.com/ahmed-saadawi-wants-to-tell-a-new-story-about-the-war-in-iraq/.
22 Sinéad Murphy, "*Frankenstein in Baghdad*: Human Conditions, or Conditions of Being Human," *Science Fiction Studies* 45, no. 2 (2018): 275.
23 Saadawi, Ahmed. *Frankenstein in Baghdad*, trans. Jonathan Wright (New York: Penguin Books, 2018), 19.
24 Warwick Research Collective. *Combined and Uneven Development: Towards a New Theory of World Literature* (Liverpool: Liverpool University Press, 2015), 7, n 16.
25 Dunmitru Radu Popa, "Globalization and Comparative Literature Revisited: An Analytical Survey," in *The Canonical Debate Today: Crossing Disciplinary and Cultural Boundaries*, eds. Liviu Papadima, David Damrosch, and Theo D'haen (Amsterdam: Rodopi, 2011) 187.
26 WReC, 12.
27 Mbembe, "Necropolitics," 23.
28 Ibid., 14.
29 Ibid., 16.
30 Ibid., 33.
31 Anna M. Agathangelou, "Bodies to the Slaughter: Global Racial Reconstructions, Fanon's Combat Breath, and Wrestling for Life," *Somatechnics* 1, no. 3 (2011): 228.
32 Ibid., 215.
33 Ibid., 242.
34 Haytham Bahoora, "Writing the Dismembered Nation: The Aesthetics of Horror in Iraqi Narratives of War." *The Arab Studies Journal* 23, no. 1 (2015): 186.
35 Luckhurst, "Iraq War," 355–72; Annie Webster, "Ahmed Saadawi's *Frankenstein in Baghdad*: A Tale of Biomedical Salvation?" *Literature and Medicine* 36, no. 2 (2018): 439–60.
36 Luckhurst, "Iraq War," 370.
37 Linda Robertson, "Baghdad ER: Subverting the Mythic Gaze upon the Wounded and the Dead," in *The War Body on Screen*, eds. Karen Randell and Sean Redmond (New York: Continuum, 2008), 64.

38 Margaret Schwartz, *Dead Matter: The Meaning of Iconic Corpses* (Minneapolis: University of Minnesota Press, 2015), 6–10.
39 Sadaawi, *Frankenstein in Baghdad*, 146–47.
40 Shelley, *Frankenstein*, 33–34.
41 Saadawi, *Frankenstein in Baghdad*, 24.
42 Mbembe, "Necropolitics," 35.
43 Saadawi, *Frankenstein in Baghdad*, 27.
44 Ibid.
45 Ibid., 280.

Chapter 5

1 See https://powerlisting.fandom.com/wiki/Frankensteinization. According to the site's homepage, "The Superpower Wiki (also known as Powerlisting) is the largest collection of superpowers known to humankind. With over 20,000 pages and climbing, the wiki aims to document and identify every single superpower that has ever revealed itself in any form of fiction. On top of being a place to spend hours of clicking and scrolling to different superpowers, the Superpower Wiki also serves as a resource to fiction writers who dabble in various extra-normal genres such as fantasy, superhero/cape punk, cyberpunk, mythology, science fiction, and more."
2 Roland Barthes' *The Fashion System* (1983; Berkeley: University of California Press, 1990) is one of the best-known applications of semiotics to popular culture.
3 Frankenstein's monster, image of Boris Karloff; from the *Wall Street Journal*, Saturday/Sunday, December 30, 2017, p. C4.
4 Alan Brookland, "The Man Who Invented Frankenstein's Monster's Bolt." Available at: http://alanbrookland.com/2009/10/27/the-man-who-invented-frankensteins-monsters-bolt/;
5 These lines begin chapter 5. In chapter 10 he also regrets his actions and wishes that he could extinguish that spark. Echoing his words, the monster himself, in the opening sentence of chapter 16, asks why he didn't immediately extinguish the spark of life as soon as he became a conscious being.
6 See, for instance, the cover of Graham Allen, *Shelley's Frankenstein* (London and New York: Continuum, 2008).
7 There was even a series of 18 Marvel comic books titled "The Frankenstein Monster."
8 See www.youtube.com/watch?v=2rXb1YVA6iA
9 Henry I. Miller and Gregory Conko, *The Frankenfood Myth: How Protest and Politics Threaten the Biotech Revolution* (Westport, CT: Praeger, 2004).
10 The advertisement for these bills says, "humorous and amazing manipulation of dollar bills by James Charles. From Star Wars to Jimi Hendrix via politicians or pop icons, James Charles did them all! Currently exhibiting at Shooting Gallery in San Francisco, they are still couple of them for sale, averaging around $70. Very worth it for these beautiful pieces of modern art"; Cyril Foiret, "Currency manipulations by James Charles". Available at: https://trendland.com/currency-manipulations-by-james-charles/.
11 Frankenstein's monster, image of Boris Karloff; from the *Wall Street Journal*, Saturday/Sunday, December 30, 2017, p. C4.

12 See the Flickery Flicks blog "The Frankenstein Concept: An Idea Ripe for Parody" Available at: https://flickeryflicks.blogspot.com/2021/08/the-frankenstein-concept-idea-ripe-for.html.

Chapter 6

1. Bruno Latour, *Reassembling the Social: An Introduction to Actor-Network-Theory* (Oxford: Oxford University Press, 2005).
2. Rafael Jean and Robert I. Lublin, "Fashioning Frankenstein in Film: Monsters and Men," in *Fashioning Horror: Dressing to Kill on Screen and in Literature*, eds. Julia Petrov and Gudrun D. Whitehead (London: Bloomsbury, 2017), 163.
3. Jean and Lublin, "Fashioning Frankenstein in Film," 163.
4. "Exclusive Interview: A History of Don Post Studios." Famous Monsters of Filmland. 4 pages. April 5, 2016. Available online: www.famousmonsters.com/exclusive-a-history-of-don-post-studios/.
5. Donald. F. Glut, *The Frankenstein Archive: Essays on the Monster, the Myth, the Movies, and More* (Jefferson, NC: McFarland, 2002), 35.
6. "Exclusive Interview," 3.
7. Glut, *The Frankenstein Archive*, 47.
8. Jean Baudrillard. "Simulacra and Simulations," in *Selected Writings*, ed. Mark Poster. (Stanford, CA: Stanford University Press, 1988), 166–84.
9. "Exclusive Interview," 2.
10. Elizabeth Enochs, "The History of Halloween Costumes Is Way Weirder Than You Could Have Guessed," *Bustle*, 18 October 2016. Available at: www.bustle.com/articles/189827-the-history-of-halloween-costumes-is-way-weirder-than-you-could-have-guessed. Accessed July 25, 2019.
11. Charles Moss, "How Ben Cooper Changed Halloween Forever." *Slate* October 31, 2013. Available at: https://slate.com/human-interest/2013/10/ben-cooper-costumes-how-the-popular-plastic-outfits-reinvented-halloween.html.
12. A photograph of this catalog page may be viewed at http://euclidboo.com/1968-ben-cooper-spook-town-halloween-costume-catalog/.
13. Julia Kristeva, *Powers of Horror: An Essay in Abjection*, trans. Leon S. Roudiez (New York: Columbia University Press, 1982).
14. Photos of this costume may be viewed at Universal Monster Army. See www.universalmonsterarmy.com/forum/index.php?topic=28046.15.
15. "Big Frank." Halloween Costumes.com. Available at: www.halloweencostumes.com/big-frank-costume.html.
16. A video featuring this mask and its history can be viewed at "2000 Don Post Studios 'Frankenstein Futura," 16 September 2019. Available at: www.youtube.com/watch?v=SOSn_TIvhFg.

Chapter 7

1. It is narrative tradition in the comics medium to use < > to indicate when dialogue is being translated from a foreign language for the reader's benefit. I have chosen to preserve this textual feature for the sake of accuracy. Victor Lavalle and Dietrich Smith, *Destroyer* (Los Angeles: Boom! Studios, 2018), 1.4.

2   Jason N. Bruck, "Decades-long Social Memory in Bottlenose Dolphins," *Proceedings of the Royal Society B: Biological Sciences*, 280, no. 1768 (2013), 1–2. Available at: https://royalsocietypublishing.org/doi/epdf/10.1098/rspb.2013.1726; Stephen E.G. Lea and Britta Osthaus, "In What Sense are Dogs Special? Canine Cognition in Comparative Context," *Learning & Behavior* 46 (2018), 335–63.
3   LaValle and Smith, 1.8.
4   Paul Bloom, *Against Empathy: The Case for Rational Compassion* (New York: HarperCollins, 2016), 178.
5   Ibid., 181.
6   LaValle and Smith, 2.2.
7   Ibid., 2.11.
8   Shaila Dewan and Richard A. Oppel Jr., "In Tamir Rice Case, Many Errors by Cleveland Police, Then a Fatal One," *New York Times* January 22, 2015. Available at: www.nytimes.com/2015/01/23/us/in-tamir-rice-shooting-in-cleveland-many-errors-by-police-then-a-fatal-one.html.
9   Goff et al., 526.
10 John J. DiIulio Jr., William J. Bennet, and John. P. Walters, *BODY COUNT: Moral Poverty . . . And How to Win America's War Against Crime and Drugs* (New York: Simon and Schuster, 1996), 27.
11 Ibid., 45.
12 An increasing number of news outlets, criminal justice reform advocates, and scholars of the criminal justice system have remarked upon the rise of "warrior culture" within U.S. law-enforcement communities. As University of South Carolina Law Professor Seth W. Stoughton has noted: "From their earliest days in the academy, would-be officers are told that their prime objective, the proverbial 'first rule of law enforcement,' is to go home at the end of every shift. But they are taught that they live in an intensely hostile world. [. . .] Fear is ubiquitous in law enforcement. As [Stoughton] has written elsewhere, officers are constantly barraged with the message that that (sic) they should be afraid, that their survival depends on it. Not only do officers hear it in formal training, they also hear it informally from supervisors and older officers. They talk about it with their peers. They see it on police forms and law enforcement publications." Seth W. Stoughton, "Law Enforcement's 'Warrior' Problem," *Harvard Law Review*, April 10, 2015. Available at: https://harvardlawreview.org/2015/04/law-enforcements-warrior-problem/.
13 In response to the prevalence of such discourse, an industry of warrior training seminars has arisen around law enforcement culture. As *Slate*'s Alain Stephens notes: "There is now a cottage industry of police consultants, which charge departments thousands of dollars to teach tactics more suited for war than civil society. Classes run the gamut of militarized policing, and are often taught by combat-tested former soldiers and SWAT officers." These courses include the mastery of such diverse skills as "the fundamentals of 'using a knife in a deadly force encounter'", "how to use a military sniper rifle in 'unique applications'," and "Law Enforcement Airborne [training]" in which SWAT team officers can learn to "parachute from planes." Alain Stephens, "The 'Warrior Cop' is a Toxic Mentality. And A Lucrative Industry," *Slate* June 19, 2020). Available at: https://slate.com/news-and-politics/2020/06/warrior-cop-trainings-industry.html.
14 Anthony Breznican, "*Destroyer* Comic Book Fuses Black Lives Matter with Frankenstein," *Entertainment Weekly*, February 13, 2017. Available at: https://ew.com/books/2017/02/13/destroyer-comic-black-lives-matter-frankenstein/.

15 ibid
16 Mary Shelley, *Frankenstein*, 3rd edition (New York: W.W. Norton, 2022), 99–100.
17 Victor LaValle, *The Ballad of Black Tom* (New York: Tom Doherty Associates, LLC, 2017), 130.
18 Breznican.
19 Ibid.
20 LaValle and Smith, 3.18.
21 Shelley, 28.
22 LaValle and Smith, 3.3.
23 Shelley, 35.
24 LaValle and Smith, 5.13.
25 Breznican.
26 LaValle and Smith, 3.15
27 Ibid., 6.4.
28 Norbert Wiener, *The Human Use of Human Beings: Cybernetics and Society* (London: Free Association Books, 1989), 61.
29 Ibid., 72.
30 N. Katherine Hayles, *How We Became Posthuman: Virtual Bodies in Cybernetics, Literature, and Informatics*, (London: University of Chicago Press, 1999), 87.

Chapter 8

1 *Presumption; or, The Fate of Frankenstein* premiered in 1823 at the English Opera House in London.
2 In June 1816, Mary Shelley participated in a now-famous ghost story contest at the Villa Diodati outside Geneva. Along with Percy Shelley, Lord Byron, and John Polidori, Mary set out to write a tale of terror. Prompted by Byron's suggestion, the competition between friends provided the impetus for Shelley to compose her most famous literary work.
3 The first recorded play that specifically focused on Mary Shelley was Mary Humphrey Baldridge's *Genesis: The Mary Shelley Play* (1978). Four years after Baldridge's play premiered in Canada, Liz Lochhead's *Blood and Ice: The Story of the Creation of Frankenstein* debuted at the Edinburgh Fringe Festival in Scotland.
4 Mary Shelley, *Frankenstein*, ed. M.K. Joseph (Oxford University Press, 2008), 351.
5 Steven Earl Forry, *Hideous Progenies: Dramatizations of Frankenstein from the Nineteenth Century to the Present* (Philadelphia: University of Pennsylvania Press, 1990), 2.
6 Nick Dear's successful reimaging of *Frankenstein* was performed at London's National Theatre and has attracted international audiences through cinema broadcasts, which have been held every year since its 2011 debut. For more on Nick Dear's *Frankenstein*, see Kelly Jones' "Adaptations of 'Liveness' in Theatrical Representations of Mary Shelley's *Frankenstein*" in *Adapting Frankenstein: The Monster's Eternal Lives in Popular Culture*, eds. Dennis R. Cutchins and Dennis R. Perry (Manchester: Manchester University Press, 2018), 316–334.
7 These include Betty T. Bennet's publication of the first volume of Mary Shelley's complete letters (Baltimore: Johns Hopkins University Press, 1980) as well as Paula Feldman and Diana Scott-Kilvert's edition of her *Journals* (Oxford: Clarendon Press, 1987).

8   *Don't Talk to Me of Love* was first performed at the Looking Glass Theatre New Works Forum.
9   *The Apology* was first produced by Rabiayshna Productions in Toronto. It was extended and received a second premiere production in 2013 at Alberta Theatre Projects in Calgary.
10 *Hideous Progeny* was produced by Livewire Chicago Theatre and staged at the DCA Storefront Theatre in Chicago. *Justified Sinners* was first staged in Edmonton at the University of Alberta and was written and staged as part of my doctoral project on Romantic Biodramas.
11 *Mary Shelley* premiered at the West Yorkshire Playhouse in Leeds and was subsequently given a touring production across England. The script was published that same year (Nottingham: Nottingham Playhouse, 2012).
12 In addition to theatrical adaptations, several twentieth-century cinematic adaptations of *Frankenstein*, such as *Frankenstein: The True Story* (New York City: Avon, 1973) and *Frankenstein Unbound* (New York: HarperCollins, 1973), feature Mary Shelley as a character within the narrative. Many biofictions connect the novel to her experiences during the infamous summer of 1816, such as Peter Ackroyd's *The Casebook of Victor Frankenstein* (New York: Vintage, 2009), Suzanne Burdon's *Almost Invincible* (Sydney: Criteria, 2014), Antoinette May's *The Determined Heart* (Seattle: Lake Union Publishing, 2015), and Sarah Stegall's *Outcasts* (San Antonio: Wings Press, 2016). As well, biopics that infer a connection between Mary's life and *Frankenstein* include Ken Russell's *Gothic* (Virgin Vision, 1986), Gonzalo Suárez's *Rowing with the Wind* (Ditirambo, 1988), Ivan Passer's *Haunted Summer* (Cannon Films, 1988), and Haifaa al-Mansour's *Mary Shelley* (HanWay Films, 2017).
13 *The Mary Shelley Opera* was written by Allan Jaffe, Deborah Atherton, and Stephen Hannock and produced by Parabola Arts and debuted at the New York Society for Ethical Culture. *Monster: An Opera in Two Acts* was written with music by Sally Beamish and libretto by Janice Galloway. It was produced by Scottish Opera and the Brighton Festival and performed at the Theatre Royal in Glasgow.
14 *Mary Shelley's Frankenstein* (2017) was created by Eve Wolf and ensemble for Ensemble for the Romantic Century in New York City.
15 The use of Shelley's name to suggest a close link between adaptations of *Frankenstein* and her novel has become a very popular choice. For example, Kenneth Branagh's film adaptation *Mary Shelley's Frankenstein* (TriStar Pictures, 1994) and the full title of Nick Dear's theatrical adaptation: *Frankenstein: Based on the Novel by Mary Shelley* (London: Faber Drama, 2011).
16 Shelley's *Frankenstein* (1818) has often been read as a coded (auto)biography. Critical readings of *Frankenstein* as an (auto)biographical text include Elisabeth Bronfen's "Rewriting the Family: Mary Shelley's *Frankenstein* in its Biographical/Textual Context" in *Frankenstein: Creation and Monstrosity* (London: Reaktion, 1994), 16–38, Anne K. Mellor's *Mary Shelley: Her Life, Her Fiction, Her Monsters* (London: Methuen, 1988), and Fiona Simpson's *In Search of Mary Shelley: The Girl Who Wrote Frankenstein* (New York City: Pegasus Books, 2018).
17 For example, the 1973 teleplay for *Frankenstein: The True Story* opens at the Villa Diodati. In this adaptation, Mary tells the group that they will play a direct role in the telling of the tale and identifies herself as Elizabeth.
18 *Frankenstein Incarnate: The Passions of Mary Shelley* was produced by Theatre Unbound and first performed in St. Paul, Minnesota at the Neighborhood House.

19 Dorset Corset was formed in 2006 by Helen Watts, Ed Burnside and Fiona Davis. See "About The Dorset Corset Theatre Company" (2019). Available at: www.mandy.com/ca/company/dorset-corset-theatre-company.
20 The Shelley Theatre, located in Bournemouth, England. The theatre was originally Boscombe Manor, the former residence of Mary and Percy's son, Percy Florence, and his wife, Lady Jane Shelley. The couple intended for Mary to move into the home, but she passed away in 1851 before it was completed. The site was converted to a theatre in 1865.
21 Carlson, *The Haunted Stage: The Theatre as Memory Machine* (Ann Arbor: University of Michigan Press, 2003), 2.
22 1816 has been referred to as "The Year without a Summer" after the 1815 volcanic eruption of Mount Tambora in Indonesia caused widespread crop failure and inclement weather through the following year.
23 The Villa Diodati group was comprised of Mary Shelley, Percy Shelley, Lord Byron, John Polidori, and Claire Clairmont, although not every member is commonly featured in *Frankenstein* Biodramas.
24 Helen Davis, *Frankenstein: The Year Without a Summer* (2010), 10, 12.
25 Ibid., 39.
26 Ibid., 30.
27 Ibid.
28 Ibid., 42.
29 Ibid.
30 Shelley, *Frankenstein*, 80.
31 *Birth of Frankenstein* was written by Adriano Sobretodo Jr, Matthew Thomas Walker, and Claire Wynveen. See "About Litmus Theatre" (2019). Available at: www.litmustheatre.com/about-us/.
32 Ibid. 3.
33 Joseph Roach, *Cities of the Dead: Circum-Atlantic Performance* (New York: Columbia University Press, 1996), 2.
34 Gary Kelly, "The Politics of Autobiography in Mary Wollstonecraft and Mary Shelley," in *Mary Wollstonecraft and Mary Shelley: Writing Lives*, eds.Helen M. Buss, D.L. Macdonald, and Anne McWhir (Waterloo: Wilfrid Laurier University Press, 2001), 25.
35 Sobretodo et. al, *Birth of Frankenstein*, 15.
36 Ibid.
37 Ibid.

Chapter 9

1 *Mary Shelley's Frankenstein* (1994), [Film] Dir. Kenneth Branagh, USA: TriStar Pictures.
2 Xavier Aldana Reyes, "Promethean Myths of the Twenty-First Century: Contemporary *Frankenstein* Film Adaptations and the Rise of the Viral Zombie," in *Global Frankenstein*, Carol Margaret Davison and Marie Mulvey-Roberts, eds. (Cham, Switzerland: Palgrave Macmillan 2018), 170.
3 Bouriana Zakharieva, "Frankenstein of the Nineties: The Composite Body," *Canadian Review of Comparative Literature* 23, no. 3 (1996), 739–52.
4 Mark Jancovich, "*Frankenstein* and Film," in *The Cambridge Companion to Frankenstein*, ed. Andrew Smith (Cambridge: Cambridge University Press, 2016), 201.

Two minor exceptions: 1999 saw the release of *Alvin and the Chipmunks Meet Frankenstein* as well as a comic, violent, sexploitative production titled *Rock and Roll Frankenstein*.
5 See Julie Sloan Brannon, "Mary Shelley's Frankenstein? Kenneth Branagh and Keeping Promises," *Studies in Popular Culture* 35, no. 1 (2012): 18, and P.J.P. García, "Beyond Adaptation: *Frankenstein's* Postmodern Progeny," in *Books in Motion: Adaptation, Intertextuality, Authorship*, ed. Mireia Aragay (Amsterdam, NY: Rodopi, 2005), 236.
6 Esther Schor, "Frankenstein and Film." in *Cambridge Companion to Mary Shelley*, ed. Esther Schor (New York: Cambridge University Press, 2003), 71.
7 Caroline Sloan Picart, "Visualizing the Monstrous in Frankenstein Films," *Pacific Coast Philology* 35, no. 1 (2000): 32.
8 Brannon, 6–7.
9 *I, Frankenstein* (2014), [Film] Dir. Stuart Beattie, USA: Lionsgate; *Frankenstein's Monster* (2014), [Film] Dir. Syd Lance, USA: First Step Cinematics; *Frankenstein vs. The Mummy* (2014), [Film] Dir. Damien Leone, USA: Image Entertainment; and *Scooby Doo! Frankencreepy* (2014), [Film] Dir. Paul McEvoy, USA: Warner Bros. Home Entertainment.
10 *The Frankenstein Theory* (2013), [Film] Dir. Andrew Weiner, USA: Image Entertainment; *Frankenstein's Army* (2013), [Film], Dir. Richard Raaphorst, USA: MPI Media Group; and *Army of Frankensteins* (2013), [Film] Dir. Ryan Bellgardt, USA: Transformer.
11 Even the earliest film versions of *Frankenstein* are significantly different from Shelley's novel, and then there are such movies as *Blackenstein* (1973) and *Frankenhooker* (1990).
12 *Frankenstein* (2004), [TV Film] Dir. Marcus Nispel, USA: Flame TV.
13 Kim Newman, *Nightmare Movies: Horror on Screen Since the 1960s* (New York: Bloomsbury, 2011), 360.
14 Brian Lowry (4 October 2004). "Frankenstein." *Variety*. Available at: https://variety.com/2004/scene/markets-festivals/frankenstein-8-1200530558/.
15 James A. W. Heffernan, "Looking at the Monster: *Frankenstein* and Film," *Critical Inquiry* 24, no. 1 (1997): 153.
16 Rafael Jaen and Robert I. Lublin, "Fashioning *Frankenstein* in Film: Brides of Frankenstein," in *Fashioning Horror: Dressing to Kill on Screen and in Literature*, eds. Julia Petrov and Gudrun D. Whitehead (New York: Bloomsbury, 2018), 78.
17 *The Frankenstein Syndrome* (2010), [Film] Dir. Sean Tretta, USA: NWR Productions.
18 Manohla Dargis, "'Victor Frankenstein' Recasts a Tale that Keeps on Giving," Review of *Victor Frankenstein*, Directed by Paul McGuigan, *The New York Times*, Nov. 25, 2015.
19 Heffernan, 147.
20 David Pirie, *A Heritage of Horror: The English Gothic Cinema, 1946–1972*, (London: Gordon Fraser 1973), 70.
21 Rafael Jaen and Robert I. Lublin, "Fashioning *Frankenstein* in Film: Monsters and Men," in *Fashioning Horror: Dressing to Kill on Screen and in Literature*, eds. Julia Petrov, Gudrun D. Whitehead (New York: Bloomsbury, 2018), 171.
22 There is only one instance in twenty-first century films in which the creation proves worse than the scientist: the monster created in *Frankenstein Vs. The Mummy* (2014) has the brain of a murderer, and when he remembers who he used to be, he pursues his evil designs with the strength of his new body. But even here, the scientist's immorality and immoral experiments are key to the film.
23 Reyes, 170.

24 Jancovich, 202.
25 Ryan Bellgardt, Plot Summary of Army of Frankensteins (2013)" *IMDB*. Available at: www.imdb.com/title/tt2620490/
26 Brannon, 14.
27 *Frankenstein* (2007), [TV Film] Dir. Jed Mercurio, UK: Impossible Pictures; FRANK3N5T31N (2015), [Film] Dir. Bernard Rose, USA: Alchemy.
28 Lissette Lopez Szwydky and Michelle L. Pribbernow. "Women scientists in Frankenstein films, 1945–2015." *Science Fiction Film and Television* 11, no. 2 (2018): 305.
29 Ibid., 326.
30 *Frankenstein's Creature* (2018) is another "Frankenstein" film presented from the viewpoint of Victor's creation. It is a cinematic staging of a one-man theatrical performance that follows the novel and provides a compelling story from his own subjective experience. *Frankenstein's Creature* (2018), [Film] Dir. Sam Ashurst, UK: Hex Studios.
31 Szwydky and Pribbernow, 328.
32 *A Nightmare Wakes: The Birth of Frankenstein* (2020), [Film] Dir. Nora Unkel, USA: Shudder.
33 Reyes, 169.
34 Picart, Caroline S. *The Cinematic Rebirths of Frankenstein: Universal, Hammer, and Beyond* (Westport, Connecticut: Praeger, 2002), xiv.

Chapter 10

1 Justin D. Edwards, *Gothic Canada: Canada: Reading the Spectre of a National Literature* (Edmonton: University of Alberta Press, 2005), 62.
2 Carol Margaret Davison and Marie Mulvey-Roberts, "Introduction: Global Reanimations of Frankenstein," in *Global Frankenstein*, eds.Carol Margaret Davison and Marie Mulvey-Roberts (Basingtsoke: Palgrave, 2018), 7.
3 Mark A. McCutcheon, "The Medium is ... the Monster? Global Aftermathematics in Canadian Articulations of *Frankenstein*," in *Local Natures, Global Responsibilities: Ecocritical Perspectives on the New English Literatures*, eds.Laurenz Volkmann, Nancy Grimm, Ines Detmers, and Katrin Thomson (New York: Rodopi, 2010), 207.
4 The second season of the show also gestures towards preoccupations with nature and the environment, but its focus seems to be placed more on matters of disease and geo-political exchanges. Although clearly salient overall, a discussion of these interactions is here saved for a different occasion.
5 Andrew Smith and William Hughes, *Ecogothic* (Manchester: Manchester University Press, 2016), 2.
6 Mary Shelley, *Frankenstein* (Oxford: Oxford Classics, 1999 [1818]), 188.
7 Ibid., 197.
8 Ibid., 176.
9 Ibid., 142.
10 Julia Kristeva, *Powers of Horror: An Essay on Abjection* (New York: Columbia University Press, 1982), 4.
11 Jean-Paul Sartre, *Being and Nothingness: An Essay on Phenomenological Ontology* (London: Routledge, 2003), 630.
12 Ibid. 629.

13 Benjamin A. Brabon "Gothic Geography, 1760–1830" in *The Gothic World*, eds.Glennis Byron and Dale Townshend (Abingdon: Routledge, 2013), 101.
14 Thomas B. Okarma, "Human Embryonic Stem Cells: A Primer on the Technology and its Medical Application," in *The Human Embryonic Stem Cell Debate: Science, Ethics, and Public Policy*, eds.Suzanne Holland, Karen Lebacqz, Laurie Zoloth, and Arthur L. Caplan (Cambridge, MA: The MIT Press, 2001), 4.
15 Claire Williams and Steven Wainwright, "Sociological Reflections on Ethics, Embyronic Stem Cells, and Translational Research," in *Contested Cells: Global Perspectives on the Stem Cell Debate*, eds.Benjamin J. Capps and Alastair V. Campbell (London: Imperial College Press, 2010), 164.
16 Kristeva, *Powers of Horror*, 4.
17 Ibid, 4.
18 Smith and Hughes, *Ecogothic*, 1.
19 Greg Garrard, *Ecocriticism* (London: Routledge, 2004), 5.
20 Brian Merchant, qtd in Elizabeth Parker, "Just a Piece of Wood" in *Plant Horror: Approaches to the Monstrous Vegetal in Fiction and Film*, eds.Dawn Keetley and Angela Tenga (Palgrave: Macmillan, 2016), 217.
21 Ibid.
22 Ibid., 218.
23 Shelby Heathcoat, "Escape to nature in Ann Radcliffe's *The Mysteries of Udolpho*," in *Global Perspectives in Eco-Aesthetics and Eco-Ethics: A Green Critique*, eds.Frederick Gordon, David R. Cole, Susan Harris, and Pramod K. Nayar (Lanham: Lexington, 2019), 203.

Chapter 11

1 Data Age, *Frankenstein's Monster* (Campbell, CA: Data Age, Inc., 1983); Tose Software, *Frankenstein: The Monster Returns* (Tokyo: Bandai Co., Ltd., 1991); Bits Studios, *Mary Shelley's Frankenstein* (Los Angeles: Sony Imagesoft, 1994); and La Belle Games, *The Wanderer: Frankenstein's Creature* (Strasbourg: ARTE, 2019). *The Wanderer* was released on Valve Corporation's Steam distribution platform and is available as well on platforms such as Android, iOS, Microsoft Windows, Linux, Nintendo Switch, Macintosh operating systems, etc. This chapter's partial critical walkthrough is based on play via the Steam platform.
2 Donna Haraway, *The Companion Species Manifesto: Dogs, People, and Significant Otherness* (Chicago: Prickly Paradigm Press, 2003).
3 Alenda Y. Chang, *Playing Nature: Ecology in Video Games* (Minneapolis: University of Minnesota Press, 2019), 10, 23.
4 Ibid., 6.
5 Ibid., 2.
6 Ibid., 32.
7 See Alyssa Wejebe, "Making *The Wanderer: Frankenstein's Creature* Closer to Mary Shelley's Vision," *Cliqist: Indie Gaming*. May 6, 2019. Available at: cliqist.com/2019/05/06/making-the-wanderer-frankensteins-creature-closer-to-mary-shelleys-vision/.
8 La Belle Games, *Frankenstein: Birth of a Myth* (Strasbourg: ARTE, 2018). This prequel game is available for play online at the following website: www.frankenstein.arte.tv/game.html.

9 Jesper Juul, *Half-Real: Video Games between Real Rules and Fictional Worlds* (Cambridge, MA: The MIT Press, 2005), 92.
10 Because the game itself depicts each new level of play as a novel chapter deriving from the advancing pages of an iconographic book, I refer to game levels as "chapters." This chapter's title most likely refers to the Latin "alba," the feminine form of the adjective "albus" ("white, light-coloured"). See the *Oxford Latin Dictionary*, s.v. "albus." All subsequent Latin to English translations are provided as notes and are based on the *Oxford Latin Dictionary*, ed. P. G. W. Glare (Oxford: Clarendon Press, 1982).
11 Mary Shelley, *Frankenstein; or, The Modern Prometheus* (1818), eds. D. L. Macdonald and Kathleen Scherf, 2nd edn. (Peterborough: Broadview Press, 1999), 82.
12 "The power or faculty of remembering, memory." *Oxford Latin Dictionary*, s.v. "memoria."
13 Chang, *Playing Nature*, 31–32. Also see thatgamecompany, *Flower* (Tokyo: Sony Computer Entertainment Inc., 2009).
14 "Nature (as the power which determines the physical properties of animals, plants, and other natural products)" or "(as the power which regulates physical requirements)" or "(as determining the span of life)." *Oxford Latin Dictionary*, s.v. "nātūra."
15 Shelley, *Frankenstein*, 128.
16 Noah Wardrip-Fruin, *How Pac-Man Eats* (Cambridge, MA: The MIT Press, 2020), 9.
17 Alexander R. Galloway, *Gaming: Essays on Algorithmic Culture* (Minneapolis: University of Minnesota Press, 2006), 90.
18 Ibid., 90–1, 91.
19 McKenzie Wark, *Gamer Theory* (Cambridge, MA: Harvard University Press, 2007), 21–22.
20 "([P]l.) the world of men, the living." *Oxford Latin Dictionary*, s.v. "homō."
21 "An unnatural event or manifestation portending a disaster, etc., prodigy" or a "monstrous event or situation, marvel" or "a monstrous person, creature, thing, etc., monstrosity; also, a wonder, marvel." *Oxford Latin Dictionary*, s.v. "prōdigium."
22 Shelley, *Frankenstein*, 139.
23 "Highest in position, topmost, uppermost" or "(applied for emphasis to things naturally high)" or "the top or summit of" or "the highest point, top, summit"; "[a] culminating state." *Oxford Latin Dictionary*, s.v. "summus"; s.v. "summitās."
24 Wark, *Gamer Theory*, 14.
25 "Diligent activity directed to some purpose, application, industry, etc." or "a particular example of diligence, a purposeful activity, etc." or "[p]urposefulness." *Oxford Latin Dictionary*, s.v. "industria."
26 Patrick Jagoda, *Experimental Games: Critique, Play, and Design in the Age of Gamification* (Chicago: University of Chicago Press, 2020), 28.
27 Ibid., 38.
28 "A smooth or level surface, expanse" or "the surface-level (of the sea)" or "[t]he sea, esp. considered as calm and flat." *Oxford Latin Dictionary*, s.v. "aequor."
29 Nintendo R&D4, *Super Mario Bros.* (Kyoto: Nintendo Co., Ltd., 1985).
30 Chang, *Playing Nature*, 33.
31 "Absence of sound, silence, quiet" or "ceremonial silence" or "[t]he fact of abstaining from speech, utterance, or other noise, silence." *Oxford Latin Dictionary*, s.v. "silentium."
32 Shelley, *Frankenstein*, 244.
33 Ibid., 243.
34 Shane Denson, *Discorrelated Images* (Durham, NC: Duke University Press, 2020), 131.
35 Ibid., 131.
36 Shelley, *Frankenstein*, 244.

37 Andrew Burkett, *Romantic Mediations: Media Theory and British Romanticism* (Albany, NY: State University of New York Press, 2016), 115–34.
38 Denson, *Discorrelated Images*, 130.
39 Ibid., 131.
40 As cited by Wejebe, "Making *The Wanderer: Frankenstein's Creature* Closer to Mary Shelley's Vision," *Cliqist: Indie Gaming*. May 6, 2019. Available at: www.cliqist.com/2019/05/06/making-the-wanderer-frankensteins-creature-closer-to-mary-shelleys-vision/.
41 Jagoda, *Experimental Games*, 38–39.

Chapter 12

1 See NewMusicNewCollege webpage "It's Alive!: A Monstrous Circus on *Frankenstein*, Available at: www.newmusicnewcollege.org/frankenstein. As situated in the full season here: www.newmusicnewcollege.org/2017-2018season.html. David Gulliver's story on the program "New College Presents the Frankenstein Story You Don't Know" is available at: https://news.ncf.edu/news/new-college-presents-the-frankenstein-story-you-dont-know/22 Jan. 2018.
2 Performed as a radio play in 1979. Available at: www.youtube.com/watch?v=bdHe4c10smY, it was first broadcast in Germany in 1979 and later performed live in Paris in 1980 (*New York Times*, 1986). Available at: www.nytimes.com/1986/10/08/arts/dance-roaratorio-at-next-wave.html. Another version in collaboration with Merce Cunningham took place in 1986. Available at: www.youtube.com/watch?v=gGHvnRtr3TI.
3 Mary Shelley, *Frankenstein*, ed. J. Paul Hunter, A Norton Critical Edition (New York: W.W. Norton, 1996).
4 Laurence Venuti, "Genealogies of Translation Theory: Schleiermacher," *érudit* 4, no. 2 (1991): 126.
5 See Courtney Hoffman's "'Now I am a man!': Performing Sexual Violence in the National Theatre Production of *Frankenstein*" in *Global Frankenstein*, eds.Carol Margaret Davison and Marie Mulvey-Roberts, (New York, NY: Palgrave MacMillan, 2018) for an interesting analysis of the ways that the play positions first the female creature as-to-be-looked at, and then enacts the creature's meeting with Elizabeth as a rape/murder scene in which child imitates creator. This latter scene is an example of the interpretive force of the translation to live performance in contrast with Elizabeth's off-stage death in Victor's own narrative in Shelley's original. Students are always stunned that Victor conceives the creature's threat to be "with him" on his wedding night as one to Victor's life, rather than a threat to Elizabeth. Hoffman's essay captures why they see that death coming and how Dear's adaptation, as realized in Boyle's production, follows the logic of what we might term "toxic masculinity."

Chapter 13

1 Holly Williams, "Why the Beatles' Yellow Submarine is a trippy cult classic" *BBC.com*, July 25, 2018. Available at: www.bbc.com/culture/article/20180724-why-the-beatles-yellow-submarine-is-a-trippy-cult-classic.

2 The director of animation, Heinz Edelmann, was responsible for the psychedelic style of the film, while the avant-garde quality of his artistry contrasts sharply with the film's closest antecedent, Disney's "Fantasia." Edelmann paved the way for Peter Max's psychedelic style as well as the brilliance of Terry Gilliam's Monty Python animation. See Melissa U.D. Goldsmith, Paige A. Willson, Anthony J. Fonseca, eds, *The Encyclopedia of Musicians and Bands on Film*, (Rowman & Littlefield, 2016), 347–55.
3 See https://en.wikipedia.org/wiki/My_Own_Version_of_You. See also the review in the British music paper *Melody Maker* of the entire album. Available at: https://melodymakermagazine.com/2021/05/11/bob-dylan-rough-and-rowdy-ways/.
4 Rona Cran, *Collage in Twentieth-Century Art, Literature, and Culture: Joseph Cornell, William Burroughs, Frank O'Hara, and Bob Dylan* (Abingdon: Routledge, 2014).
5 Graley Herren, "Mythic Quest in Bob Dylan's Blonde on Blonde," *Rock Music Studies* 5, no. 2 (2018): 124–41.
6 Available at: https://bob-dylan.org.uk/archives/15413, *Untold* Dylan, June 25, 2020.
7 Cypress trees are mourning trees in various mythic traditions. The willow was a sacred tree for the Celts; in Celtic mythology it is associated with death goddesses, and in Greek mythology with goddesses of the underworld, both of which are appropriate to the themes of Dylan's lyrics. Sharon Paice MacLeod, *Celtic Myth and Religion: A Study of Traditional Belief, with Newly Translated Prayers, Poems and Songs* (Jefferson, NC: McFarland, 2011), 108–10.
8 Dylan has explored medieval forms elsewhere, such as the *ballade*. See Elizabeth Randell Upton's "Bob Dylan's Ballade," *Postmedieval: A Journal of Medieval Cultural Studies* 10, no.4 (2019): 452–65. Upton analyzes Dylan's 1975 "Tangled Up in Blue" from the album "Blood on the Tracks" as having a musical structure that follows the scheme of a medieval song form, the ballade.
9 For how innovative Winter's synthesizer playing was for the early 1970s, see Mitchell Sigman's "Do It!: Soft Synths—Make the 'Frankenstein' Monster Lead Sound," *Keyboard* 34, no. 12 (hy): 62.
10 Loraine Alterman , "Edgar Winter: How Winter Went Glam and Created a Frankenstein Monster," *Melody Maker*, June 30, 1973, 3.
11 "It was cut up into pieces and we were trying to figure out how to put it back together," [Edgar Winter] recalls." John Law, "How Winter's Monster Was Born; Rock Jammer Who Wrote 'Frankenstein' Is Back on Tour with Ringo Starr's All-Starr Band." *Toronto Star*, June 20, 2008: E02.
12 Available at: www.rollingstone.com/music/blogs/staff-blog/the-twenty-five-best-rock-instrumentals-20071015.
13 Available at: www.richardorpheuscampbell.com/frankensteintmo. Accessed July 30, 2021.
14 Maura Judkis, "It's aliiiiive: 'Frankenstein' prog-metal opera makes its debut at GALA Hispanic Theatre," *The Washington Post*, June 6, 2013. Available at: www.washingtonpost.com/goingoutguide/its-aliiiiive-frankenstein-prog-metal-opera-makes-its-debut-at-gala-hispanic-theatre/2013/06/06/992d806a-c941-11e2-9f1a-1a7cdee20287_story.html.
15 Nick Tosches, "Transformer—Album Reviews," *Rolling Stone*, January 4, 1973. Available at: www.rollingstone.com/music/music-album-reviews/transformer-89126/.
16 Alfred Hickling, "Frankenstein's Wedding," *The Guardian*, March 20, 2011. Available at: www.theguardian.com/stage/2011/mar/20/frankensteins-wedding-review.
17 Available at: www.bbc.co.uk/pressoffice/pressreleases/stories/2011/02_february/18/frankenstein5.shtml.

18 John Baron, "Opinion: Frankenstein's Wedding—Leeds did itself proud," *The Guardian*, March 21, 2011. Available at: www.theguardian.com/leeds/2011/mar/21/opinion-frankenstein-s-wedding-leeds-did-itself-proud.
19 Liz Nicholls, "Frankenstein shakes a funnier bone; Music runs gamut from big ballads to show numbers to rock 'n' roll," *Edmonton Journal*, October 21, 1993: D3.
20 Mark A. McCutcheon, "Techno, Frankenstein and Copyright," *Popular Music* 26.2 (2007): 259–80.
21 Ibid., 259.
22 Ibid., 262.
23 Ibid., 259.
24 Angela M. Smith, "Walk This Way: Frankenstein's Monster, Disability Performance, and Zombie Ambulation," *Literature and Medicine* 36 no. 2 (2018): 412–38.
25 Ibid., 412.
26 Ibid., 416–18.
27 These kinds of performances are termed "disability drag" or "cripface" by disability scholars. Ibid., 419.
28 Luke Jennings, "Frankenstein review—a monster hash from the Royal Ballet," *The Guardian*, May 8, 2016. Available at: www.theguardian.com/stage/2016/may/08/frankenstein-royal-ballet-review-liam-scarlett

Chapter 14

1 Mary Shelley, *Frankenstein, Or, The Modern Prometheus* (New York: Oxford University Press, 1998), 9.
2 In this case, the plural pronoun "they/their" is used as a gender-neutral pronoun, one of the gender-neutral possibilities preferred by transgender persons and is therefore pertinent to cyborgs and perhaps the monstrous as well.
3 Gilles Deleuze and Felix Guattari, *A Thousand Plateaus: Capitalism and Schizophrenia* (Minneapolis: University of Minnesota Press, 1987).
4 Margaret Hart, *Untitled* (unpublished, 2016–present).
5 Rosi Braidotti, *The Posthuman* (Cambridge: Polity Press, 2013).
6 Bret McCabe, "Two Centuries of Frankenstein: John Hopkins Experts Discuss the Issues Raised by Mary Shelley's Groundbreaking Novel," *The Hub*, (October 2018). Available at: https://hub.jhu.edu/2018/10/29/frankenstein-200-years-experts/.
7 Katherine N. Hayles, *How We Became Posthuman: Virtual Bodies in Cybernetics, Literature, and Informatics* (Chicago: University of Chicago Press, 1999), 23.
8 Donna Haraway, *Simians, Cyborgs, and Women: The Reinvention of Nature* (New York: Routledge, 1991), 154.
9 Andy Clark, *Natural–Born Cyborgs: Mind, Technologies, and the Future of Human Intelligence* (New York: Oxford University Press, 2003). "Scaffolding" is described as any tool or device that extends our bodies and minds beyond a natural state.
10 College Art Association, "Code of Best Practices in Fair Use for the Visual Arts," (February 2015). Available at: www.collegeart.org/pdf/fair-use/best-practices-fair-use-visual-arts.pdf..
11 "How Gene Editing Could Break the Rules of Evolution," *WBUR: On Point with Tom Ashbrook*, [radio program, Tom Ashbrook], (November 9, 2015). Available at: www.wbur.org/onpoint/2015/11/09/gene-editing.

12 Jocelyn Kaiser, "A Human Has Been Injected with Gene-editing Tools to Cure His Disabling Disease. Here's What You Need to Know," *Science Magazine* (November 15, 2017). Available at: www.sciencemag.org/news/2017/11/human-has-been-injected-gene-editing-tools-cure-his-disabling-disease-here-s-what-you..
13 Dennis Normile, "CRISPR Bombshell: Chinese Researcher Claims to Have Created Gene-edited Twins," *Science Magazine* (November 26, 2018). Available at: www.sciencemag.org/news/2018/11/crispr-bombshell-chinese-researcher-claims-have-created-gene-edited-twins.
14 Maud Lavin, *Cut with the Kitchen Knife: The Weimar Photomontages of Hannah Höch* (New Haven and London: Yale University Press, 1993), 4–5.
15 Kristine Stiles and Peter Selz, eds., *Theories and Documents of Contemporary Art: A Sourcebook of Artist's Writings* (Los Angeles: University of California Press, 1996), 151–54.
16 Thalia Gouma–Peterson, *Miriam Schapiro: Shaping the Fragments of Art and Life* (New York: Harry N. Abrams, Inc., 1999), 13.
17 Chiwoniso Kaitano, "The Afrofuturism of Wangechi Mutu," *The Guardian*, (November 13, 2013). Available at: www.theguardian.com/world/2013/nov/13/wangechi–mutu–art–afrofuturism.
18 Trevor Schoonmaker, ed., *Wangechi Mutu: A Fantastic Journey* (Durham: Duke University Press, 2013), 38.
19 Douglas Singleton, ed., *Wangechi Mutu: A Shady Promise* (Bologna: Damiani, 2008), 146.
20 Rosi Braidotti, *Metamorphoses: Towards a Materialist Theory of Becoming* (Cambridge: Polity Press, 2002), 73.
21 Ibid., 86.
22 Ibid.
23 Kaye Mitchell, "Bodies that Matter: Science Fiction, *Technoculture*, and the Gendered Body," *Science Fiction Studies*, (March 2006). Available at: www.depauw.edu/sfs/backissues/98/mitchell98.html.
24 Ursula K. Le Guin, *The Left Hand of Darkness*, (New York: Ace Books, 1987), iii.
25 Rosi Braidotti, *Nomadic Theory: The Portable Rosi Braidotti*, (New York: Columbia University Press, 2011), 328. The term "potentia" is taken from Spinoza's theory of a body's power to persist in being; *potentia* is power that is immanent and constitutive rather than imposed from above.
26 Shelley, *Frankenstein*, 9.

Coda

1 Recent collections include *Transmedia Creatures: Frankenstein's Afterlives*, eds. Francesca Saggini and Anna Enrichetta Soccio (Lewisburg: Bucknell University Press, 2019); *Adapting Frankenstein: The Monster's Eternal Lives in Popular Culture*, eds. Dennis R. Cutchins and Dennis R. Perry (Manchester: Manchester University Press, 2018); *Global Frankensteins*, eds. Carol Margaret Davison and Marie Mulvey-Roberts (Basingstoke and New York: Palgrave Macmillan, 2018); and *The Cambridge Companion to Frankenstein*, ed. Andrew Smith (Cambridge: Cambridge University Press, 2016).
2 On Frankenfictions see Megen De Bruin-Molé, *Gothic Remixed: Monster Mashups and Frankenfictions in 21st-century Culture* (London: Bloomsbury, 2020).

3   *Victor LaValle's Destroyer* (Los Angeles: BOOM! Studios, 2018), summary.
4   "Memento Mori," *Penny Dreadful*, created by John Logan, series 2, episode 8, Desert Wolf Productions (2015).
5   Liz Lochhead, *Dreaming Frankenstein & Collected Poems 1967–1984* (Edinburgh: Polygon, 2003 [1984]), 10–11.
6   *The Mammoth Book of Frankenstein*, ed. Stephen Jones (London: Robinson Publishing, 2015 [1994]), 215.
7   Ibid., 232.
8   Ibid., 564.
9   Ibid., 244.
10 Cutchins and Perry, "Introduction: Frankenstein Complex," *Adapting Frankenstein*, 1.
11 Ahmed Saadawi, *Frankenstein in Baghdad*, trans. Jonathan Wright (London: Oneworld, 2018), 133.
12 Mary Shelley, *Frankenstein*, ed. J. Paul Hunter, 2nd edn (New York: Norton, 2012 [1996]), 102.
13 Brian Aldiss, *Frankenstein Rebound* (London: HarperCollins, 1973), 40.
14 Jeanette Winterson, *Frankissstein: A Love Story* (London: Jonathan Cape, 2019), 128.
15 Ibid., 27.
16 Ibid., 128.
17 Ibid., 127.
18 Shelley, *Frankenstein*, 118.
19 Ibid., 119.
20 Hilary Bailey, *Frankenstein's Bride* (London: Simon & Schuster, 1995), 85.
21 Ibid., 89.
22 Shelley, *Frankenstein*, 117.
23 Bailey, *Frankenstein's Bride*, 92.
24 Ibid., 93.
25 Elizabeth Hand, *The Bride of Frankenstein: Pandora's Bride* (Milwaukie OR: Dark Horse Books, 2007), 11.
26 Kate Horsley, *The Monster's Wife* (London: Barbican Press, 2014), 3, 35.
27 Ibid., 36.
28 Ibid., 70.
29 Ibid., 71.
30 Ibid., 156.
31 Ibid., 210.

Index

algorithm 29, 145–46, 225
Althusser, Louis 21, 208
antiracism 6
   see also race
ARTE 13, 141–42, 224, 149–51
Artificial Intelligence, AI 6, 11, 29–30, 34, 58, 101, 210, 211
assemblage 12, 86
Attwood, Tony
   Untold Dylan 175, 227

Babbage, Charles 11, 29–30, 32, 210
Barbauld, Anna Laetita 22–23
   Eighteen Hundred and Eleven: A Poem (1852) 22
becoming-woman 187
Bertram, Ann 116
biodrama 12, 113, 114, 121, 220–21
Boyle, Danny 5, 116, 167, 226
Braidotti, Rosi 188, 195–96, 197–98, 228, 229
Branagh, Kenneth 13, 123–26, 129, 130, 132, 205, 208, 220, 221, 222
Byron, Lord 116–18, 119–20, 212, 219, 221
   as a character 116–20, 142–43, 224

Cage, John 13, 157–59, 161, 162, 164, 165–67
capitalism 28, 60–61, 107, 228
Carey, Pauline 114
Catholicism 25
Chang, Alenda Y. 142, 144, 151, 224, 225
Cheops 24, 26–27
Church, Fredric Edwin
   Twilight in the Wilderness (1860) 149
Circus On ___ 13, 158, 226
Clairmont, Claire 115, 119, 142, 212, 221
Clapton, Eric 179
collage 84, 191, 193, 227
colonial 56–61, 64, 214
   see also postcolonial

Condorcet, Marquise de (Nicolas de Caritat) 166
Cooper, Alice 177
coquel 199
CRISPR 190–91, 229
Cunningham, Merce 226
cyborg 4, 104, 126, 186, 188–89, 195, 197, 228

Davis, Helen 116–19, 221
Dear, Nick 114, 116, 167, 219, 220, 226
Deleuze, Gilles and Felix Guattari 186, 187, 228
   A Thousand Plateaus 186, 228
Dendinger, Emily 115
Denson, Shane 153–54, 207, 225, 226
deterritorialized 188
diegetic space 33, 37, 153
disability performance 182–83, 207, 228
Dorset Corset Theatre Company 116, 119, 221
Dylan, Bob 14, 172–74, 175, 176, 178–79, 180, 227
   Blonde on Blonde 174, 227
   "My Own Version of You" 14, 172–76, 178, 227
   Rough and Rowdy Ways 173

Eckhart, Aaron 129
ecocriticism 139, 224
EcoGothic 138–40, 223, 224
Electric Frankenstein 172, 173, 176
   How to Make a Monster, see Frankenstein songs and albums
experimental games 150, 154, 225, 226

Fender, Leo 179
Frankenstein comics and related subjects
   LaValle, Victor, *Destroyer* (2017) 12, 98–99, 103–5, 109, 165, 167, 199, 217, 218, 230

Manga 7, 49, 213
Marvel Comics 7, 105, 216
"The New Creator" (1889–1890 [Japan]) 11, 40–41, 43–46, 53, 213–14
Frankenstein films and videos
  Abbott and Costello Meet Frankenstein (Universal Pictures; 1948) 73, 88–89
  Army of Frankensteins (Transformer; 2013) 124, 129–30, 222, 223
  Bride of Frankenstein (James Whale, Universal Pictures, 1935) 71, 77, 105, 119, 176, 200, 207
  Depraved (IFC Midnight; 2019) 128
  Flesh for Frankenstein (Andy Warhol, Gold Film [Italy];1973) 181
  Frankenstein (Edison Studios; 1910) 70
  Frankenstein (James Whale, Universal Pictures; 1931) 87–88, 176, 177, 181, 183
  Frankenstein (Flame TV; 2004) 124–25
  Frankenstein (Lion's Gate; 2004) 126, 127, 129
  Frankenstein (Impossible Pictures; 2007) 131
  Frankenstein, The True Story (NBC; 1973) 124
  Frankenstein Reborn (The Asylum; 2005) 127
  "Frankenstein Syndrome," also titled "The Prometheus Project" (MTI Home Video; 2010) 126, 128, 131, 222
  Frankenstein Theory (Image Entertainment; 2013) 124, 222
  Frankenstein vs. The Mummy (Image Entertainment; 2015) 10, 19–20, 28, 124, 207
  Frankenstein's Army (MPI Media Group; 2013) 124, 126, 128–30
  Frankenstein's Monster (Independent; 2014) 124, 125
  Frankenweenie (Tim Burton, Walt Disney Studios; 1984 and 2012) 9, 201
  FRANK3N5T31N (Alchemy; 2015) 13, 131–32, 223
  House of Frankenstein (Universal Pictures; 1944) 88, 207
  I, Frankenstein (Lionsgate; 2014) 13, 124, 126, 129, 222
  "I'm Not Your (Nothing)" (music video; 1999) 176–77
  Mary Shelley's Frankenstein (Kenneth Branagh, TriStar; 1994) 123–24, 125, 130, 201, 205
  Nightmare Wakes: The Birth of Frankenstein (Shudder; 2020) 132, 223
  Scooby Doo! Frankencreepy (Warner Bros. Home Entertainment; 2014) 124
  Son of Frankenstein (Universal Pictures;1939) 200
  "Thriller" (Michael Jackson, Epic Records video; 1983) 184
  Victor Frankenstein (20th Century Fox; 2015) 5, 13, 126–27
  Wayne's World (Paramount; 1992) 177
  Yellow Submarine (United Artists; 1969) 173
  Young Frankenstein (Mel Brooks, 20th Century Fox; 1974) 73, 126, 177, 182, 183
Frankenstein inspired poetry
  Dreaming Frankenstein (Liz Lochhead, 2001) 200
Frankenstein musicals, operas and ballet
  Frankenstein: The Metal Opera (2014) 14, 172, 179, 181
  Frankenstein, The Musical (1993) 172, 181–82
  Frankenstein, Royal Ballet, (2016) 182, 228
  Frankenstein's Wedding... Live in Leeds (2011) 181, 227, 228
  Mary Shelley Opera, The (2002) 115, 220
  Monster: An Opera in Two Acts (2002) 115, 220
  Rocky Horror Show (musical; 1973) 179
Frankenstein myth, defined 1, 3–4, 5–8, 10–11, 12–13, 14–15, 54, 68, 69, 113–14, 121, 123, 124, 126, 130, 172–73, 176–82, 184

Frankenstein Network 200–1, 204
Frankenstein novel adaptations
　Bride of Frankenstein: Pandora's Bride (Elizabeth Hand, 2006) 204, 230
　Casebook of Victor Frankenstein (Peter Ackroyd, 2009) 6, 201–2
　Cross of Frankenstein (Robert J. Myers, 1975) 6, 202
　Dr. Frankenstein's Daughters (Suzanne Weyn, 2013) 201
　Frankenstein series (Dean Koontz, 2004–2011) 165
　Frankenstein in Baghdad (Ahmed Saadawi, (2013; transl. 2018)) 4, 11, 54, 58–64, 165, 201
　Frankenstein Papers (Fred Saberhagen, 1986) 202
　Frankenstein Unbound (Brian Aldiss, 1973) 202
　Frankenstein Wheel (Paul W. Fairman, 1972) 5
　Frankenstein's Bride (Hilary Bailey, 2007) 203, 204, 230
　Frankissstein (Jeanette Winterson, 2019) 202
　Mammoth Book of Frankenstein (Stephen Jones, 1994) 200
　Monster's Wife (Kate Horsley, 2015) 204–5
　Slave of Frankenstein (Robert J. Myers, 1976) 6
　Son of Terror: Frankenstein Continued (William A. Chanler, 2017) 201
　Unfashioned Creatures (Lesley McDowell, 2013) 202
Frankenstein plays
　Apology (2011) 114, 220
　Birth of Frankenstein (2013) 116, 119–21
　Don't Talk to Me of Love (2001) 114, 220
　Frankenstein (Nick Dear, 2011) 5, 114, 116, 167, 219, 220, 226
　Frankenstein: The Year Without a Summer (2010) 116–19
　Frankenstein Incarnate: The Passions of Mary Shelley (2007) 116, 220
　Frankenstein's Wedding . . . Live in Leeds (2011) 181, 227, 228
　Hideous Progeny (2010) 115, 220
　Inflatable Frankenstein (2013) 115
　Justified Sinners (2017) 115, 220
　Mary Shelley (2012) 115
　Mary Shelley's Frankenstein (2017) 116
　Presumption; or, The Fate of Frankenstein (1823) 3–4, 113, 183, 219
Frankenstein songs and albums
　"Feed My Frankenstein" (Alice Cooper cover, 1991) 172, 177
　"Frankenstein" (Clutch, 2001) 179
　"Frankenstein" (Edgar Winter, 1972) 176
　"Frankenstein" (New York Dolls, 1973) 178
　"Frankenstein" (Phish, 1991) 173
　Frankenstein Baby (Phil Hammon, 2001) 178
　How to Make a Monster (Electric Frankenstein, 1999) 173, 176–77, 178, 179
　"I Put a Spell on You" (Screamin' Jay Hawkins, 1956) 175
　"I'm Not Your (Nothing)" (Electric Frankenstein, 1999) 176–77
　"Monster Mash" (Bobby "Boris" Pickett, 1962) 172, 183, 184
　"Power and Glory" (Lou Reed, 1992) 181
　"Teen-aged Frankenstein" (Alice Cooper, 1986) 172, 177
　Transformer (Lou Reed, 1972) 180
Frankenstein television shows
　Frankenstein Chronicles (2015–2017) 133–40
　Munsters (1964–1966) 7, 9–10, 73, 94
　Penny Dreadful (2014–2016) 199–200, 205, 230
Frankensteinia 10–11, 69–70, 207
Frankenstrats, 179
Frankenstein guitar 179
French Revolution 2, 10, 20, 26, 208
Friedrich, Caspar David 13, 149–50, 153
　paintings
　　Wanderer above the Sea of Fog (1818) 142, 150, 153
　　The Watzmann (1824–1825), 149

Galloway, Alexander R. 146, 225
gender 41, 42, 178, 185–95, 197–98
Gernsback, Hugo 55–56
Godwin, William
    St. Leon: A Tale of the Sixteenth Century (1799) 4
gothic 8, 13, 20, 27, 55–56, 61, 99, 113, 119, 133–34, 136–37, 139–40, 176, 180–81, 184, 205, 208

Haraway, Donna 4, 141, 154, 188–89, 195
Hart, Margaret
    Situated Becomings 185, 188–90, 196, 198
Höch, Hannah 191–92, 197
Hopkins, Lisa 24–25, 209
hybrid 6, 57, 113, 117, 122, 186–89, 191, 195, 197

ideology 20, 21, 26

Jagoda, Patrick 150, 154
Joyce, James 158, 200
    Finnegan's Wake (1939) 158
Juul, Jesper 143

Karloff, Boris 7–9, 12, 69–73, 87–91, 130, 176, 181, 183, 200–1, 204, 207, 216
Kristeva, Julia 93, 136

Larouzée, Adrien 142, 154
LaValle, Victor 12, 99, 100, 103–5, 107, 109, 167, 199, 217
    The Ballad of Black Tom (2016), 104
    Destroyer, see Frankenstein comics
Leone, Damien 10, 19, 21, 27, 28
Litmus Theatre 119–21
Lochhead, Liz, *see* Frankenstein inspired poetry
Louden, Jane Webb 10, 21, 23–25
    The Mummy! A Tale of the Twenty-Second Century (1827) 10, 19–20, 23–24, 27–28

McAvoy, James 126–27
Manga, *see* Frankenstein comics
Martin, Trayvon 98, 102
Marvel Comics, *see* Frankenstein comics

Marx, Karl 10, 20–21, 23–24, 26–28
    Eighteenth Brumaire of Louis Bonaparte, The (1852) 20–24, 27, 28, 208
mesostics 13, 158–61, 164, 166, 168
Milton, John 21, 22, 201
    Paradise Lost (1667) 22, 105
modernism 51, 158, 193, 213
modernity 31, 34, 40, 41, 43, 57, 60, 63–64
monster walk 182–83
musical groups
    Aerosmith 172, 182–83
    Alice Cooper 172, 177, 179
    Beatles 93, 172–73, 226
    Clutch 179
    Edgar Winter Group 14, 172, 177, 227
    Electric Frankenstein 14, 172, 176–77, 179
    Iced Earth 172
    New York Dolls 172, 178–79
    Phish 173, 176
    Radiohead 166
    Ramones 179
musical forms
    ballad 175, 227, 228
    chaconne 176
    dirge 175
    passacaglia 176
    sampling 182
Mutu, Wangechi 194–96
mythopoetics 173, 175

naturecultures, 141, 143, 144, 146, 152, 153, 154
necropolitical 11, 54, 58, 60–64

ontology 19, 188, 198
operational logics 145

Paradise Lost, see Milton, John
parody 1, 56, 73, 80. 106, 173, 176, 177–78, 180–82, 184
pastiche 173, 175, 202
Peake, Richard Brinsley 3–4, 113
    Presumption; or, The Fate of Frankenstein, see Frankenstein plays
Pestridge, Carol 180

Petrarch 174
photomontage 191–94
Pickett, Bobby "Boris" 1
  see also Frankenstein songs and albums
Pierce, Jack 70, 87
platformer games 151
plays-in-performance 114
Polidori, John 219 n.2, 221 n.23
  as a character 142
postcolonial 54, 55, 57, 63
  see colonial
posthuman 57, 99, 106, 108, 185–87, 188–91, 195, 197–98, 201, 205
postmodernism 6, 189
potentia 197–98, 229

race 6, 21, 23, 29, 56–57, 62, 99, 102, 108, 109, 195
  see antiracism
race traitor 106
Radiohole 115
Reed, Lou 166, 180–81
  "Power and Glory," 181
  Transformer, see Frankenstein songs and albums
revolution 2, 10, 20–25, 28
revolutionary subject 11, 19, 26–27
Rice, Tamir 98, 102, 103
Romanticism 31, 143
  legacies of 142, 154
Rousseau, Jean-Jacques 2

Saadawi, Ahmed 4, 59–60
  Frankenstein in Baghdad, see Frankenstein novels
Sartre, Jean-Paul 136
Schapiro, Miriam 193–94, 197
science fiction 2, 6, 9, 11, 14, 20, 27, 54–59, 62–64, 71, 185, 188–91, 195, 197–98, 201, 216
Shelley, Mary Godwin 1–2, 4, 12, 33, 107, 113–19, 122, 128, 132, 185, 188, 198, 212, 219
  as a character 12, 113–22, 220, 221, 132, 142
  The Last Man (1826), 23
Shelley, Percy Bysshe 6, 22, 107, 121, 182, 206, 212, 219, 221
  as a character 6, 106, 115, 116–19, 121, 132, 142, 202
  "Mutability" (1816) 22, 209
  Prometheus Unbound (1820) 6
slow reading 160

Teitel, Darrah 114–15
Till, Emmett 62, 98
time 11, 25, 30–31, 34–35, 39, 64
  representations of 6, 32–33, 35, 37–39, 56, 147, 190

Venuti, Laurence 167
video games
  Flower (thatgamecompany) 144, 151
  Frankenstein: Birth of a Myth (La Belle Games) 142–43
  Frankenstein: The Monster Returns (Tose Software) 141
  Frankenstein's Monster (Data Age) 141
  Mary Shelley's Frankenstein (Bits Studios) 141
  Super Mario Bros (Nintendo) 151
  The Wanderer: Frankenstein's Creature (La Belle Games) 13, 141–54, 224
Villa Diodati 116–17, 119, 120, 142, 219, 220, 221
Volney, C.F. 21, 57
  The Ruins, or Meditations on the Revolutions of Empires (1792) 57

Wardrip-Fruin, Noah 145
Wark, McKenzie 146, 149
Whale, James, *see* films

Zappa, Frank 165

www.ingramcontent.com/pod-product-compliance
Lightning Source LLC
Chambersburg PA
CBHW071826300426
44116CB00009B/1460